12·49

Symbol: Symbol:
Tool
or
Sy?
What

The Dyn
Symbols

P.10. the visible sign of an invisible reality

Jason Anthony Reginald Powell   Liverpool group Mtg.

* Be the change you want to see in the world (Ghandi)

* Creative Synthesis:

A Philosophical Principle that states that when several elemental components are organised or co-ordinated. — The resulting synthesis has properties + characteristics that are fundamentally different in kind from those of the separate components viewed independently.

The Dynamics of Symbols

Fundamentals of Jungian Psychotherapy

Verena Kast

Translated by
Susan A. Schwarz

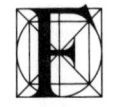

FROMM INTERNATIONAL
Publishing Corporation
New York

Translation Copyright © 1992
Fromm International Publishing Corporation, New York

Originally published in 1990 as *Die Dynamik der Symbole*
Copyright © 1990, Ammann Verlag AG, Zürich, Switzerland

All rights reserved. No part of this book may be reproduced or utilized in any form or by any means, electronic or mechanical, including photocopying, recording, or by any information storage and retrieval system, without permission in writing from the Publisher. Inquiries should be addressed to Fromm International Publishing Corporation, 560 Lexington Avenue, New York, NY 10022.

Printed in the United States of America

First U.S. Edition

Library of Congress Cataloging-in-Publication Data
Kast, Verena, 1943–
    [Dynamik der Symbole. English]
    The dynamics of symbols: fundamentals of Jungian psychotherapy / Verena Kast ; translated by Susan A. Schwarz.
        p.   cm. — (Fromm psychology)
    Translation of: Die Dynamik der Symbole.
    Includes bibliographical references and index.
    ISBN 0-88064-200-9 (cloth : acid-free paper) : $24.95
    ISBN 0-88064-201-7 (paper : acid-free paper) : $14.95
      1. Jung, C. G. (Carl Gustav), 1875–1961. 2. Psychotherapy.
3. Symbolism (Psychology) I. Title. II. Series.
RC480.K28513 1991
616.89'14—dc20   91-37673
                                                                  CIP

CONTENTS

Foreword   ix

1. ASPECTS OF HUMANITY   1

    The Individuation Process   1
    The Self   5

2. ASPECTS OF THE SYMBOL   8

    On the Concept of the Symbol   10
    The Appearance of Symbols   11
    Symbolic Acts   13
    The Symbolizing Attitude   14
    Accepting Symbols   15
    The Formation of Symbols as a Process   18
    Symbols and the Goal of Therapy   27

3. ASPECTS OF THE COMPLEX   31

    Complex Experience   33
    Definitions of the Complex   37
    Complexes with Empowering Influences   48

4. ASPECTS OF THE EGO COMPLEX   51

    The Ego Complex and the Experience of Identity   52
    The Ego Complex in Terms of Developmental Psychology   57
    The Ego Functions   66
    Constellations of the Ego Complex   68
        Compensation through Fantasies of Grandeur   70

Compensation through Idealized Powerful Parental
Figures   71
Compensation through Mirror Identification   72
Destructive Rage as a Compensation   73
Compensation through Devaluation   74
Compensation as an Attitude   76
Fragmentation   79
Therapeutic Considerations in Reestablishing
Coherence of the Ego Complex   85

5. ASPECTS OF THE ARCHETYPE   90

Bloch's Criticism of Jung's Theory of Archetypes   95
Archetypal Constellation and Relationship   97
Consequences of the Concept of Archetypes in
Dealing with Symbols   102
The Archetype of the Self and the Individuation
Process   106
    The Mandala as a Symbol   108
    The Individuation Process   112
Remarks on Synchronicity   123
    Synchronicity and Psychosomatics   130

6. TRANSFERENCE, COUNTERTRANSFERENCE AND THE FORMATION OF NEW SYMBOLS   143

Turning Points in Analysis   146
    The Experience of Being Understood in the
    Therapeutic Relationship as a Prerequisite for the
    Formation of Symbols   147
    Collusive Transference/Countertransference
    and the Formation of Symbols   157
        Thoughts on Guilt   159
        The Intrapsychic Dynamics   159
        Guilt and Responsibility   161
        The Role of Empathy   161

Dealing with Guilt Unproductively 162
Excerpts from a Course of Therapy 162
Archetypal Countertransference as a Fairy-tale Revelation 175

Notes 195
Bibliography 207
Index 212

FOREWORD

CREATIVITY is central to C. G. Jung's psychology. The goal in Jungian therapy is that individuals begin to experiment with their reality and creatively deal with their problems and personal traits. Neuroses are to be replaced by the potentials of creative change.

Jungian psychology offers the techniques necessary to make the creative potential of the unconscious accessible to consciousness and thereby transform possibility into actuality. These "techniques" are essential in an individual's therapy, both for psychic development toward autonomy and for the development of a creative lifestyle, which in turn will lead the individual to realize that his or her problems are relative not only to the environment shared with others, but also to his or her personal depth. By taking the manifestations of both sides seriously, the individual can develop creative solutions that will be expressions of her or his vital self.

Creative development becomes visible in symbols and is presented to consciousness by symbols. Working with symbols forms the core of Jungian therapy.

It is my intention to demonstrate the essential aspects of C. G. Jung's psychotherapy through symbols. At the same time I will illustrate the theoretical connections in which therapeutic considerations are rooted.

I believe it is particularly important to explain the connection between the formation of symbols and the analytic relationship, transference and countertransference.

In therapy, acknowledging and supporting symbolic processes, recognizing and working on transference and countertransference are not diametrically opposed techniques; they are mutually interwoven, just as individuation is not simply an intrapsychic process of integration, but also an external process of relationship.

I would like to thank the analysands who allowed me to use their material to demonstrate the correlation between theory and practice.

I presented most of the ideas introduced in this book in lectures at the Bern and Zurich Universities, as well as at the C. G. Jung Institute in Zurich. The audience stimulated me to present the therapeutic process as clearly and precisely as possible. Although it will never be possible to relate what really happens in therapy—too much about it is unconscious and mysterious—I do believe that whatever can be discussed should be discussed. The great interest of my students and audiences has continued to motivate me to this end.

Verena Kast

St. Gallen, September 1989

The Dynamics of Symbols

Aspects of Humanity

CHAPTER ONE

EVERY PSYCHOLOGICAL THEORY is based on an underlying concept of humanity. Jung believed that a human being should fully become the unique self that he or she is by consciously experiencing the individuation process. This is our task as human beings; this is in our power, and this also forms the theoretical basis of the therapeutic process. Jungian psychology views humanity as immersed in universally connected meaning. We are in the midst of creative transformation, oppressed by lack of transformation, and, at the same time, naturally compelled to seek an additional dimension to all occurrences beyond the obvious in an effort to preserve the mysterious aspect of reality. The reality we experience through the senses is intrinsically related to spiritual reality.

THE INDIVIDUATION PROCESS

The process of individuation is an ongoing confrontational dialogue between consciousness and the unconscious. Conscious and unconscious contents are united in symbols.

The goal of the individuation process is to become who we really are. "Become who you are," said Pindar; the idea is not new. Aristotle emphasized that every creation has its own unique nature, and that life is meant to guide us to this unique nature. Thus, the plethora of life's potentials inherent in us can be experienced to a great extent, so that what is inherent in us—and perhaps in us alone—becomes visible.

In this sense, individuation is a process that differentiates a person's singular quality, his or her uniqueness. A major part of the process is self-acceptance, acceptance not only of all of one's possibilities, but also of one's difficulties; these are essential because to a significant degree they comprise our uniqueness. Accepting oneself, one's possibilities as well as one's difficulties, is a basic virtue that is to be realized in the individuation process.

Repeatedly, the individuation process has been compared to the image of a tree: a seed falls to the ground and is to become the tree within it, which correlates to habitat, weather, and climate. When we think of trees in this context, their wounds are also characteristic.

"Become who you are" does not imply that we should become smooth, harmonious and polished, but rather that we should become increasingly aware of what we are and of what is voiced by our personality and all its rough edges. In this respect, individuation is a gradual approach, for in the end we do not really know what we are, nor does the analyst know. It is an approach; every transformation we experience is intrinsically corrigible and temporary.

Just as important, perhaps even more pertinent to psychology, and equally connected with the goal of self-realization, is the other aspect of individuation, which aims at increasing one's autonomy. Each individual is to become a singular being, detached from parental complexes and collective standards as well as from the norms and values of society, and the roles society expects. Therefore, self-realization also means a coming of age.

According to the Jungian concept of humanity, whatever is external is also internal, and whatever is internal is also external. Hence, we should try to free ourselves not only from the restraints of collective values, norms, and expected roles—which we have internalized in our persona

—but also from the restraints of the unconscious. Indeed, we should consciously interact with them. We should neither be defined by the unconscious, nor by the values our society has created. To be freed from the restraints of the unconscious means, among other things, that we do not allow our lives to be determined by an archetype without being aware of it.[1]

An example: A forty-two-year-old man was dominated by the hero archetype. Whatever the situation, he automatically wanted to be the hero and felt bad when he could not. People told him, in praise or reproach, that he behaved heroically. He was loaded with excess work because he never complained and managed well. He also dreamt about heroes. In time, he realized that he was heavily influenced by the need to be a hero. In many situations he asked himself if it really was sensible to be a hero. A dialogue between the ego and the hero began.

Heroism is not simply a problem to be overcome. The goal is to apply heroism where it makes sense. Such an approach would release this aspect from the unconscious. This is not to suggest that the unconscious factor ceases to function in the old sense, but, by relating to these aspects, we would no longer be governed by them.

When we consider both conscious and unconscious factors, it becomes clear that Jung believed we consciously experience the individuation process—in therapy—thus becoming what we actually are; that is, we are to become less and less externally dominated by the forces of the collective unconscious. This domination is replaced by a dialogue between consciousness and society, and between consciousness and the unconscious. This, according to Jung, leads to a development of increased—though temporary—autonomy during the individuation process.

On the one hand, Jung defines individuation as an internal, subjective process of integration, during which individuals become acquainted with additional aspects of themselves, make contact with them, and connect them to their self-images—e.g., by integrating projections. On the other hand, individuation is an interpersonal, intersubjective process of relationship, "because," says Jung, "relationship to the self is at once relationship to our fellow man, and no one can be related to the latter until he is related to himself."[2] Or: "The unrelated human being lacks wholeness, for he can achieve wholeness only through the soul, and the soul cannot exist without its other side, which is always found in a 'you.' "[3]

In Jungian therapy, the interpretation of symbols on a subjective and objective level is indebted to the notion that individuation is a process both of integration and relationship. For instance, if we encounter an authority figure in a dream, we may regard it as a certain aspect of an external authority. Our behavior in the dream may indicate something about our everyday reaction to authority. This would be an interpretation on the objective level. On the subjective level, the authority is seen as an inner configuration, an aspect of ourselves and, in this sense, as an authoritarian tendency within. Unless we abridge Jung, both forms of interpretation must be considered. The process of individuation should by no means cause people to become solitary individuals, but, on the contrary, should cause them to become more community oriented. According to Jung, the "process of individuation brings forth a consciousness of human community precisely because it makes us aware of the unconscious, which unites and is common to mankind. Individuation is an at-one-ment with oneself and at the same time with humanity, since the self is part of humanity."[4] Or, to put it differently: There can never be exclusive development of autonomy, for it is always accompanied by the development of the ability to relate to others.

Individuation is a goal. Becoming whole is utopian; at best we are on the way. This process fills our life with meaning.[5]

THE SELF

When we turn to the self it becomes clear that a utopian goal motivates the process of individuation, for the self motivates self-realization. Individuation is understood not only as becoming one with ourselves, but also as realization of the self. Jung says the self, which he considers to be the central archetype, is a guiding principle, the secret *spiritus rector* of our lives that causes us to be and to become.[6] Jung speaks of the drive toward self-realization. The self acts *a priori* as the creative principle that guides the structuring of the ego complex. Moreover, the self is considered the origin of the psyche's self-regulation. To Jung, the psyche, like the living body, is a self-regulating system. He sees self-regulation principally in the fact that the unconscious can be expected to react against one-sided conscious inclinations, so that even though we are capable of changing our momentary position, our essential structure remains.[7] The self is the root and the origin of individual personality, which it embraces in the past, present, and future.[8]

The symbols of the self, says Jung, arise in the depths of the body; they express both our materiality and the structure of the perceiving consciousness.[9] Symbolically, the self is often represented by the symbol of the union of opposites, or by the symbol of the lovers. It is this latter symbol that I feel to be of particular importance, because it expresses the experience of love, wholeness, the union of opposites, and the desire to do away with boundaries.[10] Repeatedly, we find that people are barely able to distinguish between the longing for love and the longing for self. When we are moved by love, we are also moved by a different longing that transcends the love relationship. In such situations the self is constellated. The self can be represented by abstract symbols, such as the circle, sphere, triangle, or cross; these figures symbolize wholeness and characteristically contain many opposites that are not necessarily merged.[11] Once we recognize the archetype of the self, we believe it pertains exclusively to us; we feel self-centered; we then have a sense of inescapable identity and the fatefulness of the situation in which this symbol is experienced. The experience of incarnation or the realization of the self represent the utopia of the entire individuation process.

Jung addresses yet another dimension of the self. The self I have discussed so far could be called "my self," or what my total being can become, what I can become in my own lifespan, and what I can develop by accepting as much as possible. The relationship between the self and the ego is based on reciprocation. The self motivates the development of the ego, and extends far beyond the ego complex; the self, in turn, can actually be realized only through the ego.

Jung speaks of "the self" as the eternal or universal human being within, *the human being* as such, "the spherical, i.e. perfect, man who appears at the beginning and end of time and is man's own beginning and end."[12] This means that realization of the self is more than a personal necessity rewarded by self-satisfaction and sensuality; it also strives for humanity on the whole.

In his last work, *Mysterium Coniunctionis*, Jung mentions a further level of individuation in connection with the self as Anthropos. This idea does not arise from his own experience, but from the works of the alchemist Dorn. I mention this concept because it serves to illustrate Jung's view of the world and humanity. The alchemist Dorn claims that the total human being can merge with the "Unus Mundus," the potentially complete world of the first day of creation. This would mean that the self, which is first of all an intrapsychic center empowered with self-regulating and self-centering abilities, is able to experience union with the cosmos as a whole. Here, the definition of the utopia becomes clear—a utopia that pertains to the ability of conscious human beings to connect with the entire cosmos, or, vice versa, to recognize the cosmos in the individual. All living things are thus seen as one organism. This idea, popular in the Renaissance, is regaining ground today through the environmental movement, which views the cosmos as an organism and humanity as an integral part of this synergistic organism. In the end, the idea of wholeness and the implied correlations are at the root of the individuation principle. This thought expresses liberation itself. Jung believes that the self motivates the development of the ego complex, while the ego and consciousness give the self the opportunity to manifest. And manifestation, or incarnation, is a form of liberation.

Individuation is utopian. It is the inner meaning of utopias to stimulate desire, give us momentum, and reveal our innermost aspirations. Individuation is utopian because it is impossible to become as whole as we intend. Jung writes in a letter to a Rudolf Jung:

> Ultimately we all get stuck somewhere, for we are all mortal and remain but a part of what we are as a whole. The wholeness we can reach is very relative.[13]

The therapeutic process, as an individuation process, essentially consists of activated areas of the unconscious and consciousness united by symbols. The creative development of the personality becomes possible through the formation of symbols.

Aspects of the Symbol

CHAPTER TWO

AN EXAMPLE: AN OBJECT BECOMES A SYMBOL. —While busy cleaning house, a woman lost her wedding ring. She thought it would turn up once she had finished cleaning. But she did not find it and became upset. Could she have dumped it with the dirty water? She asked herself, "Could losing the wedding ring mean something?" And, "How am I ever going to tell my husband?" She tried to calm herself; "It's only a ring!" But that was just the point. It wasn't just any ring, it was her wedding ring. She was afraid to tell her husband. Even though she considered her husband very understanding, she felt guilty.

A friend stopped by. The woman told her what had happened. The friend, a forthright person, said immediately, "Of course—because of all this cleaning you're destroying your relationship with your husband."

The woman thought about her relationship with her husband, and she remembered which feelings, which expectations she associated with the ring. She questioned whether she truly wanted the relationship, or if she wanted to toss it out like dirty water; and of course she also asked herself why she felt so much anxiety.

The loss of the ring could not be separated from its meaning. This was clearly indicated by the woman's dread of her partner's reaction; usually she did not fear her husband at all. She was afraid the union and the wholeness of the relationship, symbolized by the ring, might have been lost. She feared that, even if a new ring were purchased, the subject of separation would come up, and separation causes anxiety. We often project the impulse to separate onto our partner because we fear the partner's reaction more than our own impulse to separate.

In this situation, the woman did not consider any other meanings or interpretations. She might have thought of the incident as an expression of the desire to renew the relationship with her partner, that a new ring was due. After all, the old ring had become too big.

From now on the woman's life was marked by the symbol "ring." Other women told her what had happened to their rings. It is not unusual for a ring to get caught in the washing machine, or the laundry; all sorts of things happen to wedding rings. Men also talk about their rings—the ring they can't find in their vest-pocket because it is in another vest.

I have chosen this example to demonstrate that a symbol is in the first place a common object perceived by the senses, although it also signifies something mysterious; it refers to a meaning and beyond that a meaning which cannot be fully grasped at first. The ordinary object cannot be separated from its meaning. Though a ring is a common object, there also is something cryptic about it; its meaning can be related to an idea, to the general, or to the abstract.

Whenever a symbol gains importance in our lives, it reflects a current existential situation. An essential element of depth psychology is that we must examine the inherent significance of the actual, existential situation. This symbolic point of view corresponds with a human concept that incorporates our everyday reality into a greater continuity, whereby the hidden meaning influences the apparent and the apparent influences the hidden meaning.

ON THE CONCEPT OF THE SYMBOL

"Symbol" comes from the Greek *symbolon*, the word for token of identity.[1] In ancient Greece, when two friends parted, they would break a ring, a coin, or a clay tablet in half. When the friend, or someone from his family, returned, he was to present his half. If one half fit the other, he was recognized as the friend, or a relative of the friend, and was entitled to hospitality. The fitting together of two halves (*symbállein* = to compare, to fit together, to throw together) is a motif that often plays a role in fiction; for instance, the sign of recognition might be half of an oyster shell that joins perfectly with the other half.

The etymology allows us to recognize that a symbol is something put together. Not until the parts are joined is it a symbol, and, eventually, it becomes a symbol of something else. Here, it represents the spiritual reality of friendship and, beyond personal friendship, the friendship of families, and the right to hospitality. Here—and this goes for all symbols—the symbol is a visible sign of an invisible reality. Therefore, two dimensions of the symbol must be considered: the external can reveal the internal, the visible the invisible, and the physical the spiritual. Something specific can reveal the general. When we interpret, we seek the invisible reality behind the visible and the connections between the two. The symbol is marked by an excess of meaning; we will never completely exhaust its meanings.

The symbol is inherently connected with what it represents; the two cannot be separated. This distinguishes it from the sign. Signs are statements defined by common consensus; although they too are representations, they have no excess meaning. Consider the sign "knife crossed with fork," meaning restaurant. The knife and fork might conceivably be replaced by some other arrangement. We could just as well accept a bowl and a spoon. A sign depicts nothing cryptic. It has a purely representative function that indicates something. Signs can be replaced, and are replaced to suit the current trends (e.g., the sign for railroad). Symbols cannot be replaced by agreement. The color red, for instance: we associate red with blood; in this way, red comes to mean life, vitality, suffering, and passion. Aside from its tonal quality, a color suggests a meaning. It is unlikely that we could create a convention using the color green to symbolize everything associated with suffering, passion, and warm emotion. We cannot simply decide to ascribe a new meaning to a symbol, because its meaning is intrinsically connected with the image itself.

A sign can be rationally comprehended. It addresses the intellect, which is why signs are used in mathematics, science, and information processing. The symbol is much more irrational, cannot quite be grasped, and has a lot to do with emotions; it is therefore to be found in the humanities, religion, and art.

A sign, however, can assume the characteristics of a symbol. Take numbers, for example. A number is a sign. It is agreed that two is a sign for two units, and thus represents a quantity. But a number can also be considered qualitatively. The number thirteen is the sign for thirteen units, while—in terms of quality—we might say thirteen is an unlucky number. It is assigned a content, or quality. Signs can easily evolve into symbols, particularly when we approach the world with a symbolizing attitude.

THE APPEARANCE OF SYMBOLS

We experience symbols in dream images, fantasies, poetic imagery, fairy tales, myths, and art. Symbols can appear and be created quite spontaneously.

An example of a spontaneously created symbol.—During a discussion following a lecture on love relationships, a participant drew one billy goat after the other on a piece of paper. He drew with increasing fervor, very energetically. Then he sat back and contemplated his latest goat with satisfaction. Now the goat looked right to him.

When I asked why he chose this particular time to draw goats so enthusiastically, he looked at me in amazement—as if I were the first to inform him that he had been drawing billy goats. We agreed that this was a case of spontaneous formation of symbols. But a symbol for what? A symbol for the lecturer? For a participant in the discussion? For a repressed part of the lecture? (The sexual aspect had been left open.) Of course, the goat might also have been a symbol for the man at that particular moment. Perhaps he felt a bit like a billy goat. We playfully tried to relate this symbol to an actual occurrence in his life. Suddenly he said, "Now I remember—it's because I saw some illustrations from 'The Wolf and the Seven Kids' this morning." I looked at him, puzzled. I saw a billy goat, not a wolf. He noticed my confusion: "Oh, I guess it couldn't be that after all, since it isn't a wolf."

On closer examination of the fairy tale, one wonders why the nanny goat did not have a billy goat. Where was the father? He could have protected the children. I communicated these thoughts to the doodler and he told me that he had had an argument with his wife that morning. The fight had been about him, the frequently absent father. Now the doodler understood his billy-goat symbol.

Of course, he could have settled for other interpretations. However, it is typical that we are satisfied once a particular interpretation makes sense to us emotionally.

Symbols retain their significance for a certain length of time, and the symbols fill our life with their meaning. At some point these symbols recede into the background and others become important. We can reconstruct a person's background from the symbols with which he or she lives, and we will recognize a pattern, for symbols have a time of origin, of blossoming, and of passing.

Symbols arise not only during long therapeutic processes, but can spontaneously surface in real–life situations. The question is only whether we anticipate and pay attention to them.

SYMBOLIC ACTS

First, let me cite an example. A woman felt the need to have a diamond set into her wedding ring. This was a symbolic act. She and her husband had just come through a difficult crisis; they had been in therapy, where they fought it out tooth and nail. In the end, when they both realized that they wanted to live together—not simply as a lazy compromise, but because they truly cared for each other—the woman said, "Now I want to have a diamond set in my wedding ring."

This was a highly symbolic desire. But the husband said, "You always want something material."

He had little sense for symbols and symbolic gestures. To him, her desire meant that, if this relationship were to continue, he had to pay once again. He experienced her request as a repetition of a pattern and overlooked the symbolic content of the wish: "To renew the wedding ring, renew the bond—with a 'star,'" as the wife put it. To her it meant having found the way out of darkness, having a new "star" to follow. She interpreted it as understanding the old relationship under a new star.

This example illustrates that it is possible not to see beyond the concrete object. If this happens in connection with therapy, it is the therapist's responsibility to turn the emotional attention to symbols and point out their hidden message. It is foolish to claim a person has no sense for symbols without first trying to acquaint him or her with their meaning. Of course, the opposite also occurs: some individuals see symbols in everything and everyone. Symbols address our intellect much less than they do our universal perspective and our relatedness to the invisible reality that transcends us. A person who allows only visible reality to count has great difficulty with symbols and symbolic thought and attempts to make every symbol into a sign.

THE SYMBOLIZING ATTITUDE

Certain symbols arise in particular situations; we perceive them in dreams as images or fantasies we cannot suppress. But the symbolizing attitude can also be employed by the ego, as the following example illustrates.

An example for the symbolizing attitude.—A man was driving his car and at the same time discussing his career plans with his girlfriend. He was absorbed in talking and absorbed in driving. As the traffic got heavier, he started to swear; then they hit a traffic jam. He said, "Oh, now we're stuck. It's absurd to drive when you know you're going to get stuck." Suddenly he became thoughtful and said, "Why didn't I understand? It's a symbol! Now I know what it means: If I pursue the plans I've just developed, I'll get into a jam in the end, and we'll be stuck in our relationship. We'll lose our freedom. What a miserable feeling."

In a way, the traffic jam served the purpose of drawing his attention to the possibility that the plan he had formulated might have a dangerous aspect.

To symbolize is to discover the hidden meaning in a concrete situation. There is a mysterious side to concrete daily reality, and it always has something to do with us. This point of view is too extreme for some people, especially if they doubt the purpose of symbols. Symbols can indicate what the future holds in store, but tend to do so far too subtly to state in linear terms what might be good about a situation.

Nonetheless, we can certainly ask ourselves whether concrete things might not after all have a hidden meaning. The traffic jam is a viable symbol for the obstructions we create for ourselves. We should recognize collective situations as symbols for collective problems and accept that we are inevitably a part of the collective. We would consequently be able to effect change in this area. The question of hidden meaning is also a question of meaning itself.

Jungian psychology has been repeatedly called "addicted to meaning." The symbolizing attitude does indeed form the core of Jungian therapy. It is reflected in the theoretical concept of interpretation on the objective and subjective level, in the concept that what is outside is inside, and that the microcosmic is also macrocosmic. Moreover, to symbolize is a perfectly natural human attitude. When standing by the sea, for instance, we first perceive the ocean with every one of our senses. We might then perceive what we feel; and usually we discover that the sea is not just water, but can also communicate the experience of infinity. The subjects "I and Infinity," or "I and the Rhythm of Eternal Coming and Going" begin to occupy us. When we contemplate the sea for a long time we sense other aspects of our psyche, and in the end we find that a great deal can be said about the sea.

In this case the symbolizing attitude is a means of projection. We project our unconscious onto manifest reality. We cannot, however, project any subject we choose, but, depending on the symbol, only subjects that truly have an inner connection with our existence. Symbolizing implies inquiring into the hidden reality behind manifest reality, as well as observing the manifest in the mirror of the unknown, hidden reality.

ACCEPTING SYMBOLS

In order to actually experience symbols as symbols—and it is experience that counts in the end—in order to see them as more than signs, we must be prepared to respond emotionally.

An example to illustrate increasing readiness to accept symbols.—A thirty-five-year-old man, who was in therapy, said, "I had a dream-fragment about a seven-year-old child crying. I was impatient in my dream, and wanted the child to stop crying." He casually remarked that the dream had no significance, because all children cry, which was why he did not want children. He was not married. He did not want to concern himself further with this dream-fragment.

Since the dreamer had no initial affinity to the symbol, it was my responsibility to establish contact to the symbol. If the dreamer had had children of this age, I might have wondered if he was just as impatient with them. It was also conceivable that in his neighborhood there was a child of about the same age, who always cried.

In order to establish contact to the symbol, we first examine concrete life conditions and then deal with the hidden meaning.

What did the child represent? Did it stand for his own childhood, or for the idea of being a child? I established the connection to the analysand's childhood with the question, "What kind of child were you when you were about seven years old?"

> He said: "Oh, you know, I was a crybaby. I wasn't a real boy at all. I'd rather not talk about it."
> I visualized the boy and said: "I can imagine you were the kind of rejected child I'd want to buy ice cream for."
> He: "Why, do you like boys who cry?"
> I: "They make me want to comfort them and make them laugh."
> He: "Aha."

The questions and my fantasy caused him to sense the seven-year-old child inside him, and to recognize that this child still existed within him.

For weeks we attempted to keep in touch with this aspect, made possible by my intuition about the analysand's childhood. And thus we achieved contact with the symbol.

Once we relate to a symbol, everything connected with the symbol suddenly comes alive. In the case of the symbol "child," memories are activated, such as: What kind of child was I? What was it like to be a child? How do I cope with my own children? And then the awareness of life we had as children reawakens: The future is still ahead of me, just wait till I grow up. This symbol represents our personal childhood, but it also symbolizes the open future, the will to live, and constant renewal. Although we know that we are adults, and are fixed in our ideas, the symbol of the child brings up the feeling of becoming anew, of setting out, and the danger in going forth. To be aware of this feeling is of particular importance to those who have a hard time in life.

Once actively accepted, a symbol can stimulate a whole palette of psychic experiences, from memories to expectations, but only if we contact it emotionally. If we fail to do so, no matter how much mythology or how many myths of the "divine child" we discuss, the effect will be immaterial. But at least we would know we had had a very significant dream; and sometimes that can have an effect and give rise to a feeling that something meaningful is happening spontaneously in our life. However, all the force contained in the symbol, the energy inherent in it, is released only if we can emotionally accept it.

Once a symbol has gained meaning, or we have succeeded in emotionally accepting a symbol, we begin to deal with all its implications. A precise and simple definition can never be formulated. Even if one particular interpretation seems obvious, or a relatively straightforward definition is found, we can usually discover further interpretations that are justified by the evident criteria, while someone else may find yet another interpretation. This is characteristic of symbols.

A multitude of associations can be compressed within a single symbol. This is aggravating to our desire for directness. But for our need of mystery and meaning it is a gold mine.

However, symbols also awaken memories we would rather forget, and expectations that distress because we cannot incorporate them into the self–image we have created. This is why defense mechanisms are to be expected when we accept symbols or work with symbols.

Despite difficulties, despite the defense mechanisms, it is true that once a symbol is emotionally meaningful, it channels our interests, and we recognize it when we come across it in art, literature, and conversations. We begin to remember our personal history—and much of the past becomes visible in the perspective of the activated symbol—but we also remember humanity's past as we know it from mythology, fairy tales, art, and literature. Anticipation is connected with the appearance of symbols, and, contrary to reason, hope for the chance at a better life.

THE FORMATION OF SYMBOLS AS A PROCESS

Even when a fundamental symbol surfaces, it is rarely considered and experienced as a sudden major enlightenment. Frequently, a symbol approaches consciousness through a symbolic process.

To illustrate this, I am including a series of paintings by a forty-two-year-old woman. The paintings were created for the most part outside the therapeutic situation, and indicate *the formation of symbols relating to a mother complex*. I knew the woman from a series of one-week workshops on the subject "Fairy Tales as Therapy." Between the previous workshop and the one in question, the woman had lost her older sister to cancer. This triggered a serious identity crisis, culminating in the question, "Do I now have to be the woman my sister was?" Her sister's death caused her to become depressed.

When experiences of loss call forth depression rather than mourning, the question arises whether the individual exhibits depressive tendencies in other situations as well. This was confirmed by a picture the woman had painted about two years previously (cf. color plate 1).

The picture conveys a gloomy mood: in the center a woman in a dark cloak sits next to a raven, which can be understood not only as a symbol for melancholy, but also of deep wisdom and mysticism. The picture, which is composed horizontally, represents a problem related to dealing with the world, since we take a horizontal position when we settle in the world. The amount and height of sky, compared to the narrow band of earth, is striking. The picture communicates an overwhelmingly gray and powerful spiritual mood. The woman is faceless; the trees are bare. The overall impression is one of psychic winter.

Ominous clouds gather behind the tree under which the woman sits. She seems to be the center of a problem. The trees stand somewhat to the left, an area associated with the collective unconscious.[2] From that sector we might expect life to be stabilized—from the inside rather than from active, external life.

We can assume the woman has been subject to melancholy moods, and now experienced her sister's death as if a part of herself had died. Therefore, she had to go through a transformative process, which the process of mourning usually is; she had to become herself again.[3] The woman was participating in a workshop in which we examined the fairy tale "The Girl with the Little Moon on Her Forehead."[4] The fairy tale was about separation from the good mother and confrontation with the evil mother. The good mother was represented by a cow—the symbol for the maternal archetype, or the maternal in a collective form.

Once the positive maternal archetype is evoked, once an individual has experienced a positive maternal aspect, it remains present on an unconscious level, ready to become constellated in times of crisis and need.

In the fairy tale the cow is clearly a form of the mother, and thus the cow offers protection and comfort to the child; it effects a transformation by confronting the evil figures. Another key issue in the fairy tale is rejection and overcoming rejection.

In the workshops, the fairy tales are envisioned while read aloud. The participants then tell each other which passages are important to them and their experiences.[5] This woman could not visualize the cow, but she had no trouble identifying with the abandoned, rejected girl and her confrontation with the evil mother. I insisted that in this fairy tale there was not only the abandoned girl with a terrible mother, but also a helpful cow. Prompted by my very determined statement, "But there is a good, golden cow in this fairy tale," the woman painted the cow (cf. color plate 2).

In the fairy tale, the cow is yellow. Of course this leads us to think of gold; yellow and gold are solar and cognitive, while cows usually tend to be earth colored. In addition, the yellow cow was directly related to the moon on the girl's forehead and the star on her chin. This indicated that the cow was to mediate a brighter life with greater insight, which would help overcome depression.

In contrast to the first picture, the second (color plate 2) presents a better proportion between sky and earth. The girl and the golden yellow cow now replace the trees. By insisting that the cow existed, I had reminded the woman of a symbol she had repressed. I led her to accept the positive aspect of the maternal archetype in her world view; this does not mean that it would stay that way, nor that the negative aspects had been overcome. Despite a great deal of initial resistance, the woman became increasingly fascinated by the cow.

After the workshop, which I will not describe in detail at this point, the woman went home and continued to paint. At a particular phase of the workshop we had followed the fairy tale girl's path through the varied waters of the stream. The girl had to pass through green, red, black and, finally, white water. The woman, identifying with the girl, walked through the black water. She felt a strong undertow and had difficulty getting out of the water. One could say she was drawn by the "death-mother's" undertow, and, consequently, one might conjecture that the woman had a tendency to identify with her sister's death (cf. fig. 1).

Images that are mentally painful become tangible and are easier to confront once they are drawn. We can relate to the artistic product and detach ourselves from the problem by simultaneously looking at and working on it. We cease to identify with the problem and the first step toward coming to consciousness has been taken.

In her picture a bright yellow light shines into the blackness from the right, the side we associate with conscious-

ASPECTS OF THE SYMBOL

Figure 1

ness; an opening to the "you" is still present. On the lower left side we can make out fragmentary trees that may have been left over from the first picture. The painter's fear of being destroyed is apparent. On the one hand, the picture is centrifugal, while, on the other, there is a pull toward the lower left corner. It conveys the impression of a tunnel, a passage, a birth canal, which brings up the subject of rebirth and the passage from depression to light. Vital consciousness appears blackened or still black; the color of the raven is back again. But black also symbolizes beginnings, the yet undecided, and, of course, despair. This situation was recorded in Color Plate 3. The artist wrote the following:

> The girl in the black river—she's black. The river tunnel is black with a gray opening. The girl is terribly frightened that she'll be pulled back, deep into the river. But suddenly I saw the golden yellow cow look into the tunnel. I started a conversation with the girl and the cow. The cow wanted to coax the girl out, but it didn't

work. And since the cow couldn't pull her out, I thought, well, that means she can't get out.

The painter was deeply influenced by immersing herself in the symbolic process; she clearly identified with the girl and expressed the process in an imaginative form through her painting.[6] In the fourth picture the cow and the girl stand at the center. Looking at the cow is like gazing into a deep mirror; the cow's perspective transforms the entire painting. The girl is reflected in the face of the cow, in the face of the positive, maternal aspect. Thus, the despairing blackness constellated the golden cow. Or, to put it differently, the negative aspect of the archetype constellated the positive aspect as well, in an effort of self-regulation. But nothing was yet happening in the realm of experience, the woman was unaware that life can be supportive, not only threatening; beyond blackness and death there is also something that sustains life.

But then the painter remembered a magic wand from another fairy tale on which she had worked. The memory could be viewed as the influence of the positive maternal archetype. The painter remembered the transformative powers of the magic wand and suddenly saw the situation from a new perspective: as long as we live there is creative potential. This was in response to the positive maternal aspect as opposed to the negative that believes only in death. All at once, the woman knew how the girl would get out of the tunnel (cf. color plate 4).

> The cow senses that it won't work and transforms the girl into a calf. As a calf she can climb out; as a calf she has a mother of her own kind; as a girl she would have been alone.

Through the reflection the girl became a calf. Archetypal images are also effective in the sense that we see ourselves in the mirror of the archetype. In this example, although the child was carried off by the black tide, she did have a nurturing life-mother, and, in this respect, gained a sense of belonging to life. Consequently, the woman could say that the girl was no longer alone. The girl was transformed, so to speak, by being seen. A very intimate symbiosis was initiated on a symbolic level.

The painter said the next picture came to her spontaneously (cf. color plate 5). The cow is nursing the calf and licking it.

> Naturally, this picture is very embarrassing to me because of regressive desires and so on. . . . I am completely surprised at the last scene because, for the first time, I do not feel emotionally repulsed and disgusted by identifying with the drinking calf. Instead there is a very pleasant feeling. I feel warmth and skin around my nose. The fact that the girl has made her way out of the tunnel is far more important than the feeling of shame.

In this picture, the horizon has moved up considerably, there is a lot more earth, a lot more world in which to live. The birth canal is still evident. What is illustrated here is a symbiosis on an archetypal level. While the painter could now emotionally experience life as nurturing and protective, she was still ashamed of these regressive tendencies, and this was because she identified with the calf and apparently identified me with the cow.

The symbolic processes initiated in a therapeutic environment can continue to evoke transference/countertransference situations outside therapy. Transference and countertransference are even more striking when symbolic processes are perceived, experienced, and represented during the course of therapy. Although the representation of symbolic processes sometimes obscures the developing relationship, the two are never observed in isolation from each other.

When we work on symbolic processes, there are some attitudes that empower, and others that inhibit. Conscious defense mechanisms have an effect on the symbolic process. Symbolic processes move from an indefinite plane to the definite, and from chaos to significance, but they are also influenced by the relevant defense mechanisms. There are relapses to levels we thought we had already overcome.

This was clearly illustrated by another very dark picture (fig. 2). The only contrast to the blackness is provided by

Figure 2

the little yellow calf emerging from the black woman and the yellow mother cow peering through the narrow opening to the right. Perhaps the dark mother is constellated again because of our criticism of the previous picture, in which we recognized the woman's vacillation between the plane of personal transference, where she identified me with the cow, and the plane of symbolic transference. This kind of symbiosis, which is illustrated and expressed on the archetypal plane of vision, can lead us to accept desires for closeness and affection in a preverbal atmosphere, without one person being exploited or another feeling ashamed. However, if we realize that a personal transference is taking place, or that the archetypal image is being transferred onto a person, and that we have thus allowed ourselves to become dependent on a person, we activate every reaction available to us. This is why the painter felt ashamed; she had laid bare her desire to realize herself in this positive situation, and declared her aspirations to be inappropriate. But shame always implies deep insecurity. We treat our-

ASPECTS OF THE SYMBOL

Figure 3

selves the way a mother who wants us to be ashamed would treat us. This is one possible explanation of the black figure's reappearance.

The other possibility is that a counter-constellation had to take shape because the positive maternal archetype had been emphasized so much in the previous paintings. The archetypal mother can never be revealed with only her bright aspect. If life is not to be illusionary and depressive, both light and dark sides of the archetype have to come together.

The picture represented an attempt to allow the dark woman to give birth to the little calf. It was a step backward to ensure that something new had truly been created. The calf, as symbol for new and positive potential, was meant to defy the painter's black thoughts and feelings.

At first, however, as shown in Figure 3, this failed entirely. At the lower left, the black woman is sucked up into a vortex. The yellow has completely disappeared. The entire picture is black and conveys a backward pull. But still there is a counter-current pulling her toward the opening of the tunnel or birth canal. Although the opening has contracted, its presence suggests that the access to the "you" still exists. The painter, meanwhile, seemed to have come under the influence of the dark, devouring aspect of the maternal archetype; she was in despair and very depressed.

In her next picture (cf. color plate 6), it is clear that out of the darkness a birth has taken place. Dark and light aspects are experienced together. The black woman has stepped out onto the meadow; we can relate to her. The little calf looks curiously at the cow, and the cow, in turn, relates to the black woman. The painter explained that because the cow did not pay attention to the little calf, it had to leave. The entire forsaken-and-alone complex was identified with the calf, which in my opinion did not look forsaken at all, but rather bold. It is obvious that the subject of separation anxiety will be dealt with further. Moreover, this picture reasserts that a double birth has taken place: First, the little calf was born out of the light, but it was also born out of the darkness. This indicates that the maternal archetype was experienced both in its light and its dark aspects, and that, despite the dark aspect, life is possible. A first phase of the separation anxiety, with which we are familiar from the separation–individuation phase in children (sixth to thirty-sixth month[7]), has been reached; a first step toward separation has been taken—a step toward autonomy without danger of destruction. The subject "separation" is still present and will have to be dealt with further.

At this point in the creation of the picture series (the series had taken three months to paint), the woman asked to discuss it with me, because she felt an important symbolization process was unfolding.

This example demonstrated that symbols are rarely made accessible to consciousness in a single creative act. Symbols are usually brought to our conscious awareness through symbolic processes. The important thing is to experience these processes, shape them, and, finally, interpret them.

Each picture symbolized an aspect of development. Defense mechanisms, as well as situations of relationship and transference, played an essential part.

In this woman's experience, the pictures she created, the manifest as it were, also represented the thing itself in a mysterious relationship to life's hidden, supportive potentials that cannot be fully understood, but can be experienced.

SYMBOLS AND THE GOAL OF THERAPY

When we recognize symbols in a therapeutic process, we feel more alive, more emotional. A confrontation takes place between consciousness and the unconscious.

Not only our current difficulties, but also our unique potentials in life and development become visible in the symbol. Indeed, within difficulties lie the potentials of development.

Symbols communicate inhibitions; they often evoke memories repressed in earlier life. At the same time they address a motif that points to the future. The symbol, as the focal point of psychic development, is the foundation of creative development in a therapeutic process. The process of individuation can be experienced and recognized in symbols.

The basic assumption of Jungian psychology is that the psyche, a self-regulating system, has an inherent tendency to develop, to be in motion. The goal of Jungian therapy is based on the idea of development. In 1929, Jung formulated this idea in an essay as follows:

> My aim is to bring about a psychic state in which my patient begins to experiment with his own nature—a state of fluidity, change, and growth where nothing is eternally fixed and hopelessly petrified.[8]

This utopian goal illustrates what the aim of therapy should be: that people are no longer fixated; that they become flexible; that they learn to accept many possible influences in their lives. As an ideal, I believe the goal formulated above by Jung is still very inspiring. But an equally essential goal in therapy should be to learn to deal with "dry spells," to endure stagnation until it truly becomes something new, and to endure tension without counting on the promise of success.

Jung's optimistic formulation of his aim in therapy can be explained as the euphoria of a pioneer. It is a bit harder for those who follow. We have become more practical, and perhaps more modest. But in therapy, our aim is still to have direction, to cope with periods of stagnation, and to deal creatively with our lives. Above all, we aim to accept ourselves as developing beings, with all the rough edges that define us as individuals. The goal, as contained in Jung's definition, is to take on the risk of the self, to risk being ourselves. Fromm phrases the idea forcefully when he says that there are people who have not yet been born, and that you have to be born before you can die.[9] According to Fromm, we are born through creativity.

The creative development that leads to the therapeutic goal becomes visible in the symbol, and is communicated to consciousness by the symbol. In the essay "The Transcendent Function" (1916)[10] Jung wrote extensively about the formation of symbols. He described how conscious and unconscious tendencies can confront each other and be revealed in a symbol acting as a third factor; the opposing positions of consciousness and the unconscious are bridged by the symbol. Jung explained the energy of the process according to the concepts of depth psychology: when opposites collide, or conscious and unconscious intentions oppose one another, psychic dynamics come to a standstill. The psychic energy activates an image in the unconscious that unites both positions. The image is projected onto the present life and at the same time reveals which tendencies are opposed. Usually, we experience opposing tendencies as tension.

The way Jung described the formation of symbols in 1916, particularly as far as the incubation phase is concerned, is basically how we define the creative process today. In the creative process, incubation is the second phase. In the first phase, we attempt in vain to solve problems with old methods. We gather considerable information in hope of finding a solution. At some point we give up, because we know that our approach will not lead to the goal. The incubation phase begins. We lose concentration, tension. Conscious concentration is replaced by the activated unconscious while in our conscious mind we feel frustrated, anxious, dissatisfied. We indulge in amassed fantasies and remember dreams. The same incubation phase occurs when we must make small decisions. Suddenly we are indecisive; we feel frustrated, fed up; our self-esteem is considerably diminished. Everyday language has several idioms for the incubation phase, such as, "I'm mulling it over," or, "It's percolating, but I feel so undecided, so unproductive." And then, all at once, we know what to do.

In the creative process, the incubation phase is usually followed by a phase of recognition and inspiration. This inspiration may very well become accessible to consciousness in the form of a symbol.

The definition of the creative process[11] corresponds to Jung's 1916 definition of the process of symbolization. Basically, Jung's idea is that by working with symbols in multiple creative acts we finally become ourselves.

Processes of change within the psyche's self-regulating system[12] effect a transformation of the ego complex and of experience without causing us to lose our original identity. These processes are presented to consciousness through symbols and the formation of symbols. It would be wrong to consider only the moment when symbols first appear to be of importance in these processes. Though both the symbolic process and the creative process can be recognized in the first flash of a new idea, or in the experience of a new vital consciousness, they are essentially preceded by a long period of insecurity, frustration, and difficult conscious conflicts. Jung's observation that the psyche is a self-regulating system may not be true in the exclusive sense as he defines it. As long as the ego complex is sufficiently coherent, the psyche seems to function as a self-regulating system. I will deal with this subject in depth in the chapter "Aspects of the Ego Complex."

Aspects of the Complex

CHAPTER THREE

SYMBOLS ARE FOCAL POINTS of human development. They contain existential themes in condensed form, and they address themes of development, which are inevitably accompanied by inhibitions. This becomes clear when we consider that symbols represent complexes. Jung says complexes develop their own unique fantasy life. In sleep, fantasy appears as a dream, but even while awake we continue to dream beneath the threshold of consciousness "especially when under the influence of repressed or other unconscious complexes."[1]

As early as 1916 Jung had referred to content characterized by a common emotional tone as the starting point of imagination, fantasy, and image sequences, and therefore the starting point of symbolization. Complexes are energy centers clustered around an emotionally charged core of meaning, presumably called forth by the individual's painful collision with a demand or an occurrence in the environment with which he or she cannot cope. The complex determines the interpretation of each similar event and thus intensifies it. The mood and emotion that express this complex are preserved and even magnified.[2] Complexes represent those areas in an individual that are susceptible to crisis. They are, however, active as energy centers and are transmitted by emotions. They make up the greater portion of psychic life. Much within complexes hinders continued personal development of the individual, yet herein also lie the seeds of new life.[3] These creative potentials are revealed when we accept the complexes and allow them to emerge in symbols. Each of us has complexes. They are the expression of life and the problems inherent to life. They make up our inescapable psychic disposition. Therefore, symbols express complexes and at the same time can be used to work them out. Complexes, of themselves, are not visible. The corresponding emotion can be experienced, and, within the sphere of complexes, stereotypical behavior patterns can be observed. Complexes become visible in symbols through fantasy, for wherever there are emotions there are also images. One might say that complexes express their fantasies in symbols.[4]

In summary, the complex[5] may be explained as follows: A complex (from *complexus* = inclusion, enclosure, embrace) is defined as contents of the unconscious united by the same emotion and by a mutual core of meaning (archetype). The contents are to a degree interchangeable. Every emotionally charged event becomes a complex. Complexes are brought about not only by major traumatic events, but also by the recurrence of minor events that hurt us. If the contents of the unconscious are addressed on the level of emotion or meaning, their unconscious connections, along with their corresponding emotion from previous life experience and the resulting unadjusted stereotypical behavior, are activated (constellated) in their entirety. This process functions autonomously as long as the complex is unconscious. The greater the emotion and the expanse of association, the stronger the complex, the more the other forces are pushed aside or repressed. The strength of a complex can be determined by the word association test, but only in relation to those complexes a person reveals in the experiment. If the constellating complexes are not made conscious, they surface as projections. If the ego succeeds in making contact with a complex, and at the same time experiences and transforms the emerging images and fantasies, the energy inherent in a complex can vitalize the entire person. Since we experience emotion physically, and emotion is essential to complexes, we can also experience complexes physically.

Complex theory closely resembles the theory of COEX systems as described by Stanislav Grof.[6] COEX systems are "systems of condensed experience." These COEX systems have to do with specific constellations of memories from condensed experiences and fantasies arranged around a similar central theme, and charged with a strong emotion of the same quality. They influence the way in which we perceive the world, our feelings, and the formation of ideas, but they also influence our somatic processes.

Today, everyone knows we have complexes, and complexes in the realm of self-worth are the most tormenting. Self-worth is the emotion central to the ego complex. Consequently, the inferiority complex has become immensely popular. To be more precise, we ought to say that we have a complex related to self-worth, since inferiority complexes are always accompanied by superiority complexes.

Therefore, we cannot solely refer to complexes as contents of the unconscious, but must also take into account that Jung defined the ego itself as a complex, and that the ego complex is actually the central complex. In the association experiment we can bring out the landscape of a person's complex in its relation to the ego complex.

COMPLEX EXPERIENCE

Theoretically, complexes are to be viewed as the abstract structure of the unconscious. They are highly effective psychic components in the way we experience the world. How do we experience our complexes?

I would like to illustrate the typical complex experience as a reaction to being ignored. Some people, when ignored, react with a complex. They define being ignored in negative terms only and cannot comprehend that it is sometimes pleasant to be ignored. Jung says of the complex: "It obviously arises from the clash between a demand of adaptation and the individual's constitutional inability to meet the challenge."[7] Basically, only the person who raises a child can demand that it adapt. We can assume that the difficult patterns of relationship from our childhood and later life, including related emotions and stereotypical behavior, are illustrated by complexes. Within the complex of being ignored dwells the ignored child and its experience with those who raised it and who overlooked its requirements. When we examine the archetypical core of this complex, we discover a victim–aggressor theme. It is as if the ignored child were the victim, and somewhere someone—the aggressor—is ignoring the child. However, I am not referring to the victim–aggressor complex, because many other possible subjects can be addressed in this context. I would rather be precise and call this complex "being ignored."

A person with a complex related to being ignored worries constantly that he or she might once again be ignored. Their entire life is then viewed in the sense of "Am I being ignored?" Life can also be questioned from entirely different complex constellations, such as, "Am I being challenged? Am I not being challenged?" It could also be viewed in the sense of "undeserved lucky coincidences." It is fascinating to consider which and how many perspectives we normally apply to our lives. Are there variations, or are our personality and situation perhaps defined by one complex constellation providing us with only one perspective on life?

In addition to mistrust, being ignored causes the projection based on the attitude, "For the most part people purposely ignore me." Thus, because we have plainly suggested it to others, this form of transference of an early childhood situation (that is, a projection) can effect a greater likelihood of being ignored.

Individuals with this complex develop an outspoken sensitivity for situations of being ignored, not only in terms of themselves, but also in terms of others. They know when people are being ignored, and can write excellent dissertations on the subject. Complexes guide our interests and often provide us with the energy to deal with these themes. Sensitivity to everyday situations can lead to political activity induced by the urge to remedy a neglected area on a collective level. The fact that political activity also has to do with our personal complex constellation does not detract from its collective legitimacy.

So far, I have described the effect of an important complex that is present, though it has not been specifically approached or constellated. However, a complex can also be approached, or constellated, specifically—that is, internally, through a dream or a fantasy, and externally, when we confront a person onto whom we can easily project our own complexes, or when we come into a situation where the same life theme, and thereby the same old injury, are activated. In the case of the complex related to being ignored, this means that the person with this particular complex imprint is actually ignored or feels ignored. The person is then seized by a strong emotion, either anger or fear; it can also be a specific feeling, perhaps a combination of various emotions experienced in the defining situation. The affect that provided the emotional basis for the complex is reexperienced with tremendous intensity once the complex is constellated. Along with these emotions, we are bombarded by many memories; either vague, in the sense of "This always happens to me," or, more precisely, the same situations are activated that had originally called forth the emotion now experienced. This brings us to the subject of the repetition-compulsion, which also has to do with constellations of ever-returning complexes. The basic emotion —usually anger and fear connected with the feeling of insult, and the shame that the same insult is repeated and cannot be avoided—effects stereotypical behavior, or stereotypical defense mechanisms. These can also be construed as coping mechanisms, or functions that the ego employs when distressed. In this way the complex is not dealt with, but suppressed.

If a complex is touched upon, our emotional reaction is

exaggerated. We overreact, because, as long as we are unconscious of the complex, we are not reacting only to the current situation, but to all similar situations experienced within our lifetime. When couples argue they sometimes say, "You and your principles!" Of course this can mean that someone thinks in terms of principle and method, but it usually means: "You're not even reacting emotionally to what's happening, it's more as though you're reacting to your previous experiences."

When we know about complexes, we can understand that, though they may be triggered by a situation, the emotion that erupts is also directed at those who are close to us. The intensity of the emotion is a compromise between the intensity of the complex and the available defense mechanisms. In states of great excitation we cannot say that we have complexes; at that point the complexes have us, or dominate us.[8] In this condition we feel trapped and at the mercy of inner activities we cannot influence. Usually such complex constellations end up as a feeling of shame that we have lost control, that we are far less autonomous than we believed ourselves to be.

Because this complex constellation expressly subdues our free will, it is impossible to control such situations at will. The greater the excitement and the emotional intensity connected with the complex, the more our free will is diminished.

The way to confront complexes is neither by defense nor control; the idea is rather to let the complexes emerge in fantasy, to recognize and understand their role in patterns of relationship, and, finally, by working with symbols, integrate them into consciousness.

If we are sufficiently aware of our complex structure, we can anticipate complex reactions to certain situations. This conscious expectation of complexes can greatly facilitate matters. We carefully register how we react to a situation that, for instance, stimulates the authority complex. The next time the situation arises, we are able to say, "Now my body will probably react like this or that, now I will probably feel that anxiety. . . ." Optimally, this "anticipation" of the complex occurs together with making it conscious.

DEFINITIONS OF THE COMPLEX

Jung discovered complexes when he was working with the word association test, which is based on the fundamental principle that people are at all times capable of connecting ideas, and that one idea easily calls another to consciousness. Basically, a chain of associations can be initiated from any given word, and linguistically certain associations are more strongly linked than others. In the association experiment, a word is named and the subject is asked to respond as quickly as possible with a word that comes to his or her mind. Originally, this was a means to study reaction speed and reaction quality.

Jung then turned his attention to those reactions that did not follow smoothly, such as when a person did not immediately respond with another word, but gesticulated, laughed, or repeated the word. On closer inquiry, it was determined that the stimulus, the provoking word, had addressed a problematic experience, a complex.

The word association test[9] is a diagnostic possibility to determine how the complex landscape is related to the ego complex. It demonstrates that complexes are intermeshed and are in direct proportion to the ego complex. What can be worked out in experimental conditions can be experienced in everyday life. We all know that certain words provoke a reaction. Words can remind us of complex areas, words can cause us to react with a complex. Part of the complex reaction is that the emotion associated with the complex is initially experienced and later surfaces in physical phenomena or in body language such as defensive gestures, or making faces. For Jung, complexes are therefore "the *living units of the unconscious psyche*, and it is only through them [the complexes, V.K.] that we are able to deduce its existence and constitution." [Emphasis added.][10] In another passage he speaks of complexes as "focal points or nodal points of psychic life which we would not wish to do without; indeed, they should not be lacking, for otherwise psychic activity would come to a standstill. They point to the unresolved problems in the individual, the places where he has suffered defeat, at least for the time being, and where there is something he cannot evade or overcome—his weak spots in every sense of the word."[11] In this passage Jung also postulates that complexes "arise from the clash between a demand of adaptation and the individual's constitutional inability to meet the challenge."[12] He adds that the first complex is called forth by the conflict with parents; this is the parental complex.

In *Psychogenesis of Mental Disease*, Jung describes how every emotionally charged event becomes a complex.

> If it [the event] does not encounter a related and already existing complex and is only of momentary significance, it gradually sinks with decreasing feeling-tone into the latent mass of memories, where it remains until a related impression reproduces it again. But if it encounters an already existing complex, it reinforces it and helps it to gain the upper hand for a while.[13]

Jung is describing findings which are also formulated by theories of learning and upon which behavioral therapy is based. This theoretical knowledge plays an important part in the way we deal with complexes; it plays a role in all therapy, even when it is not called behavioral therapy.

In dreams, complexes appear in personified form[14] and, according to Jung, the complex plays an important part in understanding neurosis. He believes every neurosis contains a complex distinguished from other complexes in that it is highly charged and therefore forcibly influences the ego complex.[15]

This also refers to Jung's hypothesis that complexes are splinter psyches.[16] In "A Psychological Theory of Types" Jung formulates the idea somewhat less specifically:

ASPECTS OF THE COMPLEX 39

> Judging by everything we know about them, they [complexes] are *psychic entities which are outside the control of the conscious mind.* They have been split off from consciousness and lead a separate existence in the dark realm of the unconscious, being at all times ready to hinder or reinforce the conscious functioning.[17]

And this "small, isolated psyche," in turn, develops a fantasy life.

> In sleep, fantasy takes the form of dreams. But in waking life, too, we continue to dream beneath the threshold of consciousness, especially when under the influence of repressed or other unconscious complexes.[18]

This passage formulates the direct connection to symbols. However, it seems essential that we take this aspect of partial psyches or splinter psyches into account as well, even if it is not clear why something was split off. Figuratively speaking, it is equally possible that something has not been integrated with the ego complex. Since we may not necessarily be dealing with splinter psyches, but rather with psychic contents that are not yet related to the ego complex, it is indicated that, aside from consisting of repressed factors, a complex also consists of unconscious factors that may not yet be conscious. There is such a thing as age-related complexes. In mid-life (from age 40 to 55), death is experienced as a complex, possibly age and death together. People who at one time related calmly to aging and inevitable death, and who did not avoid encounters with these existential situations, suddenly react with exaggerated anxieties and depression. Not until this point can the complex be experienced existentially, and must be made conscious.

Throughout our lives, complexes can emerge in connection with the themes of development.

The idea of the splinter psyche seems important since we frequently speak of fragmentation of the ego complex, and of the ego complex losing its coherence, or of the individual losing his or her sense of identity and believing he or she is influenced by various psychic "entities." This experience could be explained by, or at least be connected to, Jung's premise that completely unconscious complexes often behave like partial psyches. The object is to relate unconscious complexes to consciousness, especially since the energy revealed in the emotional disturbance, the energy that constitutes the complex, is according to Jung precisely the energy that the suffering person needs for continued development. This points to yet another indication of the psyche's self-regulating quality—that is, as long as the disturbance is not repressed, it contains the possible cure.

However, in order to come into contact with the complexes, or with the disturbance, we must consider fantasy, dreams, patterns of relationship, and symbols in general. Since complexes can be worked out in fantasy we have an opportunity to transform them from inhibiting forces to encouraging forces. This is what happens in symbolization. In this respect, symbols are used to work out complexes. This is why dreams, images, and the realm of imagination[19] play such an important part in Jungian therapy. In practical terms, this means that we concentrate on emotions and inquire which fantasies and images are connected to them. The images can then be painted, or dealt with through imagination, or perhaps through the technique of active imagination. The important thing is that the symbol is perceived, developed, and then interpreted.

Example for the formation of symbols in confrontation with a father complex: a series of paintings by a forty-one-year-old woman. —The woman was married and had three children aged four to eight. She suffered from a very dominant father complex.

We must remember that complexes are intermeshed; this is why I speak of complex landscapes in relation to the word association test.

Since father and mother complexes are distinguished from the parental complex, we have both a father complex and a mother complex. These complexes have an inner connection. For instance, in an individual with a positive mother complex, indicative of the mother's supportive influence, a father complex will not have the same destructive effect it might have in a person whose mother complex does not display a supportive function. Father and mother complexes should be defined more clearly. Though they do have typical components, they are colored by unique encounters with the actual father and father figures, and with the actual mother and mother figures.

In her drawing, the analysand symbolized her father complex as a rooster (cf. color plate 7). She said, "Inwardly, I always retreat when father comes. The rooster still has power over me after this long conflict." She was under the impression that, although she had been dealing with her father complex all her life, she was still under his power.

As a child, the woman had been sexually abused by her father. The drawing of him as a rooster in an imposing stance displayed a sexual behavior, or a sexual fantasy, that seemed to be associated with great tension, particularly because the purple, in itself a color of tension, was in striking contrast with the orange, a color indicating erotic excitation.[20] (Of course purple might also be a color of integration, since it combines red and blue and thus indicates the overcoming of tension. But in combination with the orange this seems highly unlikely.) Emotionally, this father complex conveyed agitated tension. It was the first time the analysand had represented her situation in this way.

Our more unconscious complexes are always associated with the ego complex. In this picture, the patient herself is represented without hands or feet, pale facing her emotionally vital father. Thus a great deal of energy and vitality are bound up with the father complex, a vitality that is clearly lacking in the ego complex. The picture corresponded with the analysand's statement that when her father was present she "retreated"; she lost her identity, as it were.

A second picture, painted at the same time, illustrated perhaps more clearly than the first what it is like when this woman's father complex is constellated (cf. color plate 8). The father's head fills the right side of the picture. Should the analysand wish to move toward the right, toward the realization of life,[21] there is no way to bypass the thoughts, fantasies, and ideas that make up her father complex. Obviously, her ego feels small; its whole body is tied up. Again, there are no hands or feet, there is no opportunity to take hold of anything, no way to secure a real position in the world. With this picture the analysand is saying that when her father complex is constellated she is virtually incapable of movement; she feels defenseless, raped, and incredibly small.

The purple head again conveys tension; this, and the black, aggressive bird over his eye give the impression that her father complex is connected with considerable aggression and melancholy, an aggression that turns against the analysand.

The analysand's ego, helpless and submissive, allows us to deduce how it was influenced by the inhibitive factor of the complex. When the father complex was constellated—and only then—her ego felt weak, helpless and submissive. But complexes are not constellated at all times. In this woman's case, the father complex became constellated whenever her actual father, who at this point was a very old man, came to have coffee with her and her family. She still saw him as the brutal, abusive man of her childhood.

Complexes are projected, and therefore distort perception. This patient could not see the old man, who meanwhile would have been very grateful for a bit of attention, and with whom she might even have been able to discuss the sexual abuse. Instead she saw the father who threatened and constrained her so very much. The father image could also constellate when she dreamt about him. But as long as the complex was not addressed—either outwardly by someone else's fatherly behavior, or inwardly—she could be content as a mother and a woman. Though complexes generally determine our interests and fears, they are experienced as emotionally inhibiting or liberating only when constellated. When her father complex was constellated, the whole pattern of the relationship between the father and the childish ego was transferred. Whenever the analysand transferred her father complex, and she transferred it particularly onto men between the ages of fifty and sixty, she felt helpless. She could not see these men as they were; instead, she saw her father, and herself as a frightened, fettered child.

It is important to remember that in psychotherapy we work with transference, which distorts our perception of reality. The complex constellations are transferred onto the therapist, but not in the sense that the complex itself is transferred; since every complex is related to another ego, it is the relationship pattern that is transferred. Once these patterns are known, we can understand the painful confrontations with the environment that the individual suffered in childhood.

In this analysis, the relationship pattern between the restricting father and the restricted daughter was occasionally transferred onto me, as, for instance, when the analysand accused me of not allowing her any space, or when she took up so much space with her problem that I felt as if I were fettered. By addressing these emotional states of transference and countertransference, we are able to raise the complex to consciousness.

When I felt restrained in certain situations, the analysand may have been identifying with her father complex. We not only project our complexes, we can also identify with them. When her ego identified with the complex, the analysand was on the side of the aggressor. Actually, she was the victim, and her father was the aggressor, but once she identified with the male head, there was no way to get around her; anyone who dealt with her could easily assume the role of the crippled woman. The situation sometimes became quite heady.

When a person identifies with a complex, we can sense its incredible power. Whatever the persons actively involved with the complex did to the child, the individual identifying with the complex now transfers onto other persons close to him or her. Frequently, they become like the suffering child the individual once was. Herein lies the key both to an emotional understanding of that decisive event in our childhood that molded us, and to a transformation of the complex constellation.

Identification with complexes seems very important to me, because I believe it occurs far more frequently than projection. Complex identification implies that I can retain my identity by identifying with my main complex. Complex identification with a father complex seems to be particularly significant. Frequently, people seek therapy and complain of great misery, though the initial impression is that they function quite well in the world. It is not that they have a well-structured ego complex, but because they identify with their father complex. Consequently, they are able to master everything paternal that has to be mastered in daily life. These people usually pass unnoticed in the workaday world. Yet, there is this great emptiness; they are not living their own identity, they are living a complex-identity.

Complexes are transferred; a father complex is usually transferred onto everything paternal, and is therefore primarily transferred onto male partners. The analysand said of her third picture:

> It is a picture for my boyfriend, who devours so much of my energy. The crocodile is stealing my colorfulness, my playful balls are floating in gray space. The crocodile is consuming me with his inattentiveness and meanness, but, at the same time, the situation makes me creative. (Cf. color plate 9)

The analysand's interpretation was that the crocodile was devouring her colorfulness, which was her emotional distinction, her joy of life, and her vital ability to work. But the picture could be viewed the other way around; perhaps the crocodile was contributing colorfulness.

When constellated, a complex influences the interpretation of all other factors. Since the analysand felt her father complex to be devouring, she was, for the time being, incapable of accepting a different perspective. From an outside viewpoint, it was fully conceivable that the crocodile represented an aggressive, devouring aspect within her, which could release much vitality if she were to acknowledge it rather than project it outward.

The fourth picture was at first surprising, because the father complex is no longer quite as evident (cf. color plate 10). The analysand said: "I've drawn a magic circle around myself." This picture suggests that we are always influenced by more than one complex and are able to experience our identity when the most important activated complexes are not dominant. In any case, the picture represents a completely different identity than the one we had seen so far. This is very important, for our identity has different images. This particular identity, however, had to be protected by a magic circle. The circle was on a purple background. The analysand began to realize that the color purple was the personal coloration of her father complex. The picture conveyed spontaneous joy of physicality, of being aware of oneself. The analysand said, "Neither the crocodile, the raven, my father in the iceberg, nor the face can reach me or destroy me." The picture did give this impression. She concluded, "I'm developing the same powers as the crocodile, the raven, and the father in the iceberg. Those are incredible powers." This meant that she had withdrawn the complex factors from the projection; instead of accusing her father and mother, she realized that her complexes were a part of herself. Complexes are partial psyches within ourselves. Even if they arise out of collisions with people who are close to us, they pertain to our own selves. If we can accept this, we are able to establish contact with the complex, as, I believe, the picture shows. Though she was within the magic circle, the woman was in touch with the crocodile, the father, and the raven. She was in touch with the factors that made up her father complex; consequently, she could understand that all the energy connected with her father complex was in fact her own energy.

We should give this idea more credence. We complain about our highly charged complexes, but we are unaware that they can enrich our lives enormously, that they contain the energy we need to make our lives more colorful, providing we are able to bring them into touch with the ego complex. This is one reason why interpretation on a subjective level is so useful: it is a form of interpretation wherein everything that appears in image, symbol, or dream is seen as a part of one's personality. In this respect, we must accept a certain responsibility for ourselves. But we also get a sense that energies are present that could invigorate us.

In the next picture, the father complex once again appears, but in a changed form (cf. color plate 11). There is still something diabolical about it, and the snakes are still hissing at her. But the ego has gained definition; though it still has no feet, there is at least a suggestion of hands and a more detailed face. Another new element is the somewhat ghostly blue face with striking red lips peering from behind the curtain, which the painter identified with her mother's face. The gray curtain covering the image of her mother is slightly pulled aside. In this picture, with its intense sexual components, the particular configuration of the father complex again reminds us of incestuous childhood situations. Emotionally, much is remembered, and anger toward her mother—who somewhere in the background must have been aware of what was going on—was re-experienced.

In my opinion, these pictures illustrate how the analysand's complex has changed in relation to her ego-complex; slowly it took on a new form and became embedded in a larger life context. Aside from a greater awareness of the constraints of patriarchal and exploitative situations, her pictures still primarily conveyed the inhibiting aspect, and hardly that of support and reinforcement.

The active figures in dreams represent complexes. To illustrate this, I would like to add a few of this analysand's dreams, which she dreamt during the same period in which she was drawing the pictures.

> *Dream 1*: Father is racing along on the highway. I am sitting next to him, powerless and at his mercy. I cry, banging with my fists. I have one of my childish crying fits. I hurt my hands because I am banging them so hard. I collapse.
> *Dream 2*: Father wants to eat cake at my house. I won't give him any, and he gets incredibly angry. I give in.

Dream 3: A fatherly judge condemns me to death by drowning. A hope flashes through my mind: maybe I can swim away. But I resign myself once more. Surely, the judge will tie a stone to me so that I won't be able to swim.

The first dream did not suggest how to deal with this father complex. The father complex did not emerge in an empowering fashion. Instead, the object was once again to take stock of the situation. When she was at the mercy of her father complex, the dreamer behaved as she had in childhood: she had a crying fit, she hurt herself, she wore herself out. This meant that the complex was so destructive that when she identified with it, she had to destroy herself. Apparently, there was no solution for the ego other than identifying with the attacker.

In the second dream, however, the dream father wished to contact her; he asked her for sweet food, as children usually do. Therefore, there was an opportunity, if she could only accept it, to allow the father image to change.

In the third dream, the father was transferred. Even if we are subject to a very dominant father complex, we do not always dream of our fathers. Instead, we often dream of fatherly figures. In this case, the analysand dreamt about a judge. She experienced her father as someone who judges, and in fact the father figure condemned her to death. To offset this, there arose from her unconscious a fleeting hope that she could swim away, that the water element would be her savior. This hope lasted but a moment. Then, she again felt completely under her father's spell. The judge would arrange matters so that she could not save herself. In this dream, even the tiny, fleeting hope that there was some maternal factor over which her father no longer had any influence was nonetheless immensely important.

The self-regulation of the psyche occurs in two ways. First, by allowing the complex to emerge in fantasy, the inhibitive aspect can become empowering, mainly because the archetype is at the root of the complex. The second self-regulating factor is that a counter-reaction can occur within the complex landscape; fear, for instance, can become hope. If someone has a destructive father complex, as in the case of this patient, it would of course be appropriate for images of the positive mother archetype to constellate, as is usually possible in the therapeutic relationship.

COMPLEXES WITH EMPOWERING INFLUENCES

Since every emotionally charged experience becomes a complex, joyous experiences must also become complexes. Joy can be experienced as a mood, a feeling, or as an affect. We tend to neglect those emotions that give us wings and make us more alive. Instead, we always talk about anxiety, anger, and grief, even though there are situations that call forth joy instead of fear; and this, too, can be complex related.

Example for the emergence of a joyous complex. —A thirty-year-old man, with whom I was conducting a word association test, showed a strange reaction to the stimulus word *green*. First, his whole face lit up, then he slapped his thigh—this protracted the reaction time—then, radiant, he said, "yellow." His reaction was by no means automatic; the expressions he displayed by lighting up, laughing, and gesticulating were signs of a complex. The man had a green complex that displayed five complex characteristics, which indicated a highly charged complex. Therefore, I asked him which associations to green constellated the complex. He radiantly told me that he could think of none. I asked again, and he repeated that he could not think of anything bad. To my remark that he did not necessarily have to think of something bad, that it could also be something nice, he said, "Yes, of course, something nice!" Then he started to ramble and told me how much he liked the first green grass of spring. He remembered that he had once run away from home as a child. He had grown up in a very protective atmosphere and was not allowed to lie on the ground because you can catch a cold, etc. When he ran away, it had been the season of the first green grass. He had lain in the green grass, rolled in it, and thought it was wonderful. He said this physical feeling reoccurred whenever he recalled the green grass. He still had an intense desire to roll in that green grass.

This was a complex imagining that did not need to be warded off; it encouraged the feeling of revivification and new life. The stereotypical behavior was present. Every spring he lay down on the newly sprouting grass. Several times a year he went into the mountains to repeat the experience.

We can encounter encouraging complexes in other ways. Occasionally, we look forward to certain events so much that we forget everything else. We think only of what we really want to do, and in our fantasy we connect the imminent, longed-for experiences with memories of how good things once were. This, too, is an effect of complexes, but it disturbs us only when experience does not come up to our expectation. Usually, these complexes tend to cheer us up, so we do not take them seriously as complexes.

Falling in love is a slightly different situation. When we are in love we are also under the influence of a complex. All the signs of a complex are present. The state of being in love affects our interpretation or reinterpretation of reality. Other complexes recede into the background. From now on, our interest is focused only on the person or the object of our love, or perhaps on love poems. Being in love stimulates the memory of love and of being in love. It strongly activates fantasy. All our previous love experiences reverberate in our current experience, cause an overreaction, and even elicit extremely stereotypical behavior patterns. When we are in love, we think everything we do is completely unique, and that no one else could ever have the same ideas. But if we read someone else's love letters, we recognize the same expressions, the same terms of endearment, similar or identical "unusual gestures of love."

It becomes clear that these are stereotypical behavior patterns, not only in a personal sense, but they are also collectively stereotypical. It is hard enough for us to find new gestures for new love in our life, and collectively it seems to be even harder. When we are in love, we run the program of being in love, which, though it is very nice, is in some way always a program.

Nonetheless, being in love is a complex that greatly inspires us. It stimulates our sense of identity and encourages us to risk more, to explore more. But it can inhibit too. When we have to take care of boring, monotonous work that requires all our attention, the complex of being in love may very well inhibit our ability to work. However, in terms of vital consciousness—and this is the real criterion—this complex tends to encourage us.

There are complexes that inhibit and complexes that encourage. This is one reality. The other is that in every complex, even if it happens to be an inhibitive complex, the inhibiting factor is at the same time encouraging and, providing we accept it, it is an incentive toward development.

Aspects of the Ego Complex

CHAPTER FOUR

A WORKED-OUT WORD ASSOCIATION TEST reveals those complexes that can currently be addressed and constellated in their relation to the ego complex.

The ego complex commands a prominent position in the complex landscape. But since complexes have essentially been defined as "psychic entities which are outside the control of the conscious mind," is it even legitimate to speak of an ego complex?[1]

Jung says that the ego complex forms the "central characteristic" of the psyche, although it is still only one among many different complexes. "The others are more often than not associated with the ego complex and in this way become conscious."[2] The ego represents "a psychic complex of a particularly solid kind."[3] In another passage, Jung says:

> The ego-complex in a normal person is the highest psychic authority. By this we mean the whole mass of ideas pertaining to the ego, which we think of as being accompanied by the powerful and ever-present feeling-tone of our own body.
>
> The feeling-tone is an affective state accompanied by somatic innervations. *The ego is the psychological expression of the firmly associated combinations of all bodily sensations.* One's own personality is therefore the firmest and strongest complex, and (good health permitting) it weathers all psychological storms. It is for this reason that the ideas that directly concern our own persons are always the most stable, and to us the most interesting; we could also express this by saying that they possess the strongest *attention-tone*.[4]

In this early definition—first published in 1907—Jung still differentiates between the ego complex and the ego. In the following passage, I will describe the ego as the accumulation of ego-functions that reflect the ego complex and other complexes. This will clarify why the body and bodily sensations are considered the basis of the ego complex. Since the ego complex is the central complex, it is logical that all of the associations that compose it, or are immediately related to personality and self-worth, are most significant to the individual.

In 1946, Jung comprehensively reviewed his definition of the ego complex:

> The ego [the ego complex], as a specific content of consciousness, is not a simple or elementary factor but a complex one which, as such, cannot be described exhaustively. Experience shows that it rests on two . . . different bases: the *somatic* and the *psychic*. . . . The somatic consists, then, of conscious and unconscious factors. The same is true of the psychic basis: on the one hand, the ego rests on the *total field of consciousness*, and on the other, on the *sum total of unconscious contents*.[5]

THE EGO COMPLEX AND THE EXPERIENCE OF IDENTITY

The associations related to the ego complex revolve around identity, the development of identity, and the correlated feeling of self-worth.

The basis of identity is a sense of vitality and, closely connected to it, of personal activity. It is a feeling of being alive, and rooted in this feeling is the potential to actively involve the ego in life, and finally to realize oneself.

Vitality, ego-activity, and self-realization are interdependent. In the course of development, ego-activity becomes increasingly self-determined and less dependent. The expanding significance of personal activity, or ego-activity,

1/2

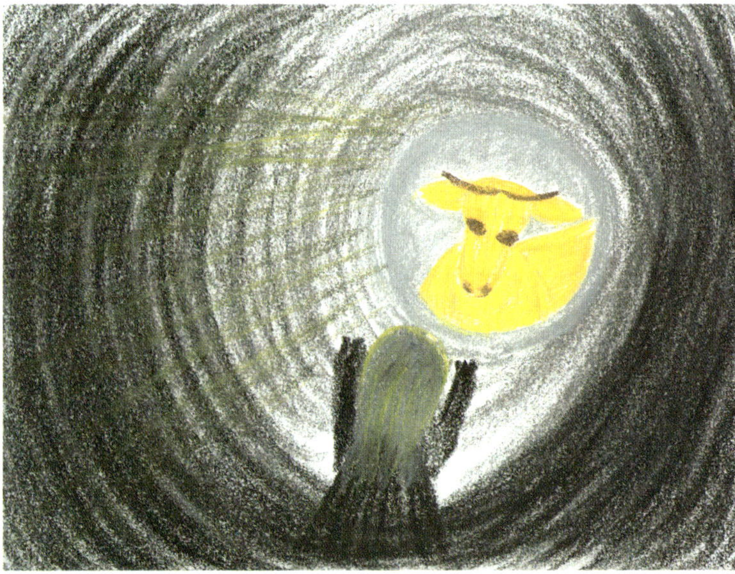

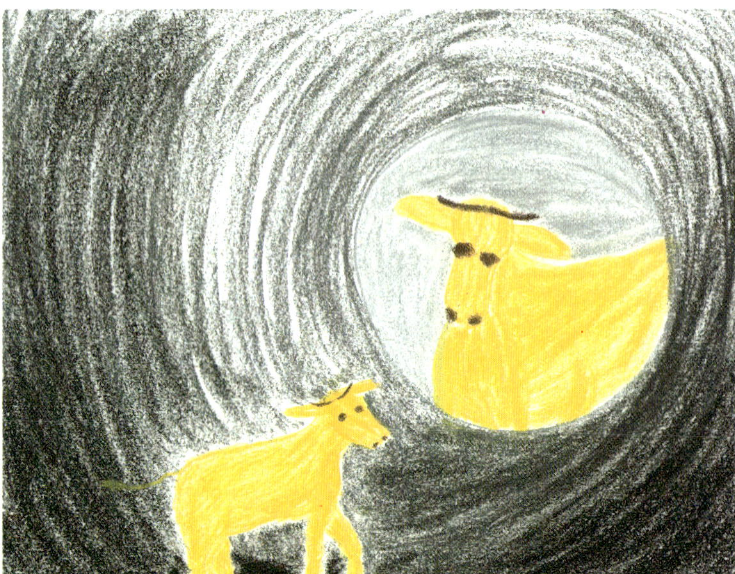

3/4

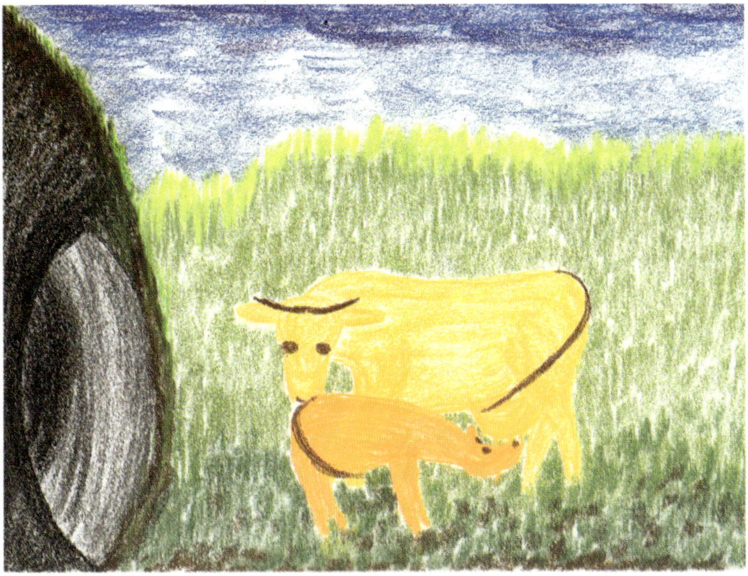

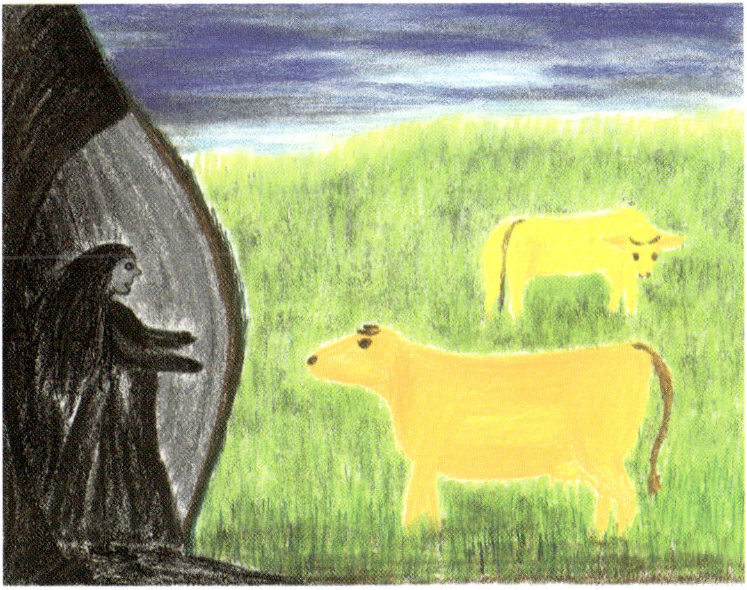

5/6

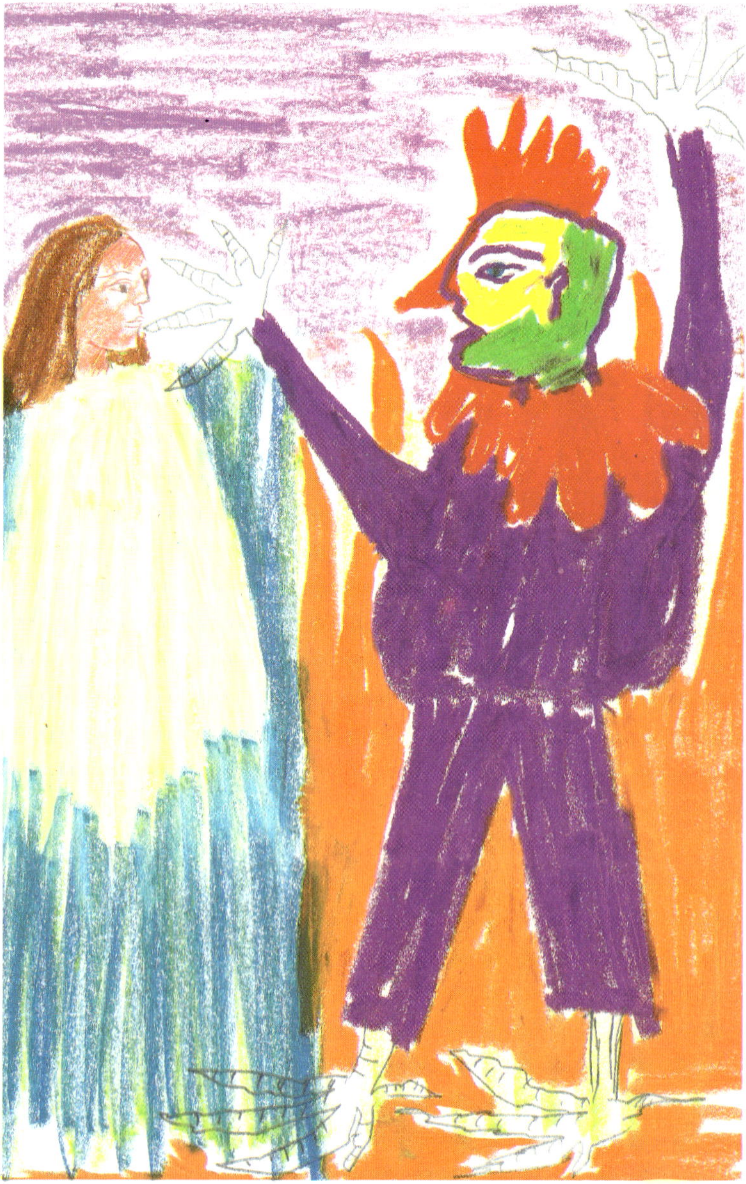

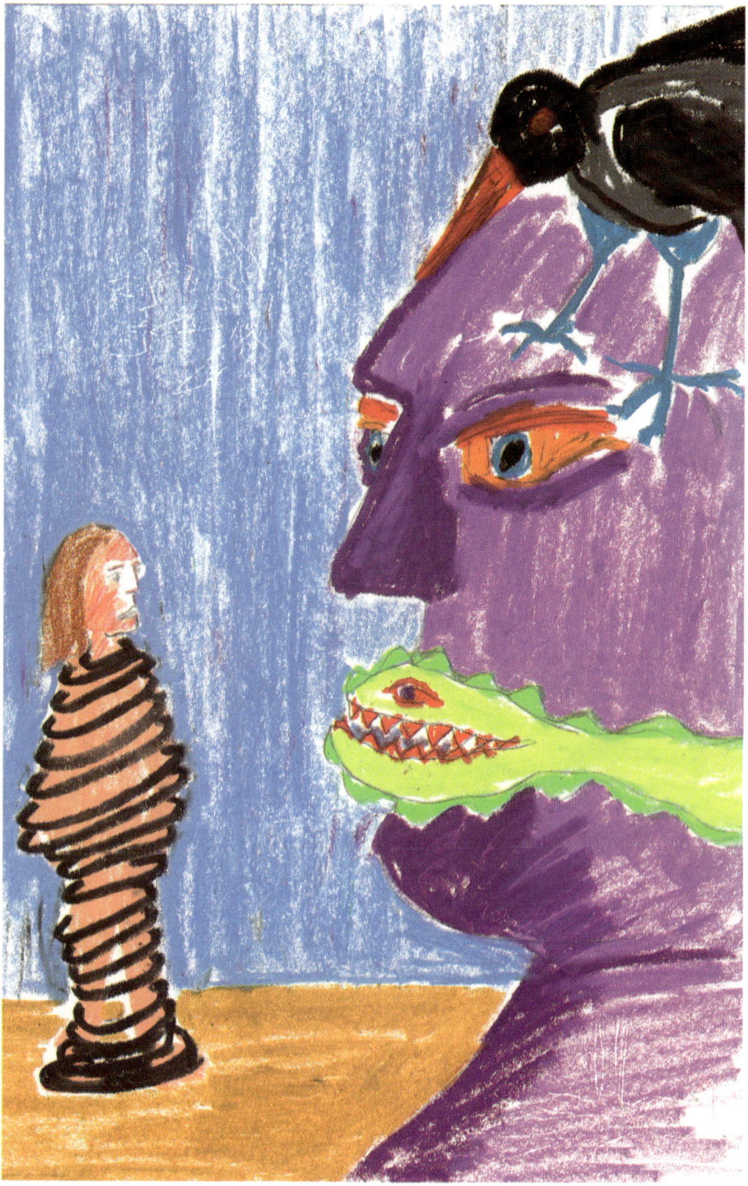

9

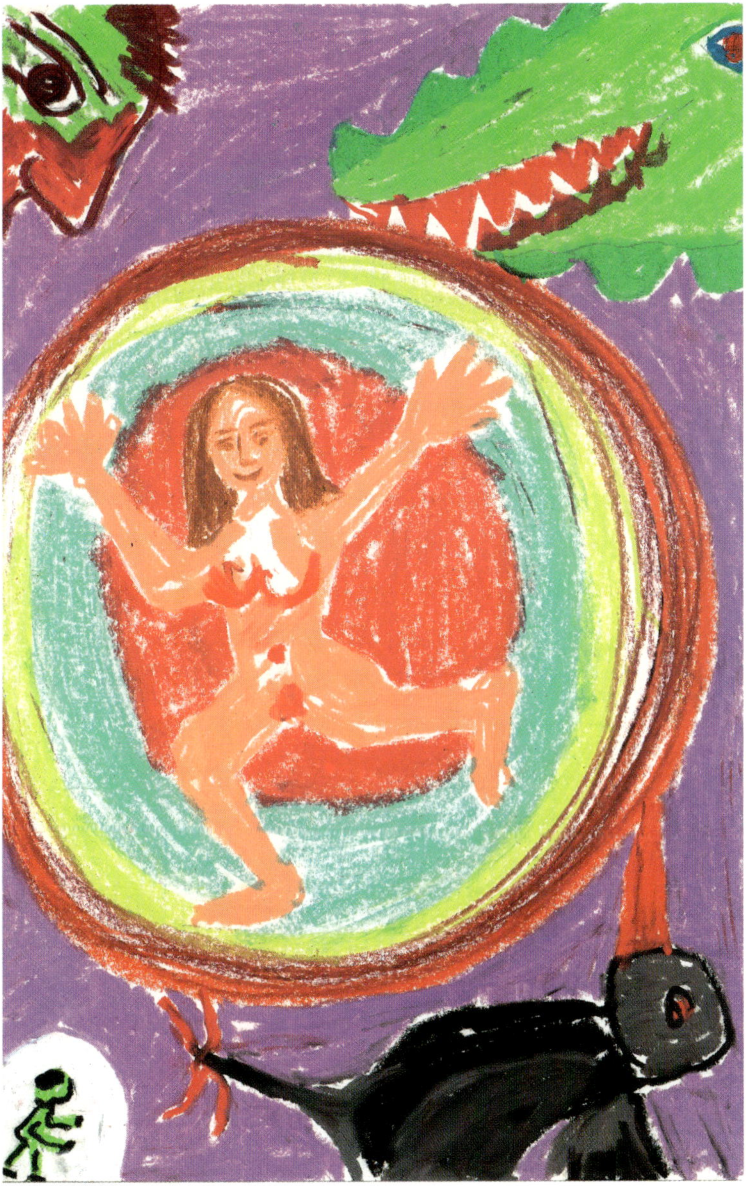

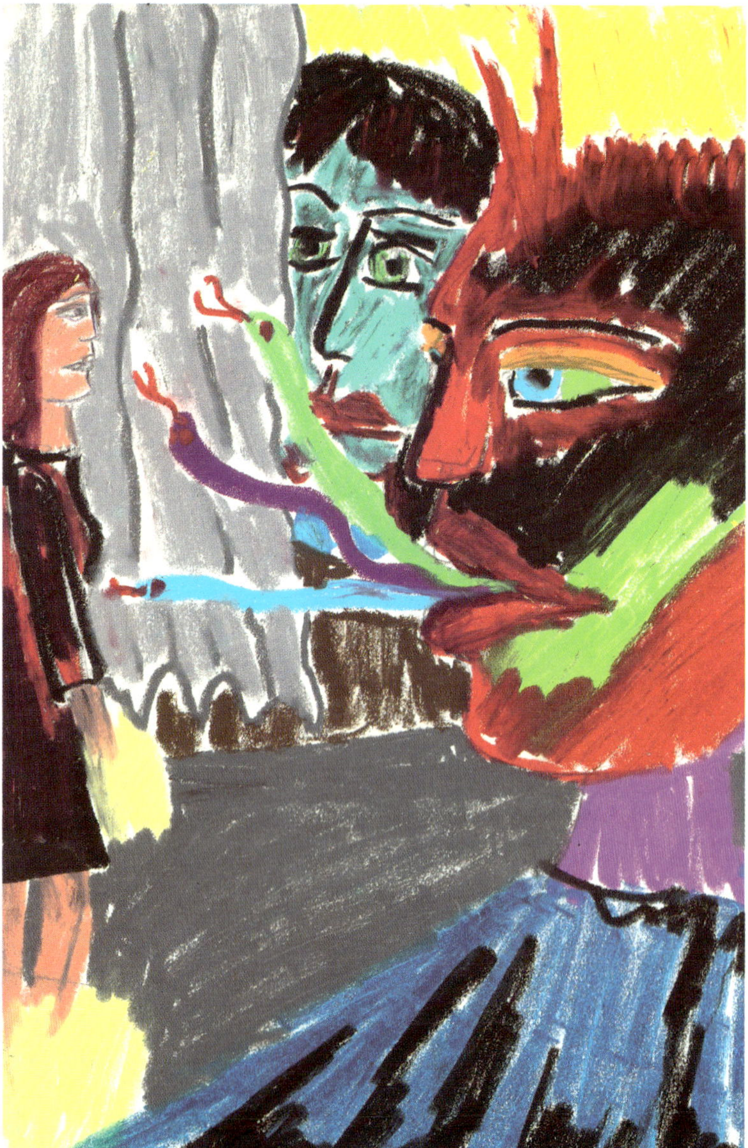

is pronounced in the development of the young child. Later, by risking personal activity and self-expression, we experience our boundaries more or less painfully; we become aware of our ego complex. The experience of identity includes the positive awareness of ourselves, the conceptions we have of ourselves, how we define ourselves, and how we confront the conceptions others have of, or project onto, us. The prerequisite for a defined ego complex is that it differentiate itself from the parental complex at the appropriate age, thereby becoming increasingly autonomous, and that we expose ourselves to relationships and experiences.

The boundaries of identity are both transient and permeable. Becoming oneself implies redefining the borders between oneself and the world, between oneself and the unconscious. Boundaries can be perceived and transversed; they are essential in any I-you relationship where the I can differentiate itself from the you. On the interior they protect us from being flooded with unconscious contents. Along with experiencing these boundaries, we must be able to rid ourselves of them. We must be able to totally identify with another person, and emotionally fuse, as we do in love and sex, and as we do when we sympathize completely with another human being.

A defined ego complex allows us to accept situations of ego loss, confident that we will be able to reorganize within our boundaries.

These definite, yet passable, boundaries imply a coherent ego complex.

A further aspect of identity is the experience of continuity, and the knowledge that throughout any change or transformation we remain developing beings. The awareness of our connection to our ancestors and descendants also contributes to a sense of continuity. If this connection becomes unimportant due to sociocultural or personal conditions, the awareness of continuity within our present lives becomes ever more central, and the question as to how we experience continuity in the development of our ego complex becomes more urgent. A lack of continuity is particularly detrimental to self-reliance.

We most often encounter continuity when experiencing emotions. Our emotions follow a biological pattern that seems to change little throughout our lives; it is the way we consciously deal with emotions that changes. In every life there is an entire palette of anxiety, anger, and joy. When, for instance, we closely examine our fits of rage, we realize they feel the same as our childhood tantrums, but we have learned to deal with them.

We experience emotions physically. Physical sensations, above all the experience of emotion, provide the basis for the ego complex and make us able to recognize continuity in our awareness of identity. Identity is interest in ourselves, in how we act, what we effect, and how it is related to our personal background. The many fantasies we have regarding ourselves are also a part of identity. Here, too, we can see the relationship to the ego complex. Since the emotion of a complex emerges in fantasy, the ego complex, as the central complex, triggers a profusion of central fantasies concerning ourselves. This should be understood as an enrichment of self-knowledge. Indeed, many fantasies revolve around what we want to be, how we want to live, and what success we desire, including all the imagined love, respect, and indulgence we wish from others. Idealized fantasies involving our self-image cause a repression of those aspects that do not agree with it; we allow them to become our "shadow," or unconscious. Other fantasies represent a less ideal self-image, and revolve around those factors that might present uncomfortable elements to our ego, or even destroy our ego. Though concealed, a very demanding ego-ideal is active here, but we no longer have the confidence to meet its requirements under our own power.

Still other fantasies do not necessarily represent ideal imaginings; they originate in those situations of our childhood that moulded our personality. For example, a thirty-five-year-old man constantly fantasized that he was second-rate; he even developed a philosophy to demonstrate why being second-rate was quite worth striving for. Yet he does extraordinarily well. After extensive analysis, a complex constellation revealed that his father wanted to be first-rate. Any son would need to limit himself to being second-rate.

The ego-ideal is a compromise between our plans for life, which are usually unconscious, but in agreement with our self, our vitality, and the fantasies others have regarding our personality and its development. The ego-ideal changes throughout our lives, just as fantasies others have about us change. At best, the ego complex can be transformed by constant confrontation between the ego-ideal and the shadow.[6] As we grow older, the ego complex separates from the parental complexes and comes into conflict with the father and mother complexes along with their collective extensions, such as authority complexes and helper complexes. The ego complex is also in conflict with demanding situations that require the realization of individual and collective values inherent to the idealized self-image. Such situations are the result of ethical demands from people who are close to us, such as parents and teachers, from collective religions, and, in later life, from our own children, who demand of the older generation the right to realize new value systems. Situations that demand the realization of values are determined in character, but not so much in content, by those persons who in our childhood prohibited and permitted. Borrowing from Freudian terminology, we could speak of the super-ego in this context, which I, however, feel belongs to the ego-ideal/shadow duality.

The experience of the autonomy inherent in the ego complex is essential to the experience of identity. We cannot become completely autonomous, but we can become more autonomous. The old dependencies remain, and new dependencies develop. In areas where we have become autonomous, i.e., where we increasingly perceive our identity as ourself, dependency is replaced by independence; we cease to be the product of the imprinting relationship with our parents. Once the ego is sufficiently emancipated from the parental complexes, which we usually project onto our parents, we can prevent the constant complex distortions that otherwise make it impossible to relate to them.

The ego complex, like every complex, is based on an archetypal core. In the Jungian sense, this is the self. Much has already been said about self-realization, self-determination, self-awareness, and self-becoming in connection with the ego complex, and finding identity. (In the Freudian tradition, what is described here as the ego complex is called the "self.") Therefore, the self is understood as the entirety of the present and future personality. It reveals our hidden goal in life through the development of the ego complex; this development is intended by the self. But becoming conscious of the ego complex is a dynamic process. Throughout life we can expect new constellations, such as described in the typical stages of developmental psychology. These are then superseded by the unique individuation process, which has to do with its very own potentials and a confrontation with those decisive situations that molded us.

Like every other complex, the ego complex is defined both by motifs of development and inhibition. The development motif is expressed in the development toward more autonomy in self-realization, self-expression, in growing self-confidence, the ability to practice self-preservation, and in accepting the risk of increasingly relating to oneself. On the other hand, the inhibition motif is recognizable in a lack of autonomy, by external dependence on social structures and concrete human relationships and internal dependence on fragmented complexes. It is often difficult to determine whether we are externally or internally dependent. Fragmented complexes are projected, and we frequently find ourselves under the impression that we are entirely governed from the outside. When we feel this way, it is certainly appropriate to determine which of our psychic difficulties are projected onto our environment, though this does not imply that we should declare the constraining structures of society to be no more than complex perceptions. They should be perceived and changed, very much as the constraining structures of our psyche.

THE EGO COMPLEX IN TERMS OF DEVELOPMENTAL PSYCHOLOGY

The self, which Jung defines as the aprioristic formative principle in an individual's development,[7] also governs the composition of the ego complex. At first, the child is unconscious of the ego complex, which gradually becomes more conscious through the experience of the physical ego—also known as the physical self—particularly when the child's reactions are perceived, accepted, and responded to by those who are close to it. In its physicality, which is the basis of the ego complex, the child attains a sense of acceptance and the right to existence. Development continues and results in the child's increasingly clear differentiation between ego and non-ego. Finally, at the completion of this stage of development, the child chooses the ego.

The stages of development in *childhood* have been described by various schools of developmental psychology.[8] The early stages of humanity and of human beings are an ideal projection surface for our fantasies about beginnings in general, the wholeness we associate with it, the subsequent separation from the whole, and the renewal of wholeness as a basic process in human life and human development. The alternating phases of separation from and re-approach to parental figures, phases of increased autonomy, and phases of security undeniably play an important part in symbiosis.[9] And yet, I feel that we often overestimate the first stage of life. Independence and the move to relate to the relevant emotions of fear, aggression, interest, joy, and love are basic motifs of the ego complex becoming conscious.

According to Jungian psychology, the self guides the

ego complex as it becomes conscious. It is a spontaneous development. The ego complex is initially expressed by physicality, feelings, and emotional demonstrations perceived by those who are close to the child. In consequence, a preverbal intersubjectivity is created. The child's reception of and response to emotion seems to confirm the child's existence and to secure the existence of the ego complex. This confirmation seems to be directly related to the feeling of being able to communicate.[10] The confirmation of existence, which initially is the emotional acceptance of the infant's physicality, and later includes all of the child's manifestations, seems to be the emotional tone that the child can later impart to its ego complex. Thus, it is the prerequisite for interest in oneself, one's welfare, and self-protection. However, I do not believe that whatever was missed in those situations of our childhood personality-molding can never be recovered. There are many points of departure in life that provide opportunities for renewed, and possibly quite profound, assurances of existence. Emotional confirmation need not come from one person alone. Usually, an infant's manifestations are perceived and confirmed differently by various people. One person may be more successful and better understood by the baby; another person may be less successful. When important manifestations are confirmed, the ego complex has a solid foundation. If the ego complex is sustained by a feeling-tone of loving interest, we will feel fine as an "ego" and will usually consider ourselves to be interesting. We will be able to lovingly observe both ourselves, with all our rough edges, and the world around us. What we call a coherent ego complex will evolve, an ego which, as a rule, is confident of its identity.

There can be many reasons for a less coherent ego complex in an adult: an early physical illness, little agreement with parental figures, a lack of other people close to the child to fill emotional gaps, and so on. I believe it is futile to exclusively blame the parents for these early disturbances. Any ideology that automatically seeks to assign guilt assumes that, were we to do everything right, we would develop without conflict and might enjoy a life without illness and death. And this "we" is easily pushed onto the mothers—"If only the mothers would do everything right!"—the very mothers who make life possible by giving birth.[11]

Developmental psychology, which is based on the observation of the way infants interact with those who are close to them, has in the last decade clearly demonstrated how much spontaneous action stems from the child—the ego complex might actually be activated by the self—and how essential it is to perceive and respond to these spontaneous actions. However, these responses cannot always be optimal, for those who raise the child have their own lives defined by conflicts, hopes, and anxieties.

According to developmental psychology, the ego complex undergoes phases of expansion and phases of consolidation as it becomes conscious. Expansion phases represent stages in which new life, new insights, or new possibilities of behavior become accessible to the individual as she or he realizes new perspectives. Consolidation phases represent stages in which new attitudes are integrated and experienced as habitual. During the development of the ego complex in childhood, phases of expansion and consolidation follow one another in rapid succession. Basically, and very generally—in the following I shall describe the ideal typical development of the ego complex in a very wide context—childhood is a time when the ego complex can be perceived with increasing clarity, initially in relation to, and interwoven with, a nurturing and supportive mother-father matrix. It is manifested as soon as the child receives a response to its emotional displays and self-expressions, and when security is provided for emotional insecurity by social interaction.[12] Furthermore, an emotional response to the child's interest in life, the necessary care, and the demarcation of limits where the child cannot itself set limits, are essential.

Initially, the ego complex is variously interwoven with the parental complexes; during childhood, parental complexes separate into father and mother complexes.

Adolescence, then, is a very typical expansion phase. At this point the ego complex is distinguished from the father and mother complexes. In adolescence we become aware that we are independent beings, separate and different from our parents. This becomes particularly evident when we absorb the shadow of the family system into our own plans for life. We begin to stand apart from the rest of our family and recognize ourselves to be detached. On the plane of complexes, we begin to realize that since we have separated from our parents, it is at times disturbing to hear their voices, and in certain situations we still wonder what Father would say about something, how Mother would react. It is not easy to intrapsychically shake off our parents. The ego complex explicitly confronts the father and mother complex, sometimes even a sibling complex. This is one way our lives are affected by complexes as they become conscious. Of course, at this particular age, the ego complex does in part still identify with the father and mother complexes.

In adolescence, the ego complex is dominated by the hero or heroine archetype. Wilfulness is emphasized, spontaneity defended. We want to become aware of our identity, as well as our relationships with other persons. Our self-chosen relationships become important, and we accept conscious responsibility for our actions more than we did in late childhood. Both anima and animus, the psyche's female and male images, are latently present and are experienced in projection as erotic and sexual fantasies.[13] The self also calls attention to itself by devising big plans for the future and personal utopias.

What strikes us externally as a fascinating, radical change, the emergence of new values, attitudes, and interests, is internally a painful process of transformation. In life, every transition follows a typical course: transitions begin with a sense of dissatisfaction that can lead so far as to bring on a massive devaluation of the current situation. We begin to take stock. This review of what life has brought so far should be understood as work of mourning.[14] We contemplate what life has been like, what is definitely lacking, and what should be incorporated into life. New values are generated as new ideals. But as yet, the values that could make possible a new quality of life have not been developed. An individual in the midst of restructuring is insecure in his or her identity. The ego complex is less coherent than usual; this triggers anxiety, but it also implies that the ego complex can be reorganized, or organized anew. In situations where our identity is expanding, where we set off toward new identities, we are initially insecure and develop anxieties. Usually, this means that old psychic and somatic disturbances flare up. But this time we can deal with them. The problematic complexes are constellated; typical problems with those who are close to us are once again experienced.

At every transition we have the opportunity to re-approach a configuration of development that we may not have faced in the best possible way before. During periods of transition, people seem more susceptible to illness. The purpose of illness is to make us take care of ourselves, to be our own father and mother matrix, and thus enable the ego complex to regenerate. Since fewer defense mechanisms function in an identity crisis, the individual is more open to new developments, which may either approach from inside or outside.[15] We try out our new attitudes on the world outside. Transitional phases follow the same principles as the creative process.

The stage of young adulthood (age twenty-five to forty) is for the most part a phase of consolidation. The ego complex is still dominated by the hero-archetype. It is essential to retain the acquired lucidity, to perceive and assert our will within the bounds of a related identity that also permits self-realization in others. Increasingly, the dream of a life worth aspiring to is replaced by the concrete formulation of everyday life and the experience of being able to effect something. Nonetheless, the hero-archetype no longer reigns supreme as in adolescence; the parent-archetype gains prominence, be it in the raising and care of our own children or caring for symbolic children. In order to let go, we must deal with our past by experiencing our growing children, and thus in our perception the past becomes present. Children also stimulate and reawaken childish qualities in adults, or even awaken them for the first time. In young adulthood we have a relatively secure sense of identity; by this time we have usually established a career and fulfilled our family responsibilities. After we have thoroughly clarified the direct cause of oppressive problems in relationships with our partners, we must once again separate from our father and mother complexes, which we tend to project onto our partners. Toward the end of this phase of relationship crises, we begin to recognize projections of the animus and anima. Hesitantly we withdraw these projections, and no longer regret that our partner does not completely fit our animus/anima image; we accept that they are human too. The yearning remains; it makes itself felt when the latent archetypes of animus and anima are constellated as an inner union that in turn stimulates a desire for deeper love and a sense of wholeness in relationship. The archetype of the divine child is also latently constellated. Sometimes, we project it too heavily onto our children.

Middle age (from forty to fifty-five) is accompanied by a distinct awakening and reassessment of values. It is a phase marked by great changes specifically related to the ego complex. Previous expansion of the ego complex was marked by the hero or heroine-archetype and the parent-archetype, but now limitations come into view. Feeling that one is in the prime of life implies that there can be no better times ahead. Out of this sense of life fulfillment, and the eminent realization of what is inherent in the ego complex, arises a vital transformation. Initially, there is still a sense of fulfillment, competence, of "being at the top," in which we revel. At first, the awareness of transformation reverberates as background music. We gain a sense of fulfillment from having called to life many things that we now have to either uphold or gradually renounce. This applies to relationships, professions, and the way in which we deal with ourselves. We do much for society or our families; this is normal, it is expected of us, and is no longer given special consideration. We no longer feel narcissistic gratification, so much easier to attain in our younger years through special accomplishments, or it goes unnoticed because we have grown accustomed to it. Whatever we do now has to be self-sustaining, otherwise we would be disturbed by the lack of narcissistic gratification. Our ego complex does not receive enough outside confirmation and therefore loses some of its coherence. We feel insecure in our identity and react with anxiety.

Middle age is also a time of truth. The grand ideas of youth have either been fulfilled, partially fulfilled, or not at all. We can no longer boost our self-worth by proposing to master at some later point whatever we have so far failed to achieve. The utopias we have proposed must become realistic utopias.

Limitations begin to be felt, particularly since we no longer have an unlimited time to live, and our aging is revealed in the ever more frequent repetition of situations; repetition is a structural element of time. Growing older is accompanied by slowing down, especially where top performance is concerned. Acknowledging that limitations are set by life, and not by incompetence, can lead us to enjoy and accept being average and mortal. We begin to sense that being average is special enough; we accept what we and our aging body have become. This means that the expansion of the ego complex has passed its zenith. If we deny this, we can expect resignation and cynicism; if we accept it—if we perform work of mourning—we can remain energetic within our boundaries.

Since the ego complex should be relatively emancipated at this age, reorientation is possible. We can anticipate conflicts with the environment, and thus our complexes cannot unexpectedly constellate. We are now familiar with the nature of humanity and our individual nature; we know that we have to reckon with aggression and jealousy, sadism and prejudice. Once we accept people as they are, and if we have experienced our shadow as at least partially belonging to the ego complex, we can deal more realistically with the everyday problems and even develop strategies to deal with them. The ego complex appears to be relatively free, and less of a complex. We will still be able to sense our basic complex constellations; they are the problems that distinguish us, though they no longer totally control us. Our relatively autonomous ego complex indicates that we accept responsibility for our lives, that we delegate less to others. We now ask what truly matters in light of approaching death. What is of substance? What is life really about? In the face of the transitory nature of life, creativity can lead us to self-realization. The archetype of the divine child gains prominence at this point. The animus and anima archetypes are better integrated than previously; and animus/anima are activated in the psyche as an archetypal union. Joined with this is a great capacity for love, but we may also sense a great longing for love which includes a longing for relationship, and inner wholeness. The self can be addressed and sensed in the union of animus and anima.[16] At this age, the raised capacity for love, and love itself, no longer aim so much for confirmation of identity or the assurance of the existence of the ego complex; what is far more important is the connection to a larger whole. I believe that a practical consequence of this love can be seen in the growing ability to care for offspring and elders, to offer assistance without expecting anything in return, and to trust in the fact that the future belongs to the young. The older individuals must now be prepared to hand over all forms of power. If they can accept this, they can rejoice in the young, and in the fact that there will be others to share the load; then they can give what they have without being bogged down by rivalry and jealousy.

Caring for elderly parents—usually another aspect of this period—awakens a sensitivity to one's own old age, portending the archetypal image of the wise old man or woman, possibly even the fearful image of senility or death. As a consequence of caring for external dimensions of life, we begin to care more for ourselves; we turn inward to the self and thus take up contact with a larger whole. This relationship now comes to the forefront; the ego remains true to itself and to what it has created, but it accepts limitations and turns inward without giving up its association with the outside world. This happens only gradually.

If individuals suffer from narcissistic disturbances, if the ego complex is less coherent and requires a good deal of external emotional response in order to be sensed as existent, they can no longer repress disturbances because aging itself is experienced as the final narcissistic insult—or as deliverance. Today, these disturbances can and must be treated by therapy.

Whereas middle age is a period of expansion, *later adulthood* (age fifty-five to seventy-five) is again a phase of consolidation. By now the dualistic sexual aspects of our personality and the related emotions and fantasies have been integrated as well as can be. A relationship to the larger whole has been established, though our influence upon it becomes increasingly fixed. In later adulthood, the individual's ego complex is influenced by the wise old man or woman archetype. All one's life experience is applied to judge situations, give ideas to younger people, and perhaps even oppose them; the younger individuals are sent upon their path, they must now act of their own accord. Still, we occasionally have authority, but this influence is exerted resolutely within the boundaries of the dignity and experience of age. We begin to retreat from the world; at the same time we look back. Excessive nostalgia is a typical problem at this point. If we idealize the past and devalue the present and future, we block the flow of life and become dissatisfied.

Finally, it is in this phase that we reassess what has been integral to the continuity of the ego complex, what has been quintessential to relationships. The archetype of death is latent.

In *old age* (seventy-five to ninety), retreat takes place. The individual must now be able to become dependent; the ego complex loses its flexibility. Stubborn egotism and an acceptance of dependency, the ability to give up both ego-will and the idea of emancipation, can be observed side by side. In old age, the individual is again dominated by his body which, to a greater or lesser extent, still permits mental freedom. Before death, we can observe a reorientation toward the physical ego.

In terms of developmental psychology, the ego complex is at first an unconscious complex that becomes conscious as we develop. We can consider it a paradigm for the way in which a complex becomes conscious; emotional confirmation is not offered by those close to us, but should and must be achieved by the ego itself.

Jungian psychology shows that the ego complex is not only the central complex, but is, as a rule, associated more or less loosely with all other complexes. In the end, all complexes are part of the ego complex. The ego complex is coherent when it develops out of the parental complexes at the appropriate age; the development of the ego complex occurs spontaneously, while new stages of development require external emotional confirmation. In other words, if we separate from the parent and sibling complexes at the appropriate age, the self and the ego will be able to communicate with each other, and we will be able to integrate the developmental influences presented to the ego by the self.

THE EGO FUNCTIONS

The ego complex is distinguished from other complexes in that it is reflected with greater clarity in the ego functions. Other complexes are reflected in the ego functions once they become connected with the ego complex and cease to be completely unconscious. The ego functions enable us to perceive our ego complex and observe our developing self-consciousness. In addition, they are those functions we normally ascribe to our ego, possibly consider to be our ego, and through which we systematize the world of consciousness. The potential of becoming conscious of ourself, our ego complex, the systemization of the world, and our awareness of the world, enable us to orientate ourselves and know what is external and what is internal. We learn to differentiate ego from non-ego, can assimilate others' reactions and accordingly modify our behavior.

Some of the primarily autonomous ego functions are: sensation, thought, attention, the ability to perceive, the capacity to remember, the formation of concepts, orientation in time and space, motor functions, and also, defense mechanisms. These ego functions may operate adequately, but they may be disturbed in various ways; this is a subject of psychopathology. If the ego complex is to some extent coherently delimited and interrelated, and charged with a feeling-tone of interest, the connection between the self and the ego complex is penetrable and we can perceive the world almost as others perceive it. We have a shared world, our memories are not distorted and our thoughts can be followed by others. However, our comprehension of the world is also determined by other complexes. The reality we believe to be true is primarily our individual reality. But as long as the ego functions work, we can share these realities with one another, and we gain the impression that we live in the same world.

When an emotionally highly charged complex is constellated, it disturbs the ego complex. Moreover, the constellated complex is projected; perception is disturbed and becomes a complex-perception.

Let us return to the father complex illustrated above by the analysand. Once her complex constellated, she perceived people, regardless whether they approached her pleasantly or simply indifferently, to be evil. This, in turn, triggered anxiety and aggression, so that her perceptions became even more distorted.

If the ego complex loses its coherence entirely, that is, if it is fragmented to the extent that the individual complexes are almost disconnected from one another, the ego functions are clearly disturbed. Memory gaps and false perceptions ensue; orientation in time and space, and particularly self-orientation, are limited.

The ego functions are often associated with the term

"consciousness." And yet, we do not truly know what consciousness is.

CONSTELLATIONS OF THE EGO COMPLEX

It is the nature of complexes to constellate, i.e., they either repress or promote consciousness. The question arises whether the ego complex can be constellated explicitly or whether it is always constellated. Experience shows that there are times when we are barely involved with our identity and concern ourselves very little with our self-image. At other times, questions of identity, injured sense of self-worth, and the related feelings of anxiety, aggression, and doubts gain agonizing prominence. This suggests that the ego complex can in fact be constellated. In such situations we see the world in terms of our ego complex and our sense of self-worth; that is, we ask what is good, what sustains or diminishes us, and perhaps what idealizes or devaluates us.

When complexes are constellated—and some complexes are always constellated in some form—they influence the ego complex. It is not unusual if, in evaluating a word association test, we determine that the subject has a complex related to self-worth; it is, in fact, normal. The question is how coherent is the ego complex and what does it look like. The ego complex can be constellated either through another complex, or in centralized form. However, these two forms of constellation are often related. The way we work out the unconscious complexes and trauma we experience is invariably connected with the ego complex. Complex reactions always influence our sense of self-worth.

Generally, the ego complex is constellated when we are ashamed that we cannot achieve an ego accomplishment that we think we should achieve. It may also constellate when others address an aspect of ourselves we would have preferred to conceal. Our deficient self is exposed, bared, we feel ashamed and insulted perhaps because someone has very directly diminished our sense of self-worth. But affronts that lead to the constellation of the ego complex are also connected with our need for acceptance. If this requirement is not fulfilled, if we are not sufficiently regarded, recognized, or appreciated, if our ego complex receives too little confirmation and appreciation from the outside, the ego complex might "erupt."

If we experience an insult, or are made to feel ashamed and limited in our ego-activity just when we were about to joyfully take risks, a feeling of self-defeat arises, perhaps even a feeling of not being worth anything—popularly known as the inferiority complex. We may experience the feeling that we are nothing; we feel destroyed or destructive. However, this reaction occurs principally in individuals whose ego complex is incoherent. The emotion would then be one of anxiety, of destructive tendencies, or even anger.

If our ego complex has not been fragmented by the insult, we react with stereotypical behavior in order to restabilize our self-esteem—above all, defense mechanisms. Perhaps we might claim that we are deeply grateful for criticism, because criticism helps us evolve. By saying this, we want to undo the affront we have experienced. Through this reversal—which is a reversal only if we were actually insulted by the criticism—we can, for the moment, regain our self-esteem. We do not have to admit the injury. We cannot, however, work out the affront.

We can also attempt to deal with the insult, providing we have a coherent ego complex, fairly solid self-esteem, and providing the insult did not hit us right in the center. We will then recognize that the injury, insecurity, and grief are caused by a disagreement between our self-image and the image the world has of us. We will realize that limitations have been defined and will ask ourselves how our mistaken behavior is related to the insult and how we can best rectify it. By remembering positive situations, potential achievements, and others who love and accept us, we regain positive self-esteem. Consequences of the insult become visible in the way we adjust our behavior and can be used in situations requiring self-assertion.

Other, less constructive but common stereotypical behavior can be recognized in the development of fantasies of grandeur and fantasies of idealized figures who are like us but who are nonetheless superior to us and can help us. Finally, it can be recognized in destruction and devaluation. These patterns should be recognized as self-regulating functions of the psyche; they are pathological only if they become attitudes that cannot be influenced. As reactions, they help maintain the coherence of the ego complex.

Compensation through Fantasies of Grandeur

To illustrate, I would like to quote a dream as described by Udo Rauchfleisch in his book on omnipotence and impotence. Rauchfleisch gives an account of a twenty-five-year-old male patient who had cut a bad figure in an insulting situation. He had experienced a common, painful insult.

> I was sitting high up in a big gymnasium, close to the ceiling, swinging back and forth on a trapeze. I looked down at the people sitting way below, and they seemed small to me. I felt free and content. A few of them tried to stop the trapeze. But I prevented this by biting each hand, forcing them to release the trapeze.[17]

This dream expresses a classic compensation or self-regulation. The dream-ego behaves like a childish "grandiose self." When we are small children we have the feeling we are omnipotent and all-powerful; we believe no one can harm us; we desperately need this at this stage in order to develop further. Later, our psyche makes use of compensation mechanisms; the grandiose self may be reactivated not only in dreams, but it may also be activated in our imagination. Many people realize they entertain fantasies of heroic deeds, or magnificent performances in situations where they have been humiliated or have not been able to achieve the desired effect. Compensation through reactivation of the grandiose self does not indicate whether the act is ethically good or bad. Clearly, the psyche's intent is to reestablish sufficient positive self-esteem.

Compensation through Idealized Powerful Parental Figures

Another form of compensation, or at least another stereotypical behavior pattern, is the activation of idealized, powerful parental figures, be it in dreams, in fantasies, or in concrete relationships.

An example: A woman in her early thirties had an insulting experience with a man who, she thought, was interested in her. When she did not comply with his desire for sex, he said he was actually relieved because he found her body too flabby, and besides, she smelled bad.

Agitated and confused, she related this experience in therapy. I asked her to concentrate on the fantasies welling up. She said:

> I'm going for a walk with Mother and Father. I'm wearing a tight dress. My father is wearing many golden chains and is a mayor or a dean at a very good university. It's obvious that he thinks I'm beautiful and attractive.

This, too, was a form of compensation. The woman was regressing; she saw herself in the role of the little girl walking between her mother and father, and felt protected. No man could attack her. The father was clearly idealized by the many golden chains and his position of mayor or dean at a university. The father complex was constellated in an idealized form, and she, as his daughter, was someone after all. She was valuable. The fear of being sexually unattractive was averted. After the fantasy, the analysand felt better; she began to speak of the way in which she experienced her body, and her fear of how men might experience her body. It became evident that these stereotypical behavior strategies, these stereotypical forms of compensation, were meant to stabilize self-esteem, in order that the conflict might be confronted. But this is not always the case.

Compensation through Mirror Identification

A mirror identification takes place when we fantasize or dream of a relationship with a person who we think to be good and who is fundamentally our equal. This relationship upgrades us narcissistically.

An example for compensation through mirror identification.—A forty-eight-year-old man had an argument with his twenty-four-year-old son, who accused him of having accomplished nothing in his life. After the conversation, the father, a man with depressive tendencies, felt worthless and destroyed; he was under the impression that his son was right, that he had achieved nothing. He considered whether under these circumstances it might not be best to commit suicide. He dreamt,

> Minister Furgler knocks on my window as if he were coming to pick me up. Since we're in the same fraternity, we're to go to a soccer match together, and afterward to a bar. We're both wearing the same fan-club sweatshirts from the St. Gallen soccer team.

He immediately felt much better after the dream. If Minister Furgler is his friend, what could possibly harm him? He would know what to do in any situation. And literally, "You know, it's really quite something to go to a soccer match with Minister Furgler; not everybody can do that." The dream reestablished his sense of self-worth. Suicide was no longer in question.

What occurred in this case was a compensation through mirror identification. The dreamer thought Minister Furgler was about the same age as himself. But he could not really explain the student fraternity. They were, however, both fans of the St. Gallen soccer team, so, he said, they had a lot in common.

Destructive Rage as a Compensation

When we feel totally *im*potent, we can be seized by *im*potent rage accompanied by fantasies of destruction. Fantasies of destruction allow the ego complex to believe itself to be in a state of virtually omnipotent activation; this is why it is so hard to reason with destructive rage. It is the only possibility for the individual to feel strong and alive in such situations. This form of compensation, however, imparts positive self-esteem for a short time only; afterward, the individual is apt to feel shame and renewed injury. Destructiveness escalates readily because the insult has to be averted with renewed destructiveness.

An example for averting insult through destructiveness. —A thirty-five-year-old man had a problem at work. His boss informed him that he could not expect any further promotions. This deeply offended the man; he thought it unfair and believed his life was over.

He had been in therapy for half a year because he was basically dissatisfied with his life. He described his insulting experience and added, "Right now a fantasy is building up inside. I want to beat up my boss and break the whole place to smithereens." I asked him to stay for a moment with this fantasy. While he sat on the chair, his hands moved as though he were smashing things to bits. That he was hurting himself was obvious. He repeated over and over, "That feels good! That feels great! He's going to have a lot to clean up!"

The rage subsided; the analysand felt neither shame, nor guilt, such as often arise after fantasies of destructiveness. Instead, he felt remarkably positive. This was very important, because in his case, after experiencing insults, to which he was sensitized, and which he all but sought out, he usually turned the destructiveness against himself. When insulted, he frequently fantasized driving into a tree, so that he might be "dead certain" he was dead.

Insults, and the fantasy that suicide can forestall a total breakdown of self-worth, play an important part in the psychodynamics of suicide cases.[18]

After this destructive fantasy, he said, "Since I just smashed the company into little bits, I can hardly work there anymore. I think I'll change jobs. Then I can think about what work I really want to do."

This example illustrates how an injured sense of self-worth is reestablished by compensation, even by destructive compensation, so that a much more realistic confrontation with the world becomes possible. We can then deal with problems with greater objectivity, and we can explore whether or not we want to take on something new in life.

Every conflict is a stimulation to either limit or develop the ego complex. If we are defensive and display stereotypical behavior, without working out the conflict, we cannot use the difficulties to advantage.

Compensation through Devaluation

Devaluation following insult is a stereotypical reaction that is common and, in my opinion, dangerous. We devalue people who get too close to us and seem to be overpowering; we devalue relationships that may be insulting to us; we devalue a world that fails to offer sufficient acceptance for the needs of our ego complex.

Example for sustaining sufficiently positive self-esteem through devaluation.—A twenty-eight-year-old woman had been in therapy for three months due to relationship problems. She was the daughter of a successful mother, who was just over fifty, and a less successful father. On the one hand, she enjoyed having such a mother, and had a good relationship with her, but at any given moment she could find her difficult. Whenever the daughter brought a man home, he—according to the analysand—would invariably be interested in her mother within half an hour. This filled the daughter with speechless rage that then turned to cynicism. In such instances she perceived her mother as a rival, dominant, and simply horrible. When she approached her mother on this subject—which the mother allowed—she answered, "It's not my fault that these young men all have a mother complex and find me attractive." After a weekend when this pattern was repeated, the analysand dreamt the following:

> I meet my mother in a seedy cafe. She looks disgusting. She's wearing false teeth, her hair is falling out, she's flabby. She looks just terrible.

She brought the dream to analysis and said, "The worst thing about all of this is that I was really happy about the dream in the morning. It made me feel positive about myself. I suddenly realized that I'll still look good in twenty years, but nobody knows what my mother will look like. That comforted me."

In the dream she compensated her negative sense of self-worth by devaluing her mother, whom she otherwise idealized; she made her mother terribly ugly. And this devaluation reestablished a sufficiently positive self-esteem.

We do not always need a dream to stabilize our sense of self-worth. Thus we are apt to deprecate successful colleagues who have aroused our envy and consequently disturbed our self-worth, perhaps with remarks such as, Oh yes, he's a hard worker, but there's nothing new in what he has to say.

That we devalue out of a secret, unadmitted jealousy indicates a need to activate our self-esteem. Our devaluation strategies are manifold. In confrontations with creative productions, such as film or theater, devaluation might take the form of criticism.

We employ these devaluation strategies to protect ourselves from jealousy, agitation, and conflict. The inherent problem is that we create an entirely devalued environment and also devalue our relationships. A certain amount of self-acceptance is absolutely necessary for positive self-esteem, but when no one and nothing is of any worth, we have devalued everyone who might have accepted us. Of course, their acceptance is then worthless, too. By devaluing the environment, we indirectly devalue ourselves.

Devaluation strategies lead to a vicious circle: the world is ultimately devalued and senseless, while we are ourselves devalued and insignificant. We fall into a depressive circle.

Compensation as an Attitude

The stereotypical behavior patterns that compensate negative self-esteem serve to regulate the psyche. They are an autonomous, methodical reaction that sufficiently reestablishes our sense of self-worth and enables a confrontation with the conflict at hand. Compensation mechanisms become pathological when they turn into attitudes, when people, in order to cope with life at all, have to permanently live with these compensations.

When a compensation mechanism becomes an attitude, i.e., if you go through life as if you were forever sitting high up on a trapeze, biting anyone who wants to reach you, if you constantly need a person around whom you can admire, or if you incessantly need an admirer, we speak of a disturbance of self-worth, or a narcissistic disturbance.

Such attitudes exist not only in the imagination; they are also brought forward as demands in relationships.

In therapy, potential compensations represent very typical situations of transference and countertransference. If you confirm your injured self-worth by reactivating a childish grandiose self, you are saying, both in relationships and in the therapeutic encounter, Prove to me that I'm exceptional! Prove that I'm above everything! The therapist will probably not affirm that you are exceptional, but will rather affirm that you *are*: that you are all right just as you are. Such narcissistic longings often arise when the expressions of the ego complex have not been emotionally reconfirmed, or possibly because one has received a message that the way one communicates and represents oneself is not acceptable.

Children, for instance, are often reprimanded for the activation of their ego complex; they are scolded when they make a mess, when they make something up; they are scolded because they express themselves, and perhaps do it a bit more noisily than rules allow. What is annoying is essentially the fact that a child is creative and dares to be itself, and perhaps oversteps its own boundaries. The child is confronted by those who raise it. On the one hand, they are jealous of its potentials, and on the other, they are intensely worried that the child might not be adequately "adjusted." Often, at the very instance when the child is remarkably sound, and senses it is doing something exceptional, something good, and presenting something very satisfying to the world, the child is made to feel that its behavior is unacceptable. If, in this situation, the child gets the message "You're not all right," it becomes uncertain of its good feeling. The emotion "I'm all right"—another way to express positive self-esteem—turns into deep insecurity.

In later stressful situations relating to self-worth, the insecurity can resurface and might be compensated with fantasies of omnipotence or grandeur. Thus, if it becomes an attitude, we might begin to seek out people who confirm and admire us. Even if we are successful in obtaining them, the confirmation and admiration is of little use, since we are left with lust for ever more confirmation and admiration. Admiration is not nurturing. Those who seek it need a great measure of emotional confirmation to believe that their existence is acceptable.

Compensation through reactivated, idealized parental figures is frequently experienced in analytical relationships. The analyst is the idealized parental figure, and the analysand the child, or vice versa. In this form of compensation, the individual identifying with the dependent role is forfeiting a considerable degree of autonomy. In return, he or she receives protection. Should this behavior mechanism become an attitude, we are faced with individuals who constantly seek someone they can admire—usually in terms of authority instead of equality—and whom they can follow. They are prepared to give up a good deal of autonomy.

In the therapeutic process, the therapist is idealized, credited with omnipotence, and admired. The analyst reacts to this form of idealized transference, which is not easy to take because it stimulates his or her own fantasies of omnipotence,[19] and in turn can cause the ego complex to become unconscious. The analyst can then no longer perceive his or her ego boundaries. Additionally, these forms of transference make us, the therapists, realize that we are no longer seen as human beings.

In the case of compensation through mirror identification, the individual is looking for someone whose opinions and values represent his or her own, and thus reaffirm his or her opinions and values, and offer affirmation in a social sense. To be eligible, this person must also be someone who has a certain amount of influence.

In terms of complex theory, such individuals separate their ego complex from the parental complexes more so than those who seek an idealized relationship. They develop more toward an I-you relationship, although they are not really after an I-you relationship; they are searching for a twin who can offer confirmation and protection through her or his power and potential mastery of life.

In the therapeutic relationship, behavioral mechanisms as attitudes become evident when analysands seek parallels between their life and the analyst's. Perhaps they find out that they were both in the same place in the same year, or that they both drive the same kind of car. But any reactions which show that things are not perceived or thought in the same manner cause a vehement response. Since these attitudes are manifested in transference and countertransference, they can be understood in light of those situations of our childhood that moulded our personality, and all the related negativity about life. However, they also contain an appeal for a very particular affirmation, which is needed by the analysand's ego complex, and which the analyst can provide.

Fragmentation

If we do not succeed in reestablishing our sense of self-worth through stereotypical behavior, or possible compensation, and are consequently unable to assure ourselves of a certain amount of self-respect, we experience fragmentation. We feel totally confused, and cannot orientate ourselves; the ego functions cease to fulfill their purpose and we are overwhelmed by a variety of emotions. We speak of fragmentation when the ego complex breaks up into its separate complexes, which then lead a separate existence. The network that normally exists is interrupted, and instead of communicating with an ego, we communicate with a father complex, a guilt complex, and so on. The ego structure disintegrates. In such situations, self-regulation is no longer possible. The self-regulation of the psyche functions only as long as our ego complex is coherent.

Coherence is lost when fragmentation takes place; the ego structure disintegrates and the ego functions fail to fulfill their purpose. This does not mean that some individuals are constantly fragmented, while others never experience the process of fragmentation, or that there are persons whose psychic self-regulation does not function while that of others always does. Fragmentation must be viewed as a process. Sudden upheaval, such as loss or death, fragments the ego complex; at such times self-regulation is not possible. Certain insults can be so central that they trigger fragmentation. Individuals with psychotic reactions have a fragmented ego complex. For a time self-regulation is not possible, but gradually the processes of restitution start up again; ego boundaries are redefined and the process of self-regulation begins anew.

Recently, Gestalt therapy has shed new light on the process of restitution in individuals who suffer from psychotic reaction. Figures, or patterns, demonstrate that neither potential compensation, nor coherence, are present: the images are fragmented. Restitution can be recognized once it is activated. Presumably, it is initiated by group work (where the group functions as a containing element), by relating to another individual, by assimilating archetypical material, which of itself is clearly structured (i.e., fairy tales), or simply by the passage of time.[20] Of course, those individuals who were able to develop only a slightly coherent ego complex tend more toward fragmentation and loss of ego structure throughout their lives—they are, one might say, structurally weak—than those who developed a coherent ego complex. Yet, we must take into consideration that some people may have very coherent ego-islands within a less coherent ego complex, while those whose ego complex is coherent may have islands that are not so coherent. There are, however, situations and events that no ego complex can truly master, nor need master, in order to function smoothly.

Example for the experience of ego-fragmentation. —A forty-eight-year-old man lost his wife and daughter in a car crash. He survived with his two sons, ages eleven and fourteen. The man was untalented as far as keeping house was concerned; in fact, he was quite impractical. He felt disoriented, confused, did not know "where his head was at," and his doctor referred him to a crisis intervention program.

During our discussion he said, "By the way, I had another dream that really finished me off." Such dreams are very typical for a lack of self-regulation. This was his dream:

> A monster tears off my hands, rips out my heart; one of my legs is lying somewhere else. I may have already lost my head. I have the impression that I'm disintegrating. And when this disintegration wakes me, I think, there's some justice in that, I wish I'd die anyway.

The man related the dream without any emotion; he might just as well have been reciting a mathematical formula.

The dream, he said, represented his situation exactly. He was totally confused, too—I sensed it in the way he spoke. He asked me, for instance, whether his wife was dead or not; if I knew where he had taken his children or if I didn't know either; if I was the therapist or the doctor who had spoken to him. The fragmented ego complex became evident in the dream. He no longer trusted his perceptions; he could not rely on his memory; he did not speak in a sequential fashion.

After a shock due to sudden loss, ego-fragmentation is relatively common. These individuals no longer want to take in the world; they want to forget. Either the wheel of time has to be reversed or they cannot find their way.

The man said that he feared he was crazy. This was an expression of his fragmentation, the feeling of being torn apart, with which we are familiar from the process of mourning.

In such cases, it is difficult to describe the therapeutic procedure, because, basically, we share the situation with the individual. We do not escape, nor do we share the panic.

I became a substitute for his ego functions. I reminded him that he had told me he brought the children to his brother's, therefore it was probably true. He had said that his wife had died two days ago; this also must have been true. Thus, I affirmed that although disoriented, he did have occasional moments of orientation. I tried to assimilate his feeling of being torn apart and the associated anxiety I sensed. At the same time I tried to communicate that these feelings, which were almost impossible to bear, were appropriate to the situation. His dream represented an archetypal motif known as the dismemberment motif; it is related to death and rebirth. When Osiris was torn into pieces by the death god Seth, Isis had to find all the pieces and put him back together. Osiris was then reanimated and became a god. In various myths, the ritual of death and dismemberment is the transitory stage necessary for rebirth and new fertility.[21]

The reference to a collective symbol for death and rebirth awakens hope and is essential to the therapist because it communicates the anxiety connected with the fragmentation. It is naked, existential fear. It is not advisable to address the transformation motif while someone feels torn apart. It is important that the therapist sense the hope connected with this motif and simultaneously assimilate the emotions inherent to dismemberment. We must realize that we are faced with a transformation myth and, finally, with a creation myth; this hope becomes the therapeutic basis wherein the ego complex can once again experience itself as coherent.

Five months after the first dream, integration took place. A dream confirmed that the ego complex, and thereby identity and self-esteem, could be freshly experienced. The boundaries that had disappeared in the first dream were back again:

> In my dream I am naked and very weak. I am at a spa. Three women and three men are wrapping me in damp linen. This immediately feels nice and warm. I feel my skin, I feel myself, I feel alive, I feel my boundaries. I have the feeling that I have some strength again.

It seems important to me that he felt his skin, felt himself again. The skin is the penetrable border of our physical ego. The dreamer was pleased with the dream and said that he felt himself once again.

When we sense our physical self, our physical ego, we gain an awareness of identity. I believe it is a good idea, if at all possible, to try to help fragmented individuals sense their bodies. The interesting thing about this dream is that the dreamer was in a spa, a place where one tends to one's body, where he was treated with a damp compress, the damp linen.

Before there was such a thing as tranquilizers, psychotics were wrapped in such damp linen cloths when they were in a very agitated state. This idea has been readopted by a university clinic in Geneva. Patients who are in an agitated or catatonic state are wrapped tightly in a damp cloth. The body reacts by producing warmth. A team continuously watches over and tends to the patient while he or she is in the "pack," thus creating a situation where attention and trust can develop, while, through her or his body, the patient regains a feeling of being alive. Thus, it could be either a situation of death and rebirth, or a restitution of the ego complex.[22]

The man had his dream before anyone called this method of "packs" to my attention. It is also interesting that he was tended by three women and three men, by both masculine and feminine aspects. Symbolically, the subject of "death and rebirth," once again at issue in his dream, specifically represented the rebirth of the ego complex.

After this dream, the man accomplished the so-called work of mourning; he was able to accept memories of the life he had shared with his wife and daughter, and to cope with the problems of his sons, who were also mourning for their mother and sister.

Thus, it became apparent that the analysand did not have a badly structured ego; his ego-coherence was perfectly satisfactory. The great loss, which had come as a shock, had caused the fragmentation of his ego complex.

Typically, individuals who have lost someone close react with total or partial fragmentation of the ego complex. This is hardly surprising when we consider that loss effects an immense readjustment of our identity, and that the process of mourning must finally lead to a transformed ego-identity. In situations of mourning, we cannot judge whether the individuals are habitually ego-strong or ego-weak. We can, however, discern this by the amount of time they take to recover, or to regain control of their ego functions. The words "ego-strength" and "ego-weakness" are popular terms for what I have previously called good, or poor, ego-coherence, which means that the ego complex reveals definite structures and clear ego boundaries.

Ego-strength connotes that, in instances when unknown

emotions are experienced or frightening fantasies surface, the ego is able to connect constellated complexes to the ego complex without having to employ too many defense mechanisms. These defense mechanisms usually cause momentary psychic balance. However, since the complex that yearns to be integrated is repressed, or split off, we can anticipate new and intense disturbances. Those who need not employ defense mechanisms quite as rigorously will find the conflict inherent to every complex easier to face. Thus, except in extreme cases, it is possible to determine ego-strength or ego-weakness, which of themselves are very difficult to diagnose, by the discernible defense mechanisms. An individual able to employ varied and modulated defense mechanisms that were adopted later in life has a stronger ego,[23] that is, a coherent ego complex that is strong enough to take on heavy burdens.

The ability to integrate constellated complexes with the ego complex means that the individual is in a position to cope with conflict and contradiction. Such individuals are prepared to keep questioning themselves and see themselves in a new light, which enables the development of the ego complex to take place. In terms of human relationships, a strong ego implies the ability to respond to other individuals, to allow them their peculiarities even if they do not suit us, to get "involved" emotionally without fear of losing oneself in the long run. To be ego-strong means to be able to risk losing face once in a while, even to lose oneself and be selfless in a relationship. I would like to stress that ego-strength is not simply habitual, for, depending on the situation, our ego can be stronger or weaker.

Ego-weakness, in contrast to ego-strength, tends to employ defense mechanisms which, for the most part, developed early in life: particularly splitting and denial. These two defense mechanisms often appear together. The most frequently experienced form of splitting is when we think ourselves to be exclusively good while we think of others as exclusively evil. These splitting mechanisms indicate the presence of great anxiety with little tolerance for anxiety, and that the anxiety therefore must be repressed at any price. Only when the ego complex is able to take on burdens, and a coherence of the ego complex is present, can the unconscious be integrated, or anything like a process of individuation begin. This is why it is important to examine the ego complex and to consider how its coherence can be reestablished in instances where it is not present.

In many passages of his works, Jung mentions that the integration of the unconscious into consciousness, or the process of individuation, is possible only when the ego is strong enough to bear the load.

It is therefore of utmost importance, providing individuation seems sensible as a therapeutic solution, to work out how one can best reestablish the coherence of the ego complex in situations where it is not present.

Therapeutic Considerations in Reestablishing Coherence of the Ego Complex

Since the ego complex is defined as the central complex, the way we deal with complexes can for the time being be applied to the ego complex.

The complex must be recognized. The self-esteem of an individual whose ego complex is constellated must be acknowledged. He or she must also be encouraged to perceive and express his or her related fantasies. This is generally not easy and demands great trust between the analysand and the analyst. As I have shown, the analysand is usually ashamed of fantasies of grandeur or destruction. Should the therapist not succeed in emphasizing the significance of these fantasies, they will have to be repressed again.

Therapists must recognize feelings; we not only assimilate them through verbal expressions, which often mask more than they reveal, but also through an awareness of body language, of the prevalent atmosphere, or of the way the analyst's own psyche responds to the given situation. The term "empathy" has been coined to denote the capacity to assimilate and sympathize. The object is not only to create an empathic atmosphere in which the individuals can communicate with themselves, but, more importantly, that the therapist formulate the feelings that are so strong they seem to fill up solid space. The situation is comparable to the development of the ego complex, when those who are close to the child perceive and respond to the feelings it expresses—though probably in a different modulation—and thus assure the child that its feelings are understandable and acceptable.

Since every complex reflects childhood relationship patterns that tend to involve two persons, the most difficult conflicts, which have either inhibited or distorted the development of the ego complex, are easily constellated in therapy. I have shown this in the passages on compensation through grandeur or idealized parental figures. If relationship patterns can be recognized and understood emotionally—and here the situation both of the former child and those who raised it must be understood—new perception and new behavior becomes possible.

Therapy does not simply repeat and repair early childhood. It is essential that someone is there who is able to conscientiously become involved in uncomfortable feelings, someone who will attempt both to understand them and make their existence understandable to the individual who feels them and is ashamed of them. It is important that the analyst does not simply take on an overprotective role—such as, this person always had a hard time in life, let me for once do something good for him—but rather provides a nurturing matrix by taking all emotional expressions seriously and formulating them. This demands emotional dependability though not necessarily continuous presence. Part of this emotional reliability is that, as therapists, we stand up for our feelings. If, for instance, we are angry and are reproached for it, we should stand up for our anger and not pretend that we just happen to be preoccupied. We must also strengthen these individuals by confirming that the emotions they perceive are correct; if they are not correct, they must be rectified. Furthermore, emotional dependability also means that the therapist clearly defines which rules are valid in this relationship, and then sticks to the rules.

Not infrequently, individuals who are in situations where the ego complex is fragmented, or under great pressure, demand the therapist's constant presence. Should the therapist give in, even more presence is demanded. The therapist need not be present at all times, no more so than those who raised us earlier in life. However, when present, the therapist must give the individual undivided emotional attention.

When ego functions fail, and confusion sets in, when memories become muddled and the mind incoherent, the therapist will provide ego functions for the analysand. I described this in the case of the man who suffered from the trauma of mourning. Ego functions must be provided only as long as needed, and only in those areas where needed.

It seems to me that we should not only provide ego functions, but also self-regulation for the psyche. When the ego complex is not coherent, or barely coherent, analysands will be incapable of regulating their psyche of their own volition. In such cases, the unconscious shared between the analysand and the analyst provides an opportunity for the analyst to become aware of the counter-regulation of the psyche and incorporate it in the analytic process.

An example of the way the analyst provides her ego functions for the analysand.—During the first session with the analysand who had lost his wife and daughter in a car accident and who seemed so very confused, I suddenly saw mathematical formulas before me, an equation with many unknowns. Since I have little to do with mathematics any more, I did not understand this image at all. It must have been a form of countertransference. My unconscious had apparently taken on something from the man's unconscious, which I formulated as soon as I was conscious of it. I said, "This seems strange to me; I see an equation with many variables. Does this mean anything to you?" And he, methodically, replied, "You know, equations with many unknowns can easily be solved." He asked me to be more precise and tell him exactly how many unknowns there were; then he suggested some solutions. Then he looked at me in surprise and said: "It still works. I'm so glad. That means I'm not crazy after all." How could I know he was interested in mathematics? The image I perceived apparently touched some healthy aspect of his ego and returned the feeling that he still functioned, a feeling that was extraordinarily important in this situation. Although his self-regulation was not functioning, mine was.

In such situations, all the analysand's dreams and imaginings are extremely important to me. Even though the analysand is usually not aware of unconscious messages when his or her ego complex does not display a certain coherence, dreams and images can illuminate the analytic relationship; they can represent patterns of relationship, indicate the analysand's emotional disposition, and thus enable the analyst to perceive the emotional disposition. It should be taken quite seriously that although individuals in these situations can hear and see the messages in their dreams, and often strong and impressive images, these dreams do not alter their emotions.

Again, this is not universally true. I believe it is important to realize that an individual does not simply have faulty ego-coherence, but that it is dependent on situations; there are situations in which weaker individuals can react just like those who have a stronger ego-coherence. As problematic as it is to be unaware of their terrible sense of nonexistence, or estrangement, it is even more problematic to declare them more ill than they really are, or to label those aspects they might use to escape, develop, and employ as autonomous structures, as sick.

The therapeutic treatment for individuals suffering from a barely coherent ego complex, or those who have temporarily lost coherence, is intrinsically connected with the way we envision the development of the ego complex. In Jungian psychology, the idea is to make individuals aware of the fact that their self controls the development of their ego, or as Neumann[24] would say, to make them conscious of their ego-self axis. This requires that the therapist does not see him– or herself as the all-powerful mother or father without whom the individuals can no longer exist. We should rather employ our mother-father functions to enable individuals to reencounter and reexperience themselves, and to enable developmental processes, which we as therapists must accept and confirm, to take place.

Aspects of the Archetype

CHAPTER FIVE

ARCHETYPES form the core of complexes.[1] This is why so many typical complexes, such as the father complex, the mother complex, the power complex, or the anxiety complex, have virtually become folklore.[2] Since complexes are worked out through symbols, Jung differentiates between personal symbols and suprapersonal symbols. For the most part, personal symbols draw their meaning from an individual's life. Suprapersonal symbols are typically human; they provide significant, fresh inspiration and affect many people. Creative works usually address suprapersonal symbols. Speaking of fantasies with suprapersonal characteristics, Jung says:

> These fantasy-images undoubtedly have their closest analogues in mythological types. We must therefore assume that they correspond to certain *collective* (and not personal) structural elements of the human psyche in general.[3]

Because of the many parallels existing between mythological, religious, artistic, and poetic motifs, Jung deduces the presence of basic structural elements, which he calls archetypes, within the psyche. The effect of these archetypes is described as follows:

> From the unconscious there emanate determining influences which, independently of tradition, guarantee in every single individual a similarity and even a sameness of experience, and also of the way

it is represented imaginatively. One of the main proofs of this is the almost universal parallelism between mythological motifs, which, on account of their quality as primordial images, I have called *archetypes*."[4]

In another passage, Jung says that archetypes effect "prenatally determined modes of behavior and function."[5] Archetypes "intervene in the shaping of conscious contents by regulating, modifying and motivating them."[6] In summary, we could say that archetypes are anthropological constants of the experience, formation, and transformation of behavior. They are, as it were, an expression of the "human quality," of the human being.[7]

The archetypal imaginings and experiences of which we become conscious must be distinguished from the archetype as such. Archetypal imaginings are extremely "varied structures which all point back to one essentially *irrepresentable* basic form. The latter is characterized by certain fundamental meanings, although these can be grasped only approximately."[8] In addition, archetypal fantasies are conveyed through our personal complexes, which explains why so many personal factors are typically enmeshed in an archetypal situation.

The archetype is a structuring factor of the psyche and the body; psychic and physical processes move within a certain human typology, and in certain situations people experience comparable images, comparable emotions, and comparable impulses. An archetype, which of itself is basically abstract and transcends consciousness, can evoke similar images, instincts, and physical reactions. Archetypes have a unique and dynamic nature.[9] Their dynamism causes potentials to become actuality and constellations to come into being; they cause us to feel a driving force. Von Franz speaks of this dynamism as a "transcendent, spontaneous motivating factor."[10] Jung uses similar terminology for this dynamism, such as "the principle of spontaneous movement and activity." The dynamics effect the independent creation of images and the sovereign manipulation of these images.[11] We can conclude that "the unconscious is not merely conditioned by history, but is the very source of the creative impulse. It is like Nature herself—prodigiously conservative, and yet transcending her own historical conditions in her acts of creation."[12]

The concept of the collective unconscious is related to the concept of archetypes. Jung differentiates between the personal unconscious, which primarily consists of emotionally charged complexes and repressed experiences of events that may or may not be conscious, and the collective unconscious and its structural elements, the archetypes. Jung says of the collective unconscious: "It is . . . identical in all men and thus constitutes a common psychic substrate of a suprapersonal nature which is present in every one of us."[13]

Thus, archetypes are regulating, modifying, and motivating influences from the unconscious, which initially are unrelated to the unconscious problems represented by complexes. Archetypal images, or suprapersonal symbols, are therefore considered "healthy signs," though, as classifiers, unhealthy and healthy do not pertain to the archetype, nor do good and evil, because the archetype is beyond good and evil, healthy and unhealthy.[14] And yet, providing our ego is sufficiently coherent, we can experience strong transformative impulses by acknowledging archetypal images. By relating personal problems to collective, archetypal processes, such as those expounded in fairy tales, an emotion of hope is awakened, the hope that problems can be solved. Additionally, the fantasies evoked, which are usually borrowed from archetypal symbols, convey a sense of increased autonomy, increased competence in dealing with life, and an increased sense of significance.

To Jung, archetypal imaginings are a timeless and basic component of the human psyche, without which we could not survive.

> There are problems which one simply cannot solve on one's own resources. Such an admission has the advantage of being honest, truthful, and in accord with reality, and this prepares the ground for a compensatory reaction from the collective unconscious. . . . If you have an attitude of this kind, then the helpful powers slumbering in the deeper strata of man's nature can come awake and intervene,

for helplessness and weakness are the eternal experience and the eternal problem of mankind. To this problem there is also an eternal answer, otherwise it would have been all up with humanity long ago. . . . The necessary and needful reaction from the collective unconscious expresses itself in archetypally formed ideas.[15]

In another passage, he says:

The impact of an archetype, whether it takes the form of immediate experience or is expressed through the spoken word, stirs us because it summons up a voice that is stronger then our own. Whoever speaks in primordial images speaks with a thousand voices; he enthralls and overpowers, while at the same time he lifts the idea he is seeking to express out of the occasional and the transitory into the realm of the ever-enduring. He transmutes our personal destiny into the destiny of mankind, and evokes in us all those beneficent forces that ever and anon have enabled humanity to find a refuge from every peril and to outlive the longest night.[16]

Here, Jung compares the effect of archetypal imaginings with the effect of the creative process. But I believe he is also addressing the therapeutic goal that suffering individuals be able to associate their problems with those of humanity. Most important, this gives rise to the hope of being able to live with the problems and to master life.

Jung's definitions illustrate how archetypal constellations are consciously experienced. Like complexes, they are endowed with intense and fascinating emotions. With regard to the extreme emotion which is triggered and made conscious by archetypal constellations, Jung uses the term "numinosity." The images evoked are enthralling, gripping, and sometimes forceful. They force their significance upon us and convey a sense of personal fate. When an archetype is constellated, we are overcome by a strong emotion accompanied by intense fantasies, visions, utopian ideals, and perhaps sexual fantasies. In any event, we cannot get the subject off of our minds; we try to understand the image, or images, that occupy us by looking for comparable images in human history. This is a method of amplification. It is an attempt to connect the dominating archetypal image, the archetypal idea, to a larger whole. By so doing, the meaning of the image may be easier to divine. This method is sensible, since the archetype of itself is not visible. Archetypal imaginings overlap in many aspects and are distorted both by complexes and cultural elements.

Amplification investigates motifs not only in isolation from others, but also in their typical combinations, in their typical environment. Lest amplification lead to the conclusion that everything is everything in the end, and humanity and life and the world are one whole—though, of course, this is true in a sense—we must take care that these motifs represent comparable emotional contents.

One archetypal motif is the "divine child." It appears, in various mythologies, as Jesus, Krishna, Hermes, or Buddha. The "divine child" is always born in a special, miraculous way, sometimes even twice, or perhaps conception is unusual (e.g., the virgin birth of Jesus). The child is then deserted and critically endangered; often there is an encounter with a demonic force that intends to destroy the child. However, the threat of an adversary serves to strengthen the child and proves it is a being who will change the world.

The mythological motif of the "divine child," and all the related structural elements, can be found in religion, art, literature, and dreams. The phenomenology is similar, as is the intense emotion it arouses. If we accept this motif, it arouses in us a hope for the future, for change, and for growth toward self-sufficiency. When we experience the "divine child" as a symbol, when the "divine child" archetype is constellated, it is accompanied by an element of possible renewal, creative change, and a confrontation between old and new. On the whole, however, it is a symbol for the experience of potential transformation, which in the end cannot be entirely explained.

Beyond implying the child within us, the symbol of the "divine child" suggests the continual potential for the renewal of all life. The motif and structural elements of the "divine child" are modified by cultural factors. Thus, Jesus is certainly not the same child as Krishna. Stories of Krishna describe how he participated in childish pranks, such as tying cows' tails together. Once he ate dirt and his friends tattled on him. When his mother called him to account, he said that his playmates were lying. His mother told him to open his mouth, and inside she saw the whole of creation: sun, moon, mountains, oceans. There are stories of Hermes stealing an entire herd of cattle—something we can hardly picture Jesus doing.[17]

But complexes also modify our perception of archetypal constellations. Our understanding of this archetype depends on which experiences we associate with being children, with childhood. And yet, I believe that even difficult childhood situations cannot eliminate, but can, at most, subdue the aspect of hope inherent to this archetypal motif. Herein lies another dimension of the archetype. It becomes apparent in persons suffering from a compulsive disorder. The psychodynamics of compulsive neurosis is to be found in the conflict between an omnipotent, prohibitive force, along the lines of a vengeful god, and the child who yearns to develop, have a future, and live. Compulsive individuals identify with the all-powerful, prohibitive force. In doing so, they are attempting to control the consequences of their actions, in particular the consequences of life and any creative transformation. When we treat compulsive illness, the archetype of the "divine child" is frequently activated, accompanied by the associated archetype of the adversary, which can be recognized by a prohibitive force. Despite the tension, the motif of the "divine child" is still experienced as a harbinger of hope.

BLOCH'S CRITICISM OF JUNG'S THEORY OF ARCHETYPES

One of the greatest critics of Jung was Ernst Bloch. His criticism is primarily directed at Jung's concept of the archetype. Bloch attacked Jung in his book *The Principle of Hope*.[18] His arguments are wonderfully emotional and unjustified. Twenty years after Jung's death, Bloch was still irate about the "Heretic from Zurich." His persistent scorn reveals his great affinity to Jung.

Bloch's contentions are that the archetype is arch-conservative and terribly regressive. Humanity would never be able to develop along these lines; there would be no political change. Bloch adds that Jung viewed the archetype incorrectly; all potential for utopia and all the visions that could change the future, says Bloch, lie within the archetype. He also speaks of "archetypally encapsulated hope."

The one aspect he chose to criticize is undeniably contained in Jung's works—the idea that humanity will remain the same, even over the course of millions of years. However, he overlooked, or rather claimed for himself, the point that the creative impulse emerges from this psychic condition, and is in fact structured by the archetype.

In several passages, Jung speaks of the fact that the unconscious is not merely "conditioned by history, but is the very source of the creative impulse."[19] Furthermore, he says that the creative process consists of the "unconscious activation of an archetypal image, and in elaborating and shaping this image into the finished work," and that "by giving it shape, . . . it is translated into the language of the present."[20] Those archetypes lacking in the spirit of the age are activated. The archetypes are then reinterpreted in the sense of the times and, consequently, the elements that had been neglected are reintroduced.

Bloch's criticism, which in my opinion is not valid, is nonetheless important, since Jungian psychology has always been denied a certain political relevance. Jung's lack of political relevance is not so much related to the concept of archetypes, but rather to the tendency to dismiss the external, political world. He tends to view individuation solely as an internal process of integration, and to neglect the fact that it is also an external process of interrelationship. If it is true that archetypal constellations can be activated as an extensive self-regulatory act, it would have to be possible to compare currently constelled archetypal images of different individuals in order to investigate the subject, say, of "threatened nature." In my opinion, archetypal constellations occur only where we have an intense relationship to another individual, an object, or to a threat. When archetypal constellations are activated as structural elements of the collective unconscious, they are presented to consciousness through the personal complex contents of the unconscious by symbols. Again, the question arises whether or not there is a connection between the personal unconscious and the collective unconscious. Szondi spoke of a family unconscious; Erich Fromm postulated a societal unconscious. These terms can easily be integrated into Jungian psychology, particularly as Jung, in diagnostic association studies, spoke of so-called "family complexes," implying a family unconscious. I believe it is typical for complexes to be relevant to a whole society, or at least to an entire generation. The "sixties" generation seems to have demonstrated a very specific collective complex constellation that motivated their actions. We might say that many people are currently working out a so-called "mother complex." I have found it is not necessarily related to the bad experiences they may have had with their mothers. When we question them individually, we often find that their mothers were good enough. We might conclude that the mother complex is a collective problem, and we all share what is collective.

The concept of a societal unconscious should pertain not only to repressed or neglected factors, but should also include new factors that aspire to come to light, that aspire to be integrated into consciousness. In this case it is the positive aspect of the mother archetype.

ARCHETYPAL CONSTELLATION AND RELATIONSHIP

When can archetypal constellations be experienced? Since they are at the root of our complexes, they can be experienced whenever complexes are constellated, although in these instances they usually remain in the background.

In this context, Jung often speaks of the regulating characteristic of archetypal constellations. Archetypes constellate when consciousness is too far removed from its foundation. I have found that archetypal constellations often occur within a relationship. In terms of developmental psychology, this would mean that the mother and father archetypes are activated through our relationship with our mother and father; they are, in turn, colored by the predominating emotion associated with the persons who are close to us. However, when these archetypes are activated, our true parents may be unable to fulfil the roles traditionally expected of them.

There may well be spontaneous archetypal constellations that are appropriate to the creative dimension of the archetype. But these archetypal constellations are frequently activated in relationships with another individual, and this requires a certain conscious attitude. I feel that the human characters in fairy tales explicitly reflect this attitude. Fairy tale heroes and heroines, after a few failed attempts, always manage to do whatever is in their power to do. They endeavor to use their ego-consciousness to master the difficulties that confront them, and accept as much responsibility as possible. In other words, they attempt to act autonomously. They come to a point where they admit they no longer know where to go, that they are at the end of their rope. Then they often fall asleep and/or have a dream (Grimm's "Jorinda and Joringel"), or someone finds them the next day and leads them to the scene of further events. Here, too, the pattern of the creative process is visible.

We encounter this perspective in Jung's works when he says there are problems we cannot solve with our own resources and that, once we admit this, a compensatory reaction can take place in the collective unconscious.[21] The suggested approach is first to expend our personal activity, then to wait for a good idea, a person who can help us, or an emotion that reawakens hope.

Children allowed to try things out on their own, while adults assist them in situations that exceed their ability to cope, are likely to trust that something positive awaits them in the world. They even believe that they are entitled to their expectations, and their desires are often fulfilled. Those who were not supported and were forced to do everything on their own need abundant faith to believe that they, too, will get what they deserve. It is a major development when they realize that they do get their share. Their first experience of the trust necessary to reveal archetypal images often occurs in a relationship with another human being.

Example for the experience of archetypal constellations.—An eighteen-year-old woman had negative mother experiences throughout her life. Her biological mother did not want her. She was sent first to one grandmother, then to the other. Finally, a foster mother was found. Thus, she was sent from one to another, and when, at the age of six, she was finally integrated in a family where she felt comfortable, her biological mother, because she had married, took her back. This was the onset of a life of conflict.

When she was eighteen, she came to therapy because she was afraid she would abuse her illegitimate child. Her overall feeling was, No one wants me, everyone sends me away, I am nothing, I can't do anything. But I'll show all of you. I'll hurt you just as you hurt me.

Her first dreams were characterized by mother figures whom she called witches: powerful, elusive figures who locked her up in dungeons, fed her poisoned food, and so on.

She transferred the archetypally toned aspect of the "witch" mother complex onto me. One day, she said, "You're the worst kind of witch. You act nice to me right now, but you'll get rid of me at the first opportunity." It was of little help that I understood she would have to feel this way with her background.

We fought it out for about one and a half years. I frequently had the impulse to send her away. But, in time, I got used to the nature of these fights; we began to battle each other out of friendship, and this affected her dreams. New female figures appeared: fat mothers with "real aprons" and pulled-back hair. They cooked with her in a kitchen. She commented, "What does this old-fashioned stuff in my psyche have to do with me?"

I addressed her highly ambivalent feelings. On the one hand, she felt quite comfortable with these maternal figures, while on the other, she feared she might lose all her autonomy. To me, it was an indication that the mother archetype was constellated in its nurturing and caring aspect, as opposed to the previous aspect as poisoner. This indicated that she could now be more motherly to herself and her child. She no longer had to see the world as a poisoning mother. Since she did not have to defend herself, she required fewer defenses.

We can basically trust that once the problematic image expressed by the complex is both experienced and understood emotionally, it becomes an expression of the supportive, permissive, or positive maternal aspects within a relationship, and enables the positive mother archetype to be evoked.

Various mother figures appeared in this woman's dreams. Initially she took on the role of the child. In her dreams, she separated from the mothers and instead related to them in friendship. Externally, she developed into a much more maternal woman, not only toward herself, but also toward her child.

In my experience, the archetypal realm is entered through relationships in which trust is possible, and where trust in one's strength is activated. The example mentioned here illustrates how the activated figures were increasingly less characterized by the original complex. Instead, they began to represent a general human potential that such individuals can then approach and apply to their daily life. This does not mean that the original problematic complex area simply disappears, but rather that the awareness of other experiences that are contrary to the complex is added to the complex experience.

The awareness of archetypal constellations does not provide concrete solutions for problems, but more often a change in the basic emotional disposition that enables the ego to deal with the current problems.

Example for a change in emotional disposition through archetypal constellations.—For two years, a thirty-four-year-old man suffered prolonged and repeated periods of depression. The most prominent symptom was apathy. He moved as little as possible and gained a lot of weight, which bothered him. He felt empty, and had a sense that his life was interchangeable, "I am interchangeable, my children are interchangeable, my wife is interchangeable, Switzerland is interchangeable, you are interchangeable, everything is interchangeable."

This feeling conveyed a sense of powerlessness, uncertainty, and fear. The man rarely dreamt, and when he did, the dreams were very concrete. He dreamt, for instance, that he was trying to tie his shoes and could not.

After two years of therapy, during which we repeatedly attempted to assimilate his feelings, to generate the emotional entanglement of his childhood through transference and countertransference, and also attempted to move his unconscious through imagination, he brought me a dream that clearly changed his situation. He described the dream as if he were reliving it in his imagination, therefore I will present it as such:

> It seems that some monster is spitting me out, maybe a whale, maybe it's one of those ultramodern submarines, the kind where people can exit from the front end. I think it's a submarine, but it's a whale, too. I'm tossed onto a beach. It hurts a lot. I have to hurry up, otherwise the waves will pull me back into the sea. I'm gasping for air, I'm breathing like I've never breathed before. (He takes a deep breath at this point.) I'm breathing as if I were just born. That's how I feel, too.

Then, with a deep, satisfied sigh, he sat back in his chair and said, "I can breathe again."

In terms of physical phenomena, it is typical that depressed individuals do not breathe properly; their breathing is shallow. This explains why, when we are depressed, it helps to do something physically strenuous, because then, if at all possible, we can breathe again. For the dreamer, it was immensely important that he could "breathe again."

He went on to tell me how he had been slammed down really hard, and he associated, "It was as if someone were saying, 'Either you're going to fall apart, or you're going to live.' But I feel alive now, I'm breathing differently, I want to live. I can live again." His associations to his dream expressed his emotional transformation.

This clearly illustrates how archetypal constellations are presented to our consciousness through symbols, in this case through the familiar motif of being swallowed by a whale, modernized by the idea of being locked up inside a submarine. To my knowledge, and to his, there are no submarines with an exit in the front, therefore the notion probably indicated torpedoes. But it is clear that he was dreaming of the mythological whale motif, the night sea journey, and rebirth, though we did not speak directly of the latter. Most important was the emotion he felt, and this—"I am born again"—both expressed rebirth better than any explanation.

None of his problems were solved. But he began to approach them with an entirely different attitude.

The dream effected a great liberation, it led him to breathe more consciously, to live.

CONSEQUENCES OF THE CONCEPT OF ARCHETYPES IN DEALING WITH SYMBOLS

Symbols work out complexes; archetypes are at the root of complexes. We may be faced with either personal symbols that tend to be related to our personal background, or with suprapersonal symbols expressing archetypal contents. But suprapersonal symbols are also presented to consciousness through complexes. Ultimately, the archetype is at the root of the symbol; it is the enigmatic factor signified by the symbol. Behind the symbol is an "archetypal image whose character is hard to define."[22]

Therefore, a symbol can never be fully explained; we are left with an excess meaning, which might be the reason why there is always potential for new fantasies and new creative impulses.

The Jungian technique of interpretation reflects these structural connections. I would like to illustrate this theory in light of the technique of dream analysis.

The dream, a symbolic expression, is examined as a series of images (first step). It is sensible, while recounting it, for the dreamer to reexperience the dream in his or her imagination,[23] and it is both meaningful and effective for the analyst to see the dream as a series of images, though undoubtedly our perceptions are never the same as another individual's. By examining the series of images, we are able to experience the symbol and recognize the related emotion, or, by experiencing it, release the emotion step by step.

Any questions that arise (second step) have to do with the spontaneous emotional reaction to the dream, the overall feeling and mood. We also look for situations that are unclear and might indicate repressed complexes. The recognition of the symbol can lead to a creative act, such as painting, that goes beyond its formation in the imagination.

The third step of interpretation is to define the context, which consists of information, association, and amplification.

The quest for information is bound to the idea that the dreamer partakes of the real world wherein problems need to be solved, and is involved in relationships that confront him or her with problems. We ask about the individual's current life situation, and problems that were most pressing at the time of the dream; we seek information about the dream figures. Where and under what circumstances has the dreamer encountered them before? What do they mean to the dreamer? We address the individual's background and fantasies.

The quest for associations is bound to the idea that symbols work out complexes. Therefore, associations should help us discover which complex patterns of relationship, or perhaps which complexes, were touched upon in the dream. By association, we compile the emotions that evoke dream figures, dream places, and dream situations. This may be determined by the dream itself or by the memories triggered by the dream. Often, emotional patterns of relationship are associated. In which situations does the dreamer behave like the dream figures? In some instances, the same relationship pattern can be identified in the therapeutic relationship.

The quest for amplification is bound to the idea that an archetype is at the core of the complex. Part of amplification is the inclusion of analogies from earlier dreams, and the inclusion of related mythological motifs from fairy tales and the like. Since the dream, as a rule, represents a symbolic process, the process within the dream is given special attention. We note the initial situation, the dream-ego's position, and which problem is represented. Next, we note where surprises and where unexpected changes occur, and who initiates them. The important factor is the relationship between the dream-ego and the dream figures, analogous to the ego complex in its central position among the other complexes. This question provides the answer in regard to the dream-ego's current status in the world and the dynamics active in the psyche.

The end of the dream discloses whether or not something new and unknown is happening, and to which goal the symbol is leading. This final developmental aspect is more important in Jungian psychology than the causal aspect, which pertains to the imprinting situation. I believe that though neither can exist without the other, the developmental dimension of the symbol is the key. The symbol presents not only memory to the individual, but also —and this is very important—the expectation of something more from life.

The idea that individuation, as it is presented to consciousness through symbols, is both a process of relationship and of integration stems from the concept of interpretation on the subjective and objective level. In interpretation on the objective level, persons and situations in the dream are related to actual persons and situations. In subjective interpretation, persons and situations are considered to indicate personal potential or aspects of personality. Since the process of individuation usually takes place in a therapeutic relationship, the question further arises whether or not the symbol is connected to the relationship between the analysand and the analyst.

Another essential question is how the body, as the basis of the ego complex, is experienced in the dream.

Finally, there are other questions relating to the current life situation. Can the process of the dream be transferred onto a current situation? Can it add anything to our knowledge of the situation? Does it inspire new action or new attitudes? This would mean that the dream, as a self-regulating activity, is an unconscious reaction to a conscious situation; the unconscious reaction can be a confirmation, an indication of antithesis, or an unconscious tendency to change. Another possible question: Does the dream represent an unfamiliar element, something that fascinates or triggers anxiety? The dream, then, would be an unconscious process unrelated to the conscious situation. It may have to do with the surfacing of old experiences, perhaps from childhood, or with archetypal constellations, or it may be only an indication that the present coherence of the ego complex does not encourage contact with unconscious constellations. In this case, meditation, imagination, and creativity are viable techniques for dealing with the dream.

The concept that symbols are presented to consciousness through symbolic processes which may extend over long periods of time, owes its existence to the recognition of dream series. The basic idea behind this is that dream-life is a continuum, made more apparent by the fact that the more dominating a particular problem, the easier it is to distinguish the connection between separate dreams.[24]

Dream series lend our interpretations a comparative context; they indicate new aspects and new perspectives, while others recede into the background. Dream series impressively demonstrate how multifaceted the symbol is, despite the fact that its emotional message is relatively straightforward.

THE ARCHETYPE OF THE SELF AND THE INDIVIDUATION PROCESS

The archetype that forms the core of the ego complex is the self. At this point, I would like to introduce a few more of Jung's definitions of the self. According to Jung, "the self designates the whole range of psychic phenomena in man. It expresses the unity of the personality as a whole."[25] In his last work, *Mysterium Coniunctionis*, Jung writes that the self is the "ground and origin of the individual personality" and embraces it in the "past, present and future."[26] In other passages, Jung speaks of the self as a numinous *a priori* principle of formation,[27] later as the energy source of the individual.[28] He also calls the self the secret "*spiritus rector*" of fate;[29] it is the "the completest expression of that fateful combination we call individuality."[30]

Since the self consists of both conscious and unconscious contents—and the unconscious is by definition not conscious—it can never be grasped entirely; like any archetype it remains mysterious. This is why the self cannot be localized within an ego complex, but instead acts as "a circumambient atmosphere to which no definite limits can be set, either in space or time."[31]

Just as the ego complex is based in the self, and draws the impulse to develop from the self as *spiritus rector*, the ego complex is also necessary for the self to incarnate. The relationship between the self and the ego complex is reciprocal. Accordingly, Jung says:

> The ego lives in space and time and must adapt itself to their laws if it is to exist at all. If it is absorbed by the unconscious to such an

extent that the latter alone has the power of decision, then the ego is stifled, and there is no longer any medium in which the unconscious could be integrated and in which the work of realization could take place. The separation of the empirical ego from the "eternal" and universal man is therefore of vital importance. . . . The unconscious can be integrated only if the ego holds its ground.[32]

This quote contains a new definition of the self as the "eternal" and universal man. It demonstrates the reciprocality of the relationship between the self and the ego, while it also states that individuation is possible only if the ego complex is sufficiently coherent. Consequently, individuation would mean incarnating the "eternal" and universal impulses in the ego complex to the extent that a constellation is present. In conjunction with this idea, Jung says:

The self, in its efforts of self-realization, reaches out to all sides beyond the ego-personality; because of its all-encompassing nature it is brighter and darker than the ego and consequently confronts it with problems which it would like to avoid."[33]

Jung also mentions that the self can be distinguished only conceptually from what has always been referred to as "God," but not practically.[34]

As psychologists, we do not refer to God, but rather to godlike images as they appear in the individual's psyche, and in what way they are experienced and shaped. When the archetype of the self is constellated, be it in dreams, fantasies, visions, or images, it is connected with a strong emotion. Symbols of the self are accompanied by an aura of numinosity. Numinosity is actually the power emanating from the deity. Jung frequently speaks of numinosity, and by using this expression, he implicitly suggests that something of the old gods' power might be hidden within the effect of archetypes. Since the archetype of the self is the central archetype, it is accompanied by a special emotion: the emotion is moving, utterly profound, and prompts a sense of natural selfness, a sense of connection to a greater whole. This archetype is repeatedly experienced and causes an unhoped-for centering of the personality. However, archetypal influences never last very long.

According to Jung, the phenomena of the self appears in the symbol of a supraordinate personality, such as a king, hero, prophet, or savior.[35] Obviously, these supraordinate personalities must also be considered in their female form.

I am very skeptical of the idea that supraordinate personalities are symbols of the self. I understand that Jung argues for it because the self is superior to the ego. But I believe that a king, for instance, can just as well signify an extension of the father complex in the archetypal realm. Those symbols of the self that represent the unity and wholeness of the personality, such as the circle, the quadrangle, the squared circle, the cross, and particularly the mandala, to which I will return later, seem more convincing to me because they are standard symbols, and signify an inexplicable emotional effect. The self can also appear as a unified duality. The Yin-Yang symbol, the two brothers, the two sisters, or the heterosexual couple are known symbols of the self. The heterosexual couple is one of the most dynamic symbols of the self.

When the self is recognized and experienced in these symbols, it effects centering and dissolves the condition of chaos; we sense an undeniable identity and the predestined nature of the situation in which the symbol is constellated.

The symbols I have mentioned above indicate the archetypal structure in which the self appears to consciousness. Then again, the dynamic aspect of the archetype is self-realization in the sense of archetypal occurrence. When the theme of self-realization is predominant, the self is represented by other symbols (e.g., the growth of a tree).

The Mandala as a Symbol

The mandala is undoubtedly one of the best-known symbols expressing the structural aspect of the self archetype. Jung repeatedly dealt with this symbol.

In Sanskrit, *mandala* means "circle." The word has become a common term in theology and, above all, in psychology as a symbol of wholeness.[36] In Indo–Tibetan culture, mandalas are represented by a circle or several concentric circles circumscribed by a square.

> In meditation, the yogi visualizes the mandala; he recognizes that it is truly the universe reflected within him. . . . Thus, the mandala is the vehicle for great transformation.[37]

In psychology, any circular shapes that emphasize the center are fundamentally regarded as mandalas. Jung says of the mandala that its symbolism embraces all "concentrically arranged figures, round or square patterns with a center, and radial or spherical arrangements."[38] The circular figure plays an important role for humanity; it is a "unique wholeness and completeness." Ingrid Riedel devoted extensive works to this symbol.[39] It has been observed that individuals undergoing periods of inner turmoil have a particular tendency to paint mandalas; either as simple, circular images, or as very complicated structures. The experience conveyed is that, despite the chaos, there is order. A center is present that can always be drawn upon, and concentration is possible. But when we look more closely at the background of mandala images, we recognize that each one expresses that the individual's inclusion in the cosmic whole.

The creation of such mandalas is a manifestation of psychic centering. Jung maintains that mandalas have a considerable therapeutic effect, but he warns us not to imitate them, since this promises no results. These days, many courses on mandala painting are being offered, and it seems to me that Jung's rigorous objection should be reinvestigated. Perhaps people who feel drawn to such a course have an inner need to deal with mandalas. Painting a mandala could reestablish the coherence of their ego complex by emphasizing the ego-self axis.

I would like to discuss a classic mandala painting from Jung's works, and another that was created in my practice. Just as Jung believed that dreams are shared between the analyst and the analysand,[40] I believe that the formation of these symbolic pictures occurs between the analyst and the analysand. Jung was excited by the classic mandalas, which is perhaps why these mandalas were created in his practice. In the chapter "A Study in the Process of Individuation" from his book *The Archetypes and the Collective Unconscious*, Jung describes the mandalas painted by a fifty-five-year-old woman. This is an example of a classic mandala[41] (cf. color plate 12), constructed with a circle and a quadrangle. The black quadrangle represents the "four quarters of life" that are experienced in the concrete environment; the circle, then, symbolizes inclusion within the more universal personality. There are four inner circles, which the painter perhaps associated with the four ego functions. I believe there are considerably more than four ego functions. But perhaps the green circle with the human figure entwined by snakes represents the underworld, the world of instinct; the figure with the birds in the yellow circle, the world of the spirit; and the riders on a horse and an elephant in the red and blue circles represent humanity as sustained by instinctual powers and able to utilize them to harmoniously create life. In all, this would be an image of the fantasized current situation of the ego complex, which is mysteriously embraced by the self.

The idea of the union of opposites is integral to this mandala, as it is also to the choice of colors. The red flower contrasts with the black, while green and red, and blue and yellow occupy neighboring fields.

In the process of individuation, the archetypal motif of the "divine child" is commonly experienced and represented, not infrequently in connection with the mandala. The child may stand in the center of the mandala, or grow out of a tree, an egg, or a blossom. Jung believes that in this case the child anticipates the being that will emerge from the synthesis of the conscious and unconscious elements of the personality. In other words, the child motif indicates that an ego-self axis is present, and the personal life is beginning to merge with the suprapersonal; this explains why Jung sees the child motif as the "savior."[42]

When the self is connected to the symbol of the "divine child," or when the child motif is integrated into a mandala, new aspects develop through this attempt at centering, this *"attempt at self-healing* on the part of nature, which. . . . springs from an instinctive impulse,"[43] and which is presented to consciousness through the mandala symbol. A new personality development is manifested, and new possibilities of realization in the concrete world are addressed. When the self is symbolized by the circle or the square, or by Yin and Yang, the formal, structural aspect of the self advances into the foreground. An ego complex that has little coherence regains its coherence through the symbol of wholeness, in the sense of self-healing. Once the mandala is combined with the archetype of the "divine child," the process of self-becoming, which is the dynamic aspect of the archetype, has been addressed.

According to Jung, the formation of a mandala is a definite sign that the coherence of the ego complex can be spontaneously reestablished through the constellation of the archetype of the self. However, since the symbols usually arise in the analytical situation, it is difficult to distinguish to what degree the relationship or the analyst's psychic self-regulation are involved.

Color plate 13 is a drawing by the same woman who drew the "cow pictures" discussed in Chapter 2. Mandala-like images such as this frequently occur in my practice.

This mandala is a transition from concrete to symbolic representation. The mandala is in the cow's stomach; thus the mandala, the aspect of centering and security, was discovered though experiencing the cow, which could be construed as the instinctual, nurturing maternal principle. The coloration of the mandala also reflects a sense of security. A child is growing out of the center of the mandala into the arms of the woman, who stands behind the mandala. The woman could be interpreted as the ego of the painter, who is devoting herself to the child. But she might also represent the analyst, implying that new factors can develop if the analyst expects and accepts them.

A new tree, another symbol for individuation, as I will later demonstrate, is growing behind the cow. The tree indicates the growth and evolution of the child.

In addition, this mandala picture also shows that the symbols for the self can appear side by side with configurations of the archetypal mother.

Finally, the painting illustrates that both self-centering and the ego-self axis have been established; the self can gradually incarnate into personal life and activate it to a substantial degree.

The Individuation Process

The dynamism emanating from the archetype of the self effects self-becoming. The theme of self-becoming is integral to humanity.

> Individuation has two principal aspects: in the first place it is an internal and subjective process of integration, and in the second it is an equally indispensable process of objective relationship.[44]

A process of integration implies that the symbols presented to consciousness are experienced, shaped, and understood, particularly in their emotional content, and then influence our action and our attitudes.

But individuation is also a process of relationship, for, according to Jung, "the relationship to the self is at once relationship to our fellow man, and no one can be related to the latter until he is related to himself."[45] Becoming oneself must not be understood as excluding the environment. On the contrary, becoming oneself, or defining oneself, defines relationship. This does not imply that our fellow man is useful to us "only" as a vehicle for projections. Obviously, since we frequently come face to face with ourself in a relationship with another person, many projections occur in relationships. Not only do archetypes activate relationships, but relationships activate archetypes. In my opinion, this is a part of any I-you relationship that is not distorted by too many projections. Beyond the I-you relationship, various relationships are possible between the individual and others, and, finally, between the individual and the world. A person on the path of individuation will invariably detect a tension between what can be perceived in symbols, what he or she senses as an inner duty, and his or her position in the world. Our experience of the world or of relationships will repeatedly alter the way we view symbols, and perhaps the way we formulate them. Relationship and individuation cannot be separated.

Since individuation is both a subjective process of integration and an objective process of relationship, two different repercussions are possible.

There are people who are capable of individuating through relationship alone; they are capable of intense devotion, can live entirely for another person, and tend to subordinate their ego. Let me illustrate this in a heterosexual couple. Symbolically, the woman accepts, attends to, and indulges her animus aspect through the man. However, since she does so as a pattern of relationship, by projection, we inevitably have the impression that the woman neglects herself and her responsibility to herself. When "women love too much," it means that the impulse toward individuation, which Jung describes as a drive, is projected onto a relationship. The relationship aspect alone is present, while the integration aspect is missing. Lacking, then, is any thought about what significance this man, to whom she is so devoted, has to her life. Is he, perhaps, an indication of some intrapsychic aspect which is desperately needed for her fulfillment? This process of introspection is lacking.

The other repercussion is individuation in an ivory tower. In this case, the process of individuation is purely internal; we make all our decisions on our own; we accept stimuli from the outside without acknowledging them as such; we use people and relationships to inspire or structure our inner life. Ideally, the tension between the internal process of integration and the external process of relationship should be maintained; then the inside would activate the outside and vice versa.

Basically, individuation is a process that cannot be predetermined; no one, not even the analyst, knows the outcome. The process as such is marked by indicators, such as the symbols we see in dreams, images, or fantasies, which we might misinterpret. In this case the symbols will present further modifications.

Jung describes the typical stages of individuation as follows. First, the shadow must be integrated. This causes problems with the persona, the image we wish to show the world, which is influenced by social values and expectations. The next step is to integrate the anima and the animus. Our confrontation with the shadow, the persona, the anima and the animus, is indeed significant. However, individuation does not necessarily occur in the sequence that Jung suggests. If the individuation process is to retain its meaning, it must be individual to each case. The only aspect common to all processes is the drive to become oneself. But the drive toward becoming oneself is also a drive toward continually going beyond limitations. On the one hand, the boundaries of the ego complex are to be traversed, and on the other, the boundaries of our relationship to the environment. They are inseparable. Individuation implies that all boundaries that are currently valid, and that define us at the moment, must be repeatedly questioned, sacrificed, and traversed. Individuation is a persistent transformation of the self and at the same time a transformation of the system. This is the emancipating aspect of individuation.[46]

The individuation process, which represents the dynamic aspect of the archetype of the self, is frequently symbolized by the growth process, particularly by the growth of trees. Trees seem to be especially suited as projection carriers for the human process of individuation. We stand upright in the world, as does the tree. It is more rooted than we are, but we, too, remember our roots. The tree rises upward, and grows until it dies. In its rising it must stand, withstand, and stand firm, just as we. It expands as its crown grows, and if it bears fruit, it is fertile and spreads out into the world. Its crown is a roof, a haven that offers birds a chance to rest. The tree is connected to the earth, to the depths, to water; it is connected to the sky. As we humans stand between above and below, so also does the tree. It changes through the seasons. The structure of the tree reveals its life history.

The symbol of the World Tree—which is often the Tree of Life, such as the World Ash Yggdrasill, a symbol of the universe and of cosmic renewal—represents both the cyclic transformation of life and the continuity of life, or eternal life. Our proverbs often equate man with trees, and there are sayings that specifically relate to parts of trees, such as, "The apple does not fall far from the tree," or "Out of the acorn grows the mighty oak." In introducing his well-known tree test, Koch says, "The growth of the psyche can be illustrated by the growth of a tree."[47] To explain Jungian psychology in simple terms von Franz, in *Man and His Symbols*,[48] compares the process of individuation with the growth of a seed into a mountain pine. At a certain time the seed falls onto a particular place. Once it sprouts, it has to contend with special climatic conditions, comparable to the environment into which a child is born. Gradually the pine grows. It would be senseless to wish that the pine might become an oak; yet, similar demands are made on human life. An integral part of individuation is the acceptance of what we are—though not in the sense that we do not want to change anything—and acceptance of basic conditions that cannot be explained away. It is the acceptance of these basic conditions that enables us to continually go beyond limitations.

A tree will also have injuries; these injuries make up its individuality.

With a few illustrations, I would like to show how trees can reflect projections of the human individuation process. At the same time, I would like to use this series to demonstrate how comparable imagery is repeatedly experienced and created in symbols at different times. I wish to demonstrate how a basically collective symbol, although it is visible in its collective aspect, is also shaped by personal factors. In the process we shall see what developmental psychology has made very clear, that the dynamic aspect of the archetype of the self is rarely experienced in its pure form, but rather in connection with other archetypes, particularly the mother archetype.

The first picture (fig. 4), "Mercurius as Virgin (Pandora) and *Arbor Philosophica*," from the year 1588, appeared in Jung's work *Religious Ideas in Alchemy*.[49]

Mercury is a symbol for the dynamics of the archetype. It is Mercury who moves everything from potentiality to actuality, and it is he who effects transformation. The alchemists often projected the process of transformation onto the tree, as a symbol for wholeness in becoming and growing.

In this illustration, the tension between the opposites is very important, as is the fusion of the opposites. It is an indication that individuation is mainly instigated by the endurance of opposing tensions and by the endeavor to integrate them. The title itself, "Mercurius as Virgin," implies the union of opposites. According to Jung, the picture also suggests a representation of the Virgin Mary.

From Egyptian mythology, we are familiar with the mother goddesses Isis, Nut, and Hathor, who are also tree goddesses; they dispense the water of eternal life, and thus guarantee that life will continue. In Greek mythology, there are tree nymphs; in Celtic mythology, the renewing powers of fairy trees can be compared to Eros.

The second picture (fig. 5, p. 118), and the third (fig. 6, p. 119), are taken from Jung's essay "The Philosophical Tree" in *Psychology and Alchemy*.[50] In Figure 5 the form concealed in the tree awakens and begins to emerge from the trunk. The snake in the treetop slithers toward the awakening woman's ear. The bird, lion, lamb, and pig evoke associations with the Garden of Eden; the pig in particular could enrich Paradise.

By its connection to the Tree of Life, this tree is, of course, also related to the Trees of Paradise, the Trees of Life and Death, and the Tree of Knowledge.

Jung's interpretation of this image is that of a self-sufficient Eve gradually emerging. He defined the picture

12

13

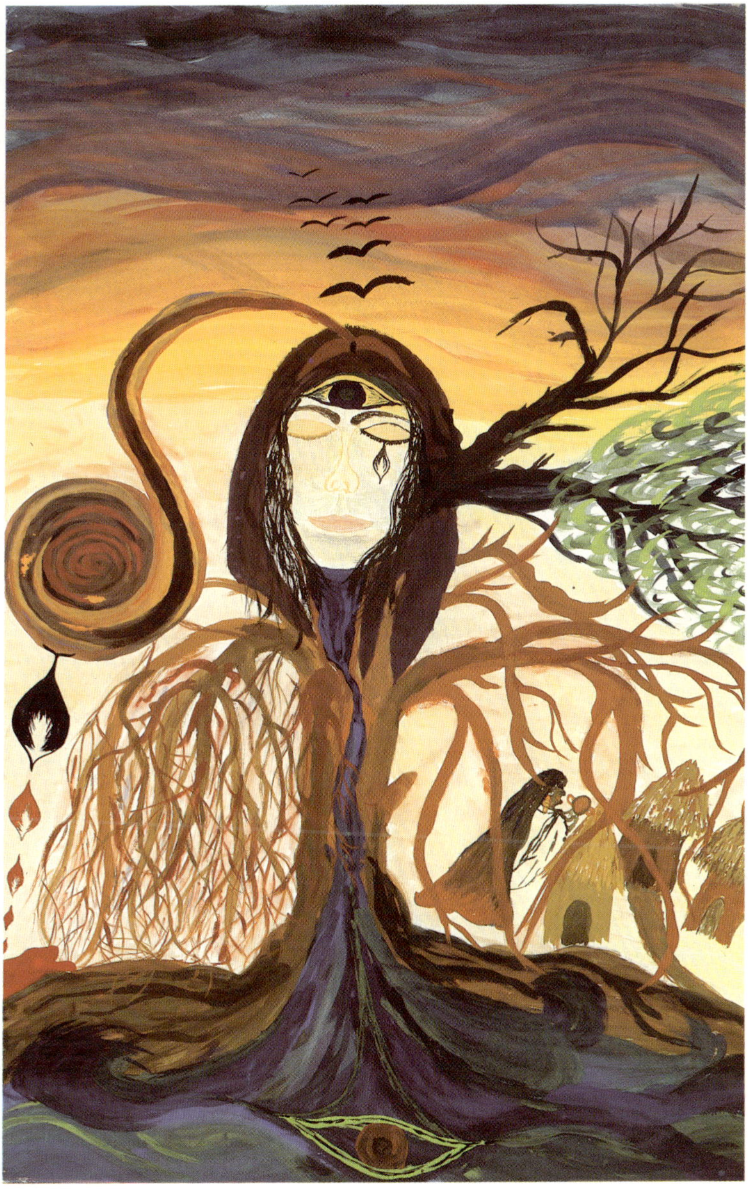

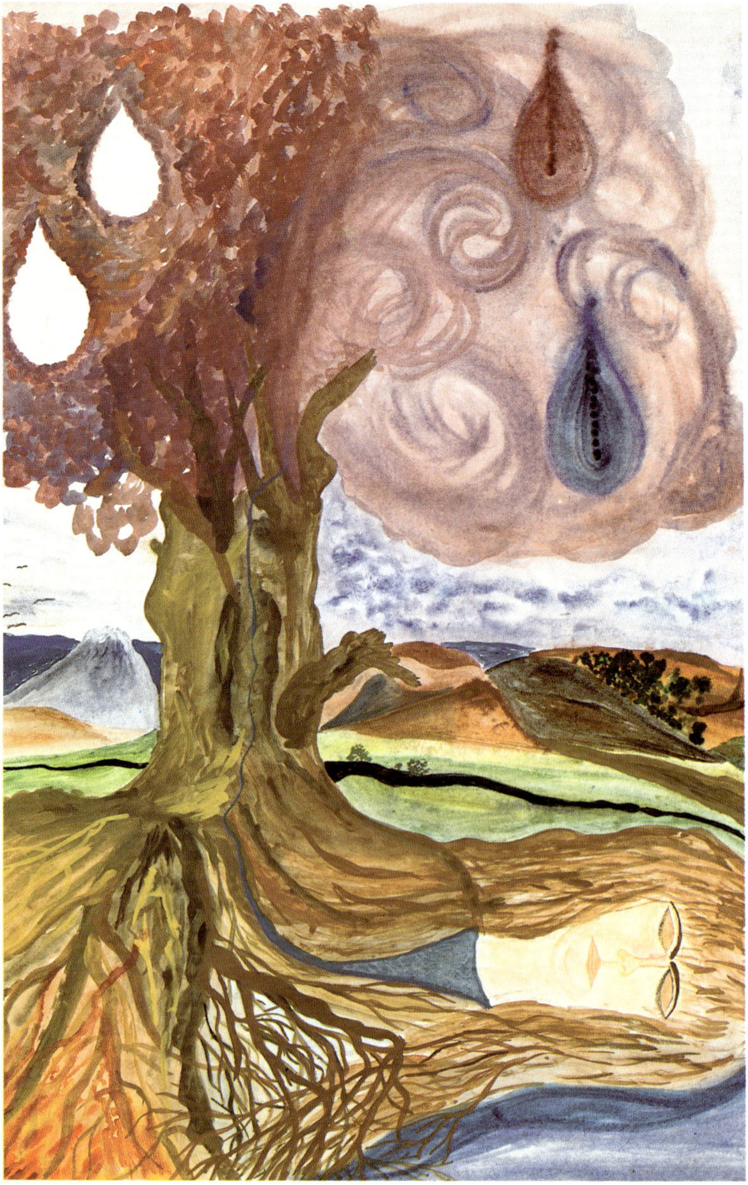

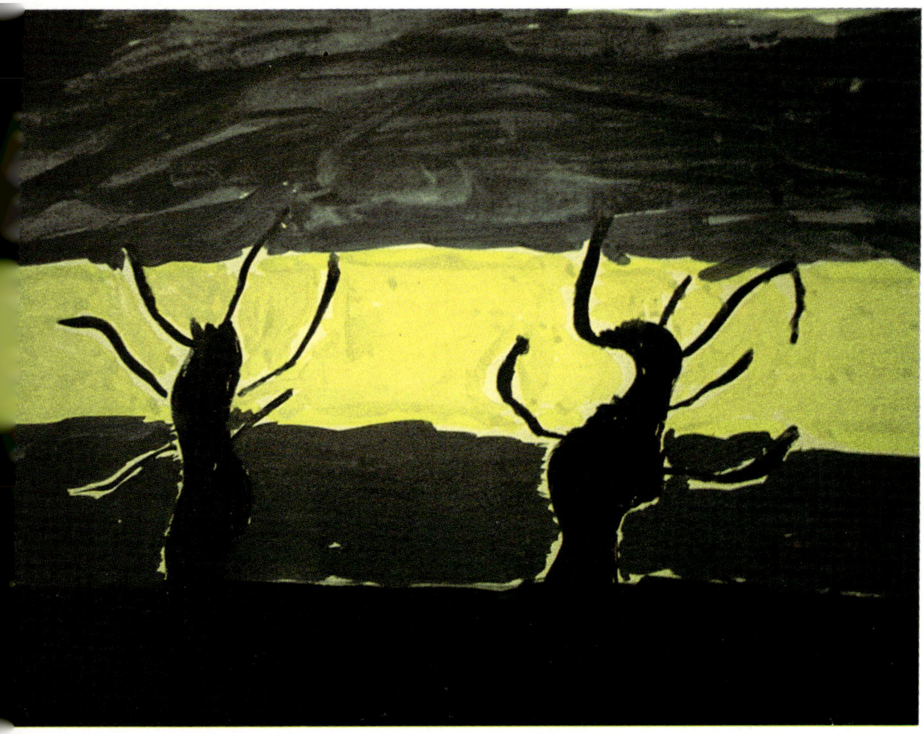

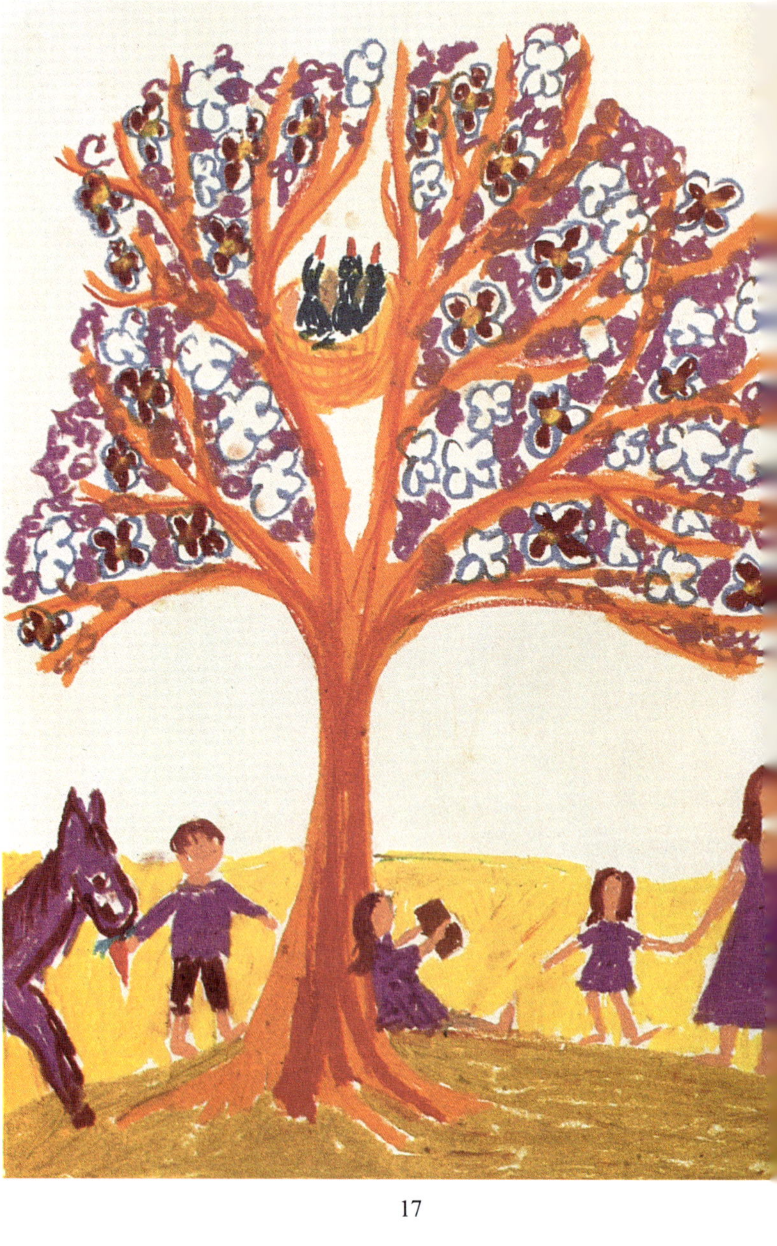

18

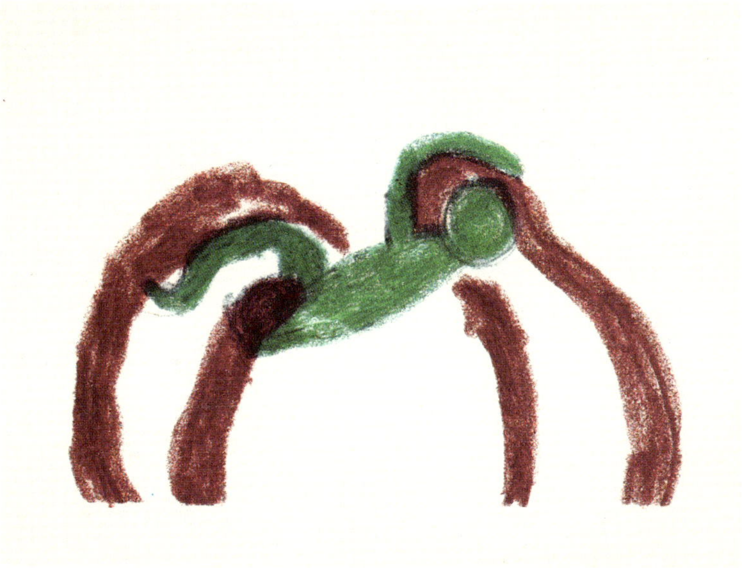

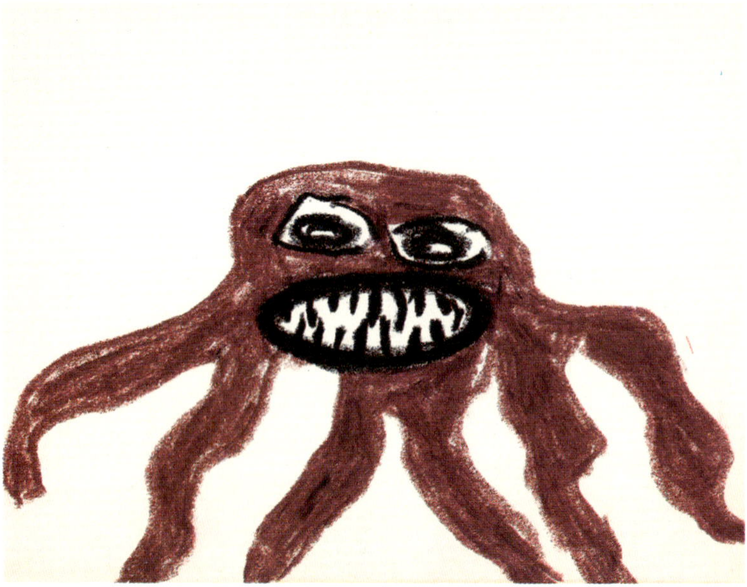

19/20

Figure 4

as a station on the path to this woman's individuation, more specifically, the point when the woman's ego complex becomes visible. She is emerging, as it were, from the mother-tree as her own being. At the same time she remains in contact with nature—a unique nature when we consider symbolism of the bird, lion, lamb, and pig.

The tree, which in its growth represents individuation,

Figure 5

is simultaneously a mother symbol, particularly the tree-trunk. Here, we have the impression that the trunk is like a mother releasing the child.

There are several fairy tales relating to this theme, such as Grimm's fairy tale, "The Old Woman in the Wood."

In Egyptian mythology, the death goddess Nut, in the form of a tree, takes the dead back into herself so that they can be reborn. In Switzerland, we still call coffins *Totenbäume*, or "trees of the dead."

Figure 6 on page 119 depicts a human figure growing out of a tree and holding the sun. Again, there are parallels in Egyptian mythology. Nut, an older form of Hathor, is also a goddess of the sky who gives birth to the sun.

The idea that the human growth process can be symbolized by a tree, and that the development of individual personality can be seen as emergence from a tree, perhaps as the emergence from a collective individuation process of humanity, is represented in every culture. Here, too, we see the interlocking of the individuation process with

Figure 6

certain symbols of the mother archetype: The tree can be seen as a maternal function releasing humanity into life, and probably taking us back into death. Such imagery is not only intercultural—we could expand these examples at will—but can also be observed throughout human history.

The next pictures are again from my current practice. Color plate 14 was painted by a twenty-eight-year-old woman during a suicidal phase. I take the female figure to be a self-portrait, an unconscious compensation, as it were, for the ego complex. She appears in the form of a wind-blown tree, which gives the impression that life has treated the woman harshly. The figure has a third eye—the eye of wisdom. She is rooted in water and drowning in sorrow. On the whole, the picture conveys the impression that, even beyond all misfortune and accident, a female identity can still be experienced, an identity which makes a developmental process possible. The picture could have been telling the painter that she was after all meant for life.

In Color plate 15, the tree is growing out of the woman, whose head is emphasized; while the head is asleep and the ego complex has given up control, the tree can continue to grow; the individuation process can be initiated. The attitude of conscious control has been abandoned, and growth in a larger context sets in.

We often have definite ideas as to how life should be, but, because life does not conform to these ideas, we are neither in agreement with it nor are we able to see what it really is. It could be that, in this case, the point has been reached where the ego complex gives up of its own impulse and volition, and that what is pushing upward from the roots to the light can now take shape. When we consider that the ego and the self mutually establish each other, and that the ego complex must incarnate the self into the world, we realize that the inspiration and impulse to life come from the self as long as communication exists between the ego and the self. If, however, the ego fixates on something, and we employ too many defense mechanisms against unconscious manifestations, the compensatory function of the unconscious might be impeded. We employ defense mechanisms because the autonomy of consciousness is valuable to us. We are not open to the unconscious until we are in a difficult situation and the ego (the ego complex) has no other way out. It is a situation of death and rebirth. This situation frequently occurs in therapy when the analysand and the therapist expect a reaction from the unconscious, be it a dream, a new feeling of vitality, or even the analyst's sense of countertransference.

Color plate 16 is a painting by a twenty-three-year-old man who since birth has had severe difficulty in walking. He sought therapy because he believed he could not cope with his disability. The trees are representations of a dream symbol.

His statement about the picture was, "These are beautiful trees, particularly because they are crippled." Despite being crippled, they were beautiful trees. He could perceive himself the way he was; he could accept himself in all his being. I asked if they were willow trees, and he answered, "Yes, but they are also crippled. This is just the way they should be." His reinforcement made it clear how important it was to him not to deny his difficulty. The trees conveyed both self-representation and self-acceptance, which enabled him to have a lighter perspective on life. The fact that there were two trees might have referred to the analytic process, but perhaps it indicates a situation where he can look at himself and see himself for what he is, and accept himself.

Finally, I would like to introduce one more tree painted by the twenty-eight-year-old woman who drew the pictures of her father complex (cf. color plate 17).

The picture represents her vision of her future life—this, too, belongs to the process of individuation. It is the vision of a family. Though at that time she had no children, she was pregnant.

Squeezed between the branches of the tree, the nest seems to lack a stable foundation. It hovers up there quite precariously. The part of the tree where the nest is situated is comparable to the uterus. Shortly afterward, the woman had a miscarriage, but she eventually gave life to three children.

Various aspects of individuation can be symbolized by the tree. It can represent the current self-image, the connection to the mother complex and the mother archetype, and the stage at which the ego separates from the mother complex and the mother archetype. Collectively, it implies a definition of position, the extent to which we have become unique beings, and the extent to which we are attached to the collective life process.

The process of individuation can also appear in a tree as a utopian vision.

With the archetype of the self, the most central archetype, I have demonstrated how an archetype can be manifested either symbolically in its structural aspect, when the self appears as a squared circle, a mandala, or a Yin-Yang symbol, or in its dynamic aspect, such as when the process of individuation is projected onto a tree. The influence a symbol has on the therapeutic situation and the developmental potential as currently presented depends on whether the symbol appears in its structural or its dynamic aspect. If we dream of a mandala, we will be very taken by this symbol; we will feel more organized than previously, and thus more energetic. We might paint the mandala. We will be interested in other mandalas.

If the structural aspect of the archetype is manifested, the time has not yet come to change anything in the outside world. But once the more dynamic aspect arises in dreams, transference, or fantasies, the time has come to realize something; what is inside must be brought out, and what is integrated must be brought into the relationship.

It is entirely possible that the structural and dynamic aspects are presented to consciousness through the same symbol, such as a child in the center of a mandala. This would represent a situation where the experience of the organizing factors, the experience of being bound in a cosmic order, and the actualization of new possibilities occur simultaneously.

REMARKS ON SYNCHRONICITY

We use expressions like "archetypes are constellated," or "to constellate archetypes." What these expressions mean is that a certain archetype has become significant in our life. Through dreams or archetypal constellations we recognize the archetype as a guiding force, and perhaps as influential even in the material world.

Archetypal constellations are energy fields that are expressed by emotions; they are accompanied by the interpretations we associate with them.

When we remember important situations in our life, we usually notice that "everything fit together," or that certain hoped-for events could not take place because the constellation as a whole was not appropriate, and life was governed by other influences.

We feel we could describe a group of events and experiences that coincide with each other. For the therapist, who is able to participate in developmental processes concerning another individual, it is fascinating to observe how life is characterized by certain themes at certain times, such as the theme "departure," and how difficult the situation becomes if the individual resists this theme.

Constellations can also be experienced in a different form. Perhaps someone has to attend an event which he has absolutely no desire to go to; but he must go, for lack of a good excuse. The situation is highly ambivalent, and emotionally charged. He gets into his car and it will not start. More aggravation! A friend stops by and looks under the opened hood. The problem cannot be located; half relieved, half with a bad conscience, he has to cancel his appointment. And to top off the situation, someone else comes along, looks at the engine, and asks: "Didn't you notice that one of the plugs is loose?" There can hardly be a conclusive causal explanation for this series of events. Two things, whose concurrence cannot be explained causally, coincided. How should the car know the man did not want to drive just then, and, by not functioning at the right moment, do him a favor?

This brings up a subject that is difficult to grasp and judge: synchronistic phenomena.

Jung defines synchronicity as the temporal coincidence of two or more events of comparable significance, which are causally unrelated. I quote:

> Synchronicity . . . consists of two factors: *a*) An unconscious image comes into consciousness either directly (i.e., literally) or indirectly (symbolized or suggested) in the form of a dream, idea, or premonition. *b*) An objective situation coincides with this content.[51]

In the case of the car that will not start, the unconscious image is the desire not to have to go to the party. The image is repressed as soon as it comes into consciousness, and this causes the ambivalence. The objective situation is the car that does not start.

Jung also speaks of synchronicity when comparable dreams are dreamt by different people in different places.

He speaks of synchronicity, and not simply synchronism, because the situations happen both simultaneously and are characterized by the same content. Aside from causal structure, Jung also postulates an acausal order.

An example for synchronicity.—A twenty-eight-year-old man was very worried because he had applied for a position he very much wanted. Up to that point, he had not received a reply. Being otherwise fairly apprehensive, he felt very tense and obsessed by this problem. He dreamt:

> I'm talking to the director of the new company on the telephone. Somehow another director is there, who says over the phone, "I would be delighted if you would accept this position." I say, "I will gladly accept it." I wake up feeling happy.

At eight in the morning he came to analysis with this dream from the previous night. We tried to understand it.

The analysand was very happy. I considered whether the dream might have been related to wish fulfillment, as a form of compensation, a self-regulation to placate his fears. I also considered that, if this were the case, and should the opposite of the dream's message occur, the result would be a severe narcissistic injury. It became clear to me that it was important how the dream was interpreted. If I responded to his emotional mood, I would have indirectly confirmed that the dream was prophetic, and if he were not to get the job, his world would collapse. Initially, I did not make a commitment. Instead, I tried to find out who the other director might have been. The analysand knew nothing of him and we speculated whether or not the dream might have been related to various aspects of his authority complex, because he might well have had the need to be accepted by an authority higher than the director. We associated and gathered ideas. Our work was interrupted by a message from the analysand's wife, who had just received a call from the company and asked that he phone back. Rather than wait, he immediately went to the telephone—I was glad I was there to deal with the situation, in any event. The director, with whom he had always negotiated, and who also appeared in the dream, said, "I would be delighted if you would accept this position." He added that he said this in the name of his father as well.

Until this moment, the analysand had been unaware that the director's father also worked for the company.

This was a synchronistic event. The job was very important to the man, and he faced a major decision in his life.

Generally, we experience synchronicity when we must master an emotionally charged situation, such as in times of upheaval when new archetypal constellations become manifest. We frequently experience synchronicity in connection with death.

An example for a synchronistic incident connected to death.—In the same night, a brother and sister dreamt. The brother dreamt:

Father says good-bye. He's laughing. I call after him not to forget something. As a rule, Father always forgets something. In the dream, he says, "For me there is no more forgetting."

The dreamer woke in an agitated state. In the middle of the night, the man, who thought little of dreams, called his sister three hundred kilometers away. She was the first to speak, "I'm glad you called. I think we should go see father right away. I dreamt he's lying in bed and I can't wake him anymore. I'm really worried."

They drove to see their father. He died a week later.

We repeatedly hear such stories. We tend to reject and dismiss them by declaring that they were made up afterward. But, nonetheless, these things do happen and need to be explained.

Synchronicity occurs when archetypal structures constellate not only in our psyche and body, but also, to a certain extent, in the material environment.

Time and again, Jung has been held responsible and reproached for this definition of synchronicity. But it actually has a long philosophical tradition; Jung introduced the idea to psychology. At this point, I cannot discuss the subject in detail, but I would like to mention a few main points.

Chinese thought was and is familiar with the idea of synchronicity. We Westerners are more interested in particulars, while to the Eastern mind details serve merely to complete the whole. The *I Ching*, a very old Chinese book of oracles, has to do with synchronicity. The way our hands toss coins or sort yarrow stalks in a particular emotional situation corresponds with our inner disposition. Chinese thought, exemplified by the *I Ching*, does not question what should be done in the given moment, but rather how our actions are related to life. It judges our actions according to the circumstances affecting them. Chinese thought asks which archetypal structure is currently active, and how we can arrive at decisions enabling us to live in concord with, rather than in contention to, that structure.

The therapeutic process aims to recognize the constellated archetypal structures so that we may go with the flow of life and not against it. But experience shows that, except in times of crisis and upheaval, many different archetypes are usually active at the same time, making it difficult to attune to the flow of life.

An example for the simultaneous effectiveness of various archetypes.—A fifty-three-year-old woman was presented with her first grandchild. She had looked forward to the event. She was going through menopause and interested in the change of life. She also had a very old mother who was quite ill and seemed to be nearing the end of her life. Suddenly, she was responsive to the archetypal image of the wise old woman; she looked for fairy tales where the wise old woman appears; she complained that, despite their age, old people were not wise.

The archetypal structure activated here was revealed in the motif of the grandmother and the wise old woman.

But the woman also wanted to finish, as quickly as possible, her studies in two subjects, because she was under the impression that the time for studying was coming to an end, and that something else was about to begin. This came from the archetypal constellation—something else *was* beginning.

She sought therapy because, for the first time in her life, she had difficulty working and could not study for her exams; she was exasperated, because all her life she had been able to study whenever she wanted, and now it was suddenly a problem.

When considered in terms of archetypes, it was evident that she wanted to force something that did not agree with the archetypal structure currently activated. Passing tests has more to do with the archetype of the hero or heroine. It is a battle. The trickster archetype may also be involved. In special cases, an exam could be influenced by the wise old woman or man archetype, but less so the preparations for an exam.

I presented these correlations to her. We both realized that, though it was sensible for her to take the exams, it had little to do with her developmental process. She decided to complete only one subject and to accept that she could not invest all her energy in taking the final exam.

By no means does this imply that a fifty-three-year-old cannot take an exam. The hero archetype can also be constellated at the age of fifty-three, but it is equally possible that a different constellation is present. Essentially, these constellations follow the transitional phases I attempted to present globally in connection with the development of the ego complex.

However, individuation does not necessarily follow a collective typology; the hero archetype can constellate in some individuals who are sixty-five to seventy-five years old.

Synchronicity was thought of not only in China. Around 300 B.C., Hippocrates spoke of the sympathy between all things; he said all things together make a whole, and the reaction of each part influences the whole. He formulated the modern theory of systems. Plotinus took up the idea again, and Avicenna, who lived from 980 to around 1040 and established the basis of medical studies, proposed the hypothesis that the human soul has a unique power to alter the material world when seized by a great excess of love or hate; that is, by strong emotions. This explains why synchronicity is so carefully scrutinized; the ability to change even material things when in a state of excess love, or hate, or a similar emotion, would be magic.

The idea of synchronicity might explain why acts of magic are possible. Alchemy followed similar lines of thought—another reason why Jung refers to alchemical writings to explain his ideas. Synchronistic thought is founded on the supposition that the psyche and the material world are expressly *not* non-equatable, but, rather, they are perhaps attributes of one and the same being. In his book *The Turning Point*, F. Capra states dryly that synchronicity implies the acausal relationship between the symbolic images of the psyche and the events in external reality. In other words, there is an acausal order of mind and matter, which today, thirty years after Jung had postulated the idea, seems to be confirmed by various developments in physics. Physicists differentiate between causal and acausal order and call them local and non-local orders. "At the same time patterns of matter and patterns of mind are increasingly recognized as reflections of one another."[52] Capra, too, is unaware that synchronicity is an old idea reintroduced by Jung.

In this respect, one of the most famous precursors of Jung is Leibniz (1646–1716) and his idea of preestablished harmony. He opposed Geulincx, who proposed that the world of the spirit and the world of the body are completely separate entities, like two clocks that God occasionally connects. He is, therefore, called the representative of occasionalism. Leibniz, on the other hand, countered that though both clocks run their course from the start, they are crafted with such great art and skill that they are certain to be in concord. This is the law of preestablished harmony. Body and soul each follow their own laws, but they do agree with each other, because they are representations of the one universe. The soul, as much as the body, represents the universe.

According to Leibniz, synchronicity can be experienced at any given moment. Jung conjectured that it occurs only in exceptional cases, as when a special archetypal constellation can be experienced. This seems implausible, for in a sense archetypes are always constellated. Of course, there are situations related to death, love, and upheaval in general, wherein archetypal constellations are considerably more evident than in times of great tranquility. Most experiences of synchronicity accumulate in times of upheaval, but I believe we notice them only in extreme situations. One consequence of Jungian thought would be to propose an acausal order next to the existing causal order.

What does synchronistic thought mean to Jungian psychology? First of all, it explains parapsychological events that can occur in times of great emotion. It explains how oracular methods, such as the tarot or the *I Ching*, work; why the cards that are drawn or the arrangements of the yarrow stalks have something to do with us, and why they are appropriate surfaces for the projection of our unconscious constellations. In therapy, the idea of synchronicity influences interpretation on the subjective and objective level, and particularly the tendency to formulate symbols. The man who was in a traffic jam might have thought in causal terms, At this time of the day a lot of cars are heading the same way, therefore a jam is likely. But he can also think synchronistically and ask himself what this means to him. Both questions are justified.

A man who has had three typewriters break on the same day does not take the third machine to be repaired. Instead, he sits down and wonders what could be wrong with his writing. Synchronistic thought is holistic. The world, as we perceive it, would then also be symbolic for our inner life. Synchronistic thought might also explain certain phenomena of countertransference, such as why in certain situations the analyst reacts with a sudden stomach ache. Of course, we all know that physical symptoms are one of the possible countertransference reactions. The idea of synchronicity offers an explanation for such phenomena.

Synchronicity becomes critical whenever it moves into the realm of solid matter, although the body is in fact also solid matter.

I have had my practice for eighteen years, and my heating system broke down once in all this time. The heater failed precisely when I was having a session with a man who dreams of polar bears and ice significantly more often than others do. In addition, his name had something to do with the word "cold." But even if such situations could be explained in the sense of synchronicity, it is not easy to pinpoint the meaning that is, or might be, behind it.

Synchronicity and Psychosomatics

I believe that synchronistic thought is most consequential in relation to a comprehensive psychosomatic approach.

Von Uexküll defined a physical-psychosocial model in connection with psychosomatics.[53] He believes that the body, the psyche, and the environment are interrelated within a dynamic balance. The dynamic balance can be disturbed now and then; any illness is a dynamic imbalance. The disturbance is a change in the self-organized system that embraces the body, psyche, and environment, and can reveal itself on various planes: in the body, the psyche, or the environment. If, for instance, something new is unleashed internally, we might become physically ill, we might become depressed, we might irresponsibly retreat from the rest of the world, or destroy our environment. Thus, things are not the way we have long thought or said them to be, "I become physically ill because I fail to accept something psychically." This concept unjustly places the psyche before the other elements; actually, illness is a part of us. It can manifest equally on the psychic, physical, and even the social plane. This revises the elementary idea: We do not become ill because we have done something wrong, instead we might become ill when life enters a new situation.

On the whole, synchronistic thought relativizes our concept of guilt, an elementary idea that is indebted to causal thought: it is not because we have done or failed to do something that things happen the way they do; we live within circumstances where changes occur with which we can deal either well or badly. Of course, it is difficult to apply these ideals to our daily lives. Although Jung did not speak of synchronicity in terms of the reciprocal relationship of the body and the psyche, the idea can nonetheless be detected throughout Jungian psychology. He did say that the formation of symbols is frequently associated with physical disorders of a psychic origin.[54] Jung was perhaps less attentive to the fact that the formation of symbols frequently has to do with collisions in the external world, with the destruction of objects or the creation of new objects. Consequently, every symptom would be a symbol, as would our handling of objects; whatever happens when we deal with objects would be understood as a symbol.

Basically, the psychosomatic viewpoint of Jungian psychology could also be deduced from complex theory. Emotion is a major aspect of symbols. We experience emotions physically and they influence our body. However, I believe that archetypes and complexes can at best be differentiated in theory; in practice their effects are commingled. Therefore, the idea of synchronicity offers a psychosomatic explanation beyond the theoretical definition of complexes and their emotional influence.

What is essential to the new psychosomatic idea according to von Uexküll or Overbeck,[55] and implicit in Jung's concepts, is that it enables us to escape the blame that is almost inevitable in connection with physical illness. The idea has already been applied in certain instances. But some people still believe that "the wages of sin is death." The general sentiment has always been that illness is somewhat indecent; to a great extent it is associated with the idea that illness is caused by some transgression. If we were to think in terms of synchronicity, that is, according to the new psychosomatic parameter, and not in purely causal terms, those thoughts focused on the guilt factor would recede into the background. Illness would then indicate that something new had entered our life, which presently can be mastered only through illness. Thus, illness would be an attempt at dealing with fate.

Nonetheless, the new psychosomatic parameter has not done away with humanity's guilty conscience. On the contrary—although the new model is acknowledged to be pertinent, we remain confined to causal thought. In addition, we are no longer solely concerned with basic psychosomatic illnesses, such as bronchial asthma or stomach ulcers. Today, all illnesses are considered to be psychosomatic—people seek an explanation for every cold; they want to know what they have done wrong. In this instance, a system that is not purely causal is still understood in exclusively causal terms.

However, what can remain in relation to guilt is responsibility. We must handle life responsibly, regardless whether a conflict arises on the physical, psychic, or social plane, or in our relationship with the world around us. Instead of simply indicating the what and why of our wrongs, feelings of guilt could lead us to realize that we must deal responsibly with the prevailing situation. In the end, such questions are motivated by the idea that, if we did everything right, life could be lived without illness and death. If we were to take synchronicity seriously, we would anticipate a dynamic imbalance in situations of upheaval. Indeed, we would recognize situations of upheaval by this dynamic imbalance. The resulting illness would be a problem to be solved or with which we would have to live. The question, then, regardless in which area the illness manifests, ought to be, "How do I deal with it, and live with it?" This implies that no one area susceptible to conflict is more significant than another. In theory, this may be plausible, but in practice we react otherwise. Psychotherapy is a form of therapy requiring emancipation; it aims at empowering humanity with increased consciousness and autonomy. This viewpoint will invariably clash with the notion that at a certain stage of development some people resolve their problems through physical illness. They might, for instance, retreat and take care of themselves—which is absolutely sensible—and then continue life as before. I believe that in this instance psychotherapy's requirements for emancipation must at all costs be modified; we must accept that certain changes occur unconsciously and are not made conscious.

It is even more difficult in the case of chronic illness that can be accompanied by immense problems. Although it is both meaningful and necessary to clarify and become consciously aware of the motivations behind conflicts when illness becomes chronic, I nevertheless believe it is time to see humanity and individuals more realistically without giving up the requirement for change.

Even if we manage not to elevate any one area susceptible to conflict above the others, the question remains why some individuals tend to deal with conflicts psychically—though accompanied by physical symptoms, and perhaps even social eccentricity in behavior toward their environment—while others express them primarily physically. There are many explanations and an extensive literature on psychosomatic illnesses. Overbeck pragmatically interprets the preponderance of physical disease; he says psychic illness is less acceptable in our world than physical illness, for which we receive the required care. We also tend to accept this care more readily.[56] However, Overbeck's rationalization does not explain why an individual might become psychically, rather than physically, ill; it simply explains why physical illness is prevalent in our society.

Another interpretation is that we are inclined to repress the body and bodily functions in daily life; we virtually "desomatize." When we have an emotion, we seldom act spontaneously, as children do, from the depth of the emotion; instead we control the emotion, weigh the situation, and decide what should be done. In other words, we do not simply act, we attempt to negotiate. However, when the body is afflicted with illness, the excessive tendency to negotiate yields to action. Perhaps illness is motivated by the challenge to once again identify with the body; the initial purpose of every illness is that we pay more attention to our body.

From the perspective of Jungian psychology, whenever a complex "erupts," it is connected to a physical reaction. Assuming the body is the basis of the ego complex, we might expect physical illness in situations when the ego complex is no longer coherent. More so than complex theory, the idea of synchronicity maintains that the body is co-reacting at all times. Whether we exhibit physical, psychic, or social eccentricity, then, is far more determined by what we have learned in the course of our life. We might learn that conflicts can be solved through illness. If someone in our family gets a headache over every conflict, it is likely that in future arguments we, too, will get a headache in order to retreat from a situation.

The many exciting theories on this subject demonstrate the abundance of perspectives from which it can be approached. We realize what immense efforts have gone toward developing new perspectives on this problem, and how difficult it is to understand the equal importance of psyche, body, society, and environment. In Jungian psychology, the interlocking of the various planes of experience and reaction is expressed by the idea of synchronicity. But in the end, Jungian psychology gives precedence to the psychic or even the spiritual, and seeks the spiritual idea behind the entire range of events. I believe we should take the event and everything connected with it at least as seriously as the idea behind it. Idealism still plays a fairly major part in psychotherapy. However, the attempt to see life holistically, as suggested by Jung's symbolic definition of the self, as expressed by synchronicity, and as propagated by other forms of psychotherapy, is at extreme odds with the old and familiar concepts.

When we treat individuals who tend to experience their conflicts on a physical plane, or, in other words, who experience them most clearly in their body, it is of utmost importance to create a climate of attention. We should attempt to use the attention that is required in the analytical situation to evoke a relaxed and expressive atmosphere.[57] At this point, we focus our work less on confrontation, and more on support and concern for the problem; it is also recommended that creative methods be employed. Here, imagination comes into play, even when imagining is very difficult. If the therapist is qualified, "soft" breathing exercises may be employed.[58] The idea is to lead the individual back to the images that represent the physical symptoms, and, finally, to translate the images into language.

According to Jungian perspective, symptoms are also symbols; and these are the symbols that psychosomatics bring to therapy. Such symbols are extremely physical, yet they are symbols. Although these individuals' fantasies revolve almost exclusively around their body and physical well-being, they have no less imagination than others. Since psychotherapy is easily accused of being intangible, people often speculate whether they might be better cured by the doctor who originally referred them rather than by the psychotherapist. The object is to recognize the symbols offered by those who come to therapy; in this case they are symptoms. Repeatedly, we hear that so-called "psychosomatics" lack the ability to formulate symbols; this is true, if we consider the formation of symbols only in the abstract sense. But when we recognize symptoms as symbols, it becomes clear that psychosomatic individuals can formulate symbols.

The allegation that "psychosomatics" are virtually unimaginative, that they are less emotional than others and have superficial minds,[59] seems equally unjustified. Individuals who tend to "settle" their conflicts through the body can be highly emotional, although they have difficulties expressing their emotions.

If the goal of therapy is to arrive at a symbol and its linguistic formulation and interpretation through the symptom, it is basically because the physical symptom is a deeply unconscious expression of symbols and their formation.

Even if we accept symptoms as symbols, it is recommended that we apply the same approach as with other symbols. The symptom must first be perceived emotionally, then we can continue with formation and interpretation.

An example and images for the formation of symbols in psychosomatic disturbances.—During the course of therapy, a thirty-two-year-old man consulted his doctor concerning several functional complaints, and a general psychovegetative syndrome. His circulation was not satisfactory and he had pains in his lower abdomen. Since examinations revealed no somatic findings, he and I were to approach the symptoms through psychotherapy. The analysand described his complaints very objectively.

In one session he reported that he had acute pains in his lower abdomen, a diffused, stabbing pain. He had cramps, too, and some diarrhea; but most uncomfortable was the mysterious, stabbing pain. First, I asked him if something special had occurred. I addressed the most important areas of his life. No, nothing special had happened. He was married and was very attached to his child. He had a good job and was an above average achiever. Neither in his family, nor in his relationships, nor at his place of work had anything special occurred. I gave him some crayons and asked him to draw his pain.

My intention was to make the symptom into a symbol by having him formulate it. Symptoms involving the lower abdomen are generally thought to be related to the ability to give, to elimination or to holding back and, in the extended sense, with separation processes. However, this is only a general indication, and rarely reflects the unique situation.[60]

The analysand drew his first picture and said, "This is a green man on an obelisk." (Cf. color plate 18.) Then he fell silent. I wondered if at that moment he might have had a fantasy of grandeur. Sitting on an obelisk would mean he was high up, and enthroned above everything. I noticed the upper body was green and the lower body was barely present. There was no stomach to speak of, and no abdomen or genitals at all. The black wedge reached almost to the neck and seemed to impale him. He was no longer on the ground; he was enthroned.

We looked at the picture for some time and exchanged our thoughts about it. Then the man said, "I'm incapable of functioning up here." This corresponded with the fact that he had drawn no hands or feet.

Of course, hands imply more than action alone; they are also organs of relationship. With our hands, we sense our relationship to others; we sense attraction, or repulsion. With our hands we express tenderness and can establish a very basic emotional contact. If we believe hands are no more than a symbol for action, we have become a victim to our ideology of "do-ability."

The painter was unable to take hold of himself, nor was he likely to communicate his sense of contact. The choice of colors was interesting. We tend to associate the color green, a very dark green, with the calm of the forest, with vegetative life. This possibly indicated that he was afflicted in his vegetative system.

The black wedge moving up from the bottom was threatening. Black can be associated with night, dark, evil, or repression, and perhaps with beginning stages. Apparently, he was very actively and aggressively threatened—as the triangle indicates—by something that came out of the darkness, out of the night, out of the unconscious.

Black, he said, is the color of death. In other words, the pains in his lower abdomen were related to a fear of death. Fear of death is not only a fear of dying, it can also mean one is afraid to live. In any case, the drawing conveyed the idea that his pain had to do with the subject of life and death. Black can be the color of death; the goddesses of the underworld tend to appear in black.

The masculine triangle pushed upward with intense force. It drove a wedge into his life. He said it was a pain that put him out of commission. Naturally, this caused us to question the source of this dynamism that gave him the feeling he was skewered.

The analysand suggested he would like to represent the pain differently (cf. color plate 19). Again, the green man floats on the page without support. He has no bed, no ground, nowhere to rest. This is odd, for when we are in pain, we should at least have a mattress. He, too, was puzzled by his drawing and said, "I am nothing but feet, legs, and arms." Interestingly, the feet were not even defined.

The pain was now dark red mixed with some brown.

When I looked at the drawing, I sensed immense fear. I asked him if the picture expressed fear. "No," he replied, he did not see that, he saw only the arms.

Basically, these signs of pain were an attempt to ground him.

I continued to fantasize and said that they might be spider legs, or the legs of some other animal. He said, "That's not what it is."

Now both of us were dissatisfied, so I asked him to make a picture focused on the red "arms and legs" (cf. color plate 20).

In the previous picture, the pain had become red instead of black. Red is of course the color of suffering, but we would rather expect a stinging red for a stinging pain.

This red was stale; it resembled a menstruation red. It is the color of the all-devouring Kali, the Indian Mother Goddess.

The third picture was of an octopus; its black mouth was contained in the red. The analysand said: "Something like this beast is sitting in my intestines . . ." I added, ". . . and it's frightening."

He: "Yes, it's incredibly voracious."

I said only: "It has six tentacles."

He, "But I am not thinking about sex, I am thinking about cancer." Then he added, "But of course that's not a crab;[61] it really is an octopus, even if it has only six tentacles."

It was no coincidence that the subject of sexuality was touched upon. In the first picture both the sexual organs and the elimination organs were attacked by the wedge. For the moment it was not sexual fear, but the fear of cancer, the fear of dying from cancer.

The octopus lives in the sea under rocks, and is considered an underworld monster. This black monster sprays ink to obscure its surroundings. Symbolically, it suggests the powers of darkness and resembles the spider. But since the analysand's octopus was not black, but dark red, I believe that whatever was frightening him must have been related to life. The toothy mouth was particularly menacing. It suggested a *vagina dentata*, which castrates and swallows men. With this mouth, the octopus became a symbol for the fear of being caught, of being imprisoned, swallowed, and disempowered. Basically, we could say the death-mother had constellated here. This might indicate that the analysand had an aggressive tendency or a fear of being victim of aggression. However, he did not represent himself as a prisoner; he felt threatened, he was frightened, he was resisting capture. Although his ego complex sensed the approach of a devouring something, he was still able to defend himself.

It became clear that, in some form, his autonomy was breaking away; it was threatened. Theoretically, this meant that he was threatened by regression; he could have lost his self-sufficiency. The mother archetype and the mother complex were constellated in their devouring and sexual aspect. It is conceivable that he was reacting to the threat with a compensation in the form of a male protest, as evident in the first picture, though it was lacking a foundation. To protest without standing on the ground with both feet easily becomes groundless and inflated.

Though I say the mother archetype was constellated in its devouring aspect, it had little to do with his actual mother. In this area of psychotherapy, things tend to get confusing. We have fantasies regarding our mothers, and we have experiences with our mothers. Experiences and fantasies are not the same thing. This is why I believe the idea of the archetype is very important. In this connection, we begin to realize that our fantasies regarding our mothers have a lot to do with our primordial fears relating to the maternal, to our primordial and unfulfilled longings and needs for the maternal. Nor is it valid in this case to say the analysand's mother was obviously consuming him and he therefore was projecting her onto the therapist. This might have been true, but it was not likely.

Because of the nature of therapy, we cannot conclude what a person's parents are really like. We talk about images of people, and fantasies. If the therapy flounders, we are in danger of making rash statements about real parents, or real mothers and fathers. We are inclined to place guilt on the mothers, who are far more susceptible to accusations than fathers.

In this case, the mother archetype was constellated in its devouring, threatening, inhuman aspect; the relationship between the ego and the unconscious had entered a phase wherein the ego was losing much of its autonomy and the analysand was becoming more unconscious. He was terrified of this phase.

Though I realized his fear was wordless, as we had sensed in the prevalent atmosphere, I attempted to address it in relation to his everyday life. I asked him if at the time he perceived anything to be threatening, or consuming.

He mentioned his job, his lack of free time, the stress, and his wife's demands. It was quintessential to each of these notions that he permitted himself to be consumed.

In light of synchronicity, or other holistic, psychosomatic theories, the illness was related to his social environment, which he believed was consuming him. We usually allow ourselves to be devoured when we cannot say "no" to our fellow beings, when we cannot limit ourselves out of fear that we will lose others' love and will then be cut off. Thus, we lose the autonomy we ought to have. We become guilty of neglecting the responsibility to be ourself.

The painter continued to project the octopus onto people who were close and important to him, who wanted to "eat him up," and who gave him a sense of being devalued. But since the octopus was his picture, it must have also represented a psychic content of his own and the related behavior. The analysand succeeded in imaginatively identifying with the octopus; he identified with the greediness for food, the desire to have, and to destroy. Instead of limiting himself, he identified with the octopus and had to destroy. This was precisely what he did not do in life; his destructive impulses were, for the most part, unconscious and turned against himself through his somatic complaints. The picture he drew made him aware that he would have liked to destroy, but he could not, and did not want to, for moral reasons.

The pictures indicated the presence of a psychic constellation of the negative, devouring mother archetype. Great fear was developing, and a proportionate amount of aggression was required to counter the fear.

I explained that he had developed a definite aggression by identifying with the octopus, and that, at this point, the aggression was absolutely necessary to prevent him from being swallowed from all sides. I then asked him to imagine relaxing images,[62] which have the purpose of conveying something sustaining in life, a place where one can feel safe. Such relaxation images are particularly important when we are about to face a conflict with destructive forces.

Above all, the relaxing image of well-being, and feeling well physically, is absolutely necessary for individuals who react to conflicts with physical complaints.

After we practiced relaxing images and he felt better, I told him that we now had to deal with three further areas of conflict. The relaxation allowed him to compose himself. He felt elevated and protected by a supportive, maternal aspect. Thus, his ego complex gained coherence, and I could remind him of the conflicts we had to solve. In doing so, I also expressed my faith in the ability of his ego complex to face conflicts; I addressed him on the level of his autonomy. The main problem was his insecurity in relationships. A pattern of relationship was illustrated by his identification with the octopus; when he felt challenged by those who were close to him, he had to challenge them, and destroy them. He tended to do this with cynical remarks.

Another area of conflict was his career; and the third was the question to what extent he experienced me to be overdemanding and disempowering as a therapist. These subjects occupied us for about three weeks; then the pains in his stomach were gone. It was never clear whether they disappeared thanks to psychotherapy or in spite of psychotherapy.

Symptoms can be worked with in this way until creativity shapes them into symbols, which, if they are perceived emotionally, reveal both the conflicts and the strategies behind everyday actions.

Transference, Countertransference and the Formation of New Symbols

CHAPTER SIX

IN JUNGIAN THERAPY, it is important to activate the unconscious and its symbols so that individuals are enabled to deal creatively with their problems and their personal disposition.

If the ego complex is not sufficiently coherent, coherence must first be made possible.

Symbols are activated in a therapeutic relationship when the analyst shows interest in the analysand's total personality, in his uniqueness, his potentials, and his inhibitions.[1] This interest usually activates the unconscious; symbols emerge which are perceived as meaningful. They must then be shaped and interpreted.

The goal of therapy is to assimilate the developmental impulses awakening in the psyche. This enables the individual to gain competence in dealing with himself and others. He will understand himself better, even his darker aspects, those projections will subsequently be easier to recognize. The overall goal is increased autonomy, increased ability to relate, and increased authenticity.

The activation of the unconscious takes place in an analytic relationship, in an I-you relationship, or in any situation where one individual can learn from another. In such a concentrated encounter, new aspects can be activated and developed. The analytic relationship is distinguished from everyday relationships in that great attention is paid to transference and countertransference.

144 THE DYNAMICS OF SYMBOLS

```
      ANALYST                                    ANALYSAND
      EGO           RELATIONSHIP                 EGO
```

Diagram (Figure 7): Analyst Ego (top left) and Analysand Ego (top right) connected by "Relationship" at top; Personal Unconscious below each; Collective Unconscious at bottom. Diagonal arrows labeled "Transference—Countertransference—Projection" cross between Analyst Ego and Analysand's Personal Unconscious, and between Analysand Ego and Analyst's Personal Unconscious. Note at left: "The contents activated by transference and countertransference become conscious through a creative act."

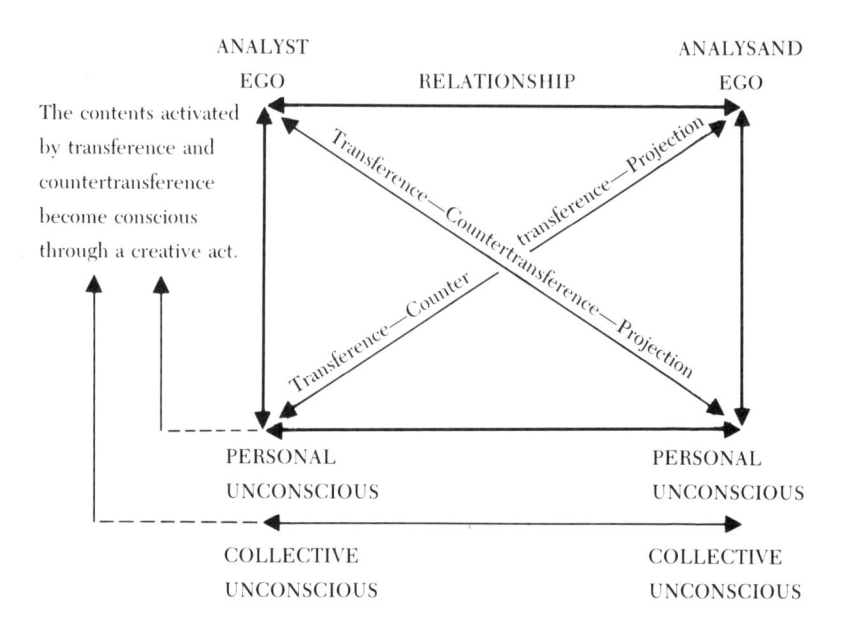

Figure 7

As early as 1946, Jung dealt extensively with transference and countertransference in his work *The Psychology of the Transference*, which I consider the most complete theory of transference, countertransference, and relationship ever published. As a matter of fact, he had already introduced the term countertransference to therapy in 1929.

My schematic for transference/countertransference (cf. fig. 7) is borrowed from Jung, though his is based on an alchemical text.[2]

A relationship takes place between the analyst's and the analysand's egos. In my view, an analytic relationship includes all areas of the encounter where the analyst is perceived as a real person and in this capacity enters into contact with the analysand.[3] Transference is understood as the distortion of perception in relationships; earlier patterns of relationship (complexes) are transferred onto the analyst or onto the relationship between the analysand and the analyst. Transference is usually a compromise between the original complex content and defense. Not only complex contents and patterns of relationship are transferred, but also archetypal images.

I define countertransference as the analyst's emotional reaction to the analysand, and, in particular, to situations of transference. A mysterious relationship or fusion seems to exist between the unconscious of the analyst and the unconscious of the analysand. The mutual unconscious can be sensed in analysis as the atmosphere of the relationship. It might also explain the possible factor of "contagion," when, for instance, the analyst physically senses the analysand's unperceived and unexpressed fear. The unconscious relationship is a prerequisite for what we call countertransference, and, at best, is an opportunity for the analysand to participate in the analyst's self-regulation, assuming that it functions in the analyst. These unconscious processes, and perhaps each person's unconscious identity, make it possible for the analyst's psyche to consciously perceive archetypal and complex constellations. The analyst will then be able to find an image—be it archetypal or personal—for these emotional vibrations, and thus a significant symbolic situation can be made conscious by the analyst's creative act. In such situations, the analysand feels understood; an important emotional experience has been affirmed, grasped in a sense, and the analysand is reassured that it can contribute significantly to his understanding both of himself and of his situation. And, most importantly, he gains the impression that he can be understood.

An essential aspect of countertransference is that an image, a memory, a fairy tale, an emotion, or an intuition of the analyst cannot be explained by the course of events between the analyst and the analysand, nor is it a logical consequence of their communication. Instead, it seems to run counter to occurrences on the conscious plane. Another typical possibility in countertransference is that feelings and reactions provoked in the analyst are similar to the original interaction between the analysand and people close to him. This type of countertransference can contribute diagnostic clues regarding problematic relationship patterns. Not infrequently, these are situations of transference/countertransference that are collusively assigned, that is, one person plays a role, the other a counter-role, and, despite the fact that we realize it is role-playing, we cannot prevent it. This special situation of transference and countertransference has to do with the resurfacing of difficult relationship patterns from childhood, which are readily reassigned to two persons in contrapuntal roles.

There is also a type of illusionary countertransference, such as when the analyst sees things in the analysand that are barely present, or at least not to the extent he believes them to be. I am referring to transference from the therapist onto the analysand.

The analyst's countertransference is also a compromise between the images and emotions he perceives and his defense mechanisms. If, for instance, the analyst intuits aggressive images, he will have difficulty in uniting them with his self-image; he will fend them off. The same goes for sexual images.

TURNING POINTS IN ANALYSIS

I speak of turning points when a new formation of symbols becomes possible, when symbols appear that formerly could not be perceived; they encourage different emotions and foster new behavior, insights, and hopes. The appearance of new symbols in analysis, which often occurs after long periods of "fiddling around," has to do with special situations of transference and countertransference that are conducive to deeper understanding. The theoretical key to understanding this connection is concealed in the concept of complexes.

A complex is expressed in the activity of fantasy; it can become the turning point from captivity to liberation. Within this fantasy lies the energy necessary for the individual's continued development. As long as complexes are unconscious, or not understood emotionally, they can be experienced in transference/countertransference, frequently in the sense of collusive transference/countertransference. I will illustrate this later with an example.

I will present three concentrated therapeutic situations that were turning points in analysis, where the symbols were clearly perceived as focal points in development, and where memories and expectations clearly constellated within the symbols. At the same time, I would like to explain why transference/countertransference and the activation of symbols do not compete with each other, but complete each other.

The Experience of Being Understood in the Therapeutic Relationship as a Prerequisite for the Formation of Symbols

Due to a restructuring of his company, which was taken over by the younger generation, a sixty-three-year-old man was forced into early retirement. He had been the branch manager. He had the choice of either retraining or retiring. Since he could not decide *for* either, it was assumed he had chosen to retire.

Two decisive insults were apparent: The son-generation made changes that left no room for him, the father, and since he apparently could not decide—he felt very blocked—he was not asked; action was simply taken. Indirectly he was made to feel that his collaboration was no longer important.

After retirement, he sat around at home and read the paper. He was tired and without energy. His wife insisted something was wrong with him. Their relationship became increasingly tense. There were more arguments; he was bored with the arguments. He was no longer interested in his grandchildren. He said he had no interests. He felt empty, he had difficulty sleeping, and he was uninterested in sex; he felt shut out from everything, useless. All this had been going on for four months. He had retired six months ago. In other words, he reacted to his retirement with depression. In addition, he felt under pressure: now he finally had the time to do all those things he had planned. He could organize his slides, read all the news clippings and put them in order. . . . But now that he had the time, he had no energy.

The course of therapy proceeded as follows: In the first encounter, I found an extremely polite man was seated across from me. He said he was not feeling well, then he told me the story of his retirement and how he could not deal with it.

The goal of therapy was clearly defined: he wanted to cope with his retirement.

He told his story very succinctly. But he kept repeating that he was not feeling well. When I asked if he believed his company had treated him badly, he looked at me, astonished, "Well, yes . . ." but actually, he said, he could understand the company's position. I felt a sprawling emptiness, and I fended it off; I did not wish to be emptied. Since I was not yet sure how coherent his ego complex was, I did not yet address this feeling of emptiness, which probably had a lot to do with the insult and the disappointment he had repressed—an indication that it was perhaps easier for him to live with depression than with anger. I perceived these feelings of countertransference within myself. In our conversation, we agreed on the goal of this therapy: to cope with the insult caused by retirement.

I explained why it was important for him to contribute dreams so that I might work with fantasies and images. This would have enabled us to illuminate his situation through the unconscious as well as through consciousness; his psyche could have provided indications of how his life should continue.

The basic theme of depression is the necessity to be oneself; only our psyche—or perhaps the therapist as mediator—can present to consciousness what this means.

In the following sessions we spoke of his life story. He lived in the town where he had grown up. He was an only son and had three older sisters. He and his father had worked for the same company. Toward the end he held the same position as had his father. He described his family as very normal, with a good mother. He said he grew up like everyone else: obeyed, worked, and did his duty. That was about it. He was then apprenticed at *the company* and advanced at the usual pace. He married at twenty-six. He had a good wife and three children, two sons and a daughter. None of the children worked for the company, a good thing, he said, the way things were. He already had grandchildren; he used to enjoy them, but no more.

While he clearly and concisely related this information, I had the impression that, though I got information, I did not really have any contact with him as a human being. This caused me to conclude that he probably had too little contact with himself as well. For several weeks things remained this way. I saw him twice a week. He told me his problems, and quite a bit about his life, but I hardly felt him as a person.

When the objective is to understand another person, and to give him emotional confirmation, it is of course essential to grasp the person emotionally. Individuals who have a good sense of themselves can easily be sensed by others. When individuals have difficulties in this respect, it is often a long process to reach that point.

The analysand's presence was strongest when he complained, when he said he could not sleep, when he asked what would become of him if the therapy failed to help. I sensed his fear that the therapy would fail, but even more I sensed a fear of addressing the fear. I made it clear that I understood his fear very well, and I asked if he sometimes wondered if the therapy could advance more rapidly. He replied: "I think you're doing your best."

In light of the situation, I once again considered what I could do. I, too, was discouraged, and I recognized my despair. Then an image surfaced in my imagination: I suddenly saw myself as a lifeguard. I was under water, and although I could see the drowning person—my analysand —somewhere, I could not get hold of him because the distances were distorted under water. And soon I, too, would be running out of air. A real lifeguard would exhale and reach for the other person again, but then she would come back to the surface to save her own life.

This countertransference reaction, which took place in the thirty-second session, about a half year after the therapy began, was very important to me. Naturally, I was compelled to employ other methods, to become active, to respond to the analysand's understandable impatience. However, I was aware that this was not the path to the goal. All my efforts would have been condemned to failure, because the object was not my activity, but his. This is why the image of the lifeguard was so helpful. Exhale, reach out one more time, it meant I should again attempt to grasp him. And in any case, I would not try any new swimming techniques on someone who is drowning.

Once I perceived the countertransference image, I decided not to wait much longer. In the thirty-third session, he brought me a little dream, "I see a meadow. It's been too long since the grass has been cut." I asked him to imagine the dream once again, and he said, well, the grass was bent, it had been trampled on. It hadn't been cut in a long time; the harvest hadn't been brought in. We agreed that it was a shame the harvest had not been brought in; he could not connect the dream to his life.

The symbol offered was still perceived in its concrete sense. He mentioned that the dream reminded him of today's young people; they just didn't care. Grass had a value, didn't it, the same thing was happening in the Alps. Everyone emigrated; only the old people stayed behind.

Some anger at young people could be sensed in this projection, and I asked myself if he might have been directing the anger at his young boss. But I also considered whether the anger might have been aimed at me. To clear up the matter, I asked what it meant to him that I was twenty years younger than he. He looked at me kindly, as if he saw for the first time how young I was, and said he had not yet given my age any thought. He said he was not upset with young people in general; he was upset only with people who acted irresponsibly. I remarked that his new boss had been young, too. "Yes, young, but not irresponsible." That was one thing you couldn't say about him. I deliberately guided him away from this complex theme and asked if he had brought in his harvest. He smiled shrewdly, "Yes, I have." He had already put his share aside, but with the decline of money these days, it was a very risky business. He talked for a long time about how one can become poor in today's world, and how he was in danger of becoming impoverished. Then he looked at me and said: "And for your generation, it's much worse; no one is going to pay your pension. . . ."

I commented how difficult it must be when, from one day to the next, the young people cause one to be no longer needed. I asked him to tell me once more—we had already discussed this several times—what his work had meant to him. In a way, I was trying to encourage a process of mourning.

He said his job had meant little to him, "Everyone has to work, that's what we're paid for." Sometimes he had a good feeling when everything went well, but actually nothing ever turned out as well as it could have. A constant and subtle devaluation of his work and personality ensued, in the sense of: Everything was alright, but everything actually could have been much better, and this was the real reason why they did not want to retrain him. It was his own fault! As he devalued himself in this way, I sensed a burning impulse to offer him the other side of the story, but I knew this would probably be counterproductive. I felt powerless, angry, and I sensed that I was about to internally devalue the analysand. I caught myself contemplating under which conditions analysis is plausible and under which it is not. In other words, I became aggressive in the countertransference. I sensed my tendency to devaluate and attempted to address the same tendency in him by saying it was inconceivable to me that someone could endure a life of work, and yet always sense it was no good. Again, he looked at me pleasantly and said, "Aren't most people dissatisfied with their work?" Again I felt I could not understand him at all, nor did I feel understood. I asked myself if I should have let him know directly that I was slowly running out of breath.

He said the good thing about his job had been that life was organized, which had been comforting to him. And now he did not have this routine anymore. If he had a routine again, he would immediately feel much better.

I asked, "You think if I were to tell you exactly what to do, you would feel better?"

He: "We would advance quickly. I'm sure you know what I should do."

I: "Then it's out of pure cruelty that I don't tell you."

He: "I can hardly imagine that would be true."

I finally sensed some aggression in his transference, but I also sensed his request to give him more structure for his everyday outside life. In therapy itself, I actually provided quite a bit of structure for him while I repeatedly advised him that a new order must come from his own psyche, that he was in a situation of upheaval, and that there was little sense in his doing what I believed to be right.

I was aware of the reason for my hesitation. He had once told me that he read a lot of newspapers. Although they were depressing, he would go to the newsstand and buy another paper, which was no more satisfying than the first. Besides, he usually forgot what he had read. I had said that I hoped he did not buy the paper at the closest newsstand, and that, since a little movement would do him good, he should rather buy it at the stand on the other side of the swimming pool, then he could stop off and swim a lap. As a consequence, he brought a list to every session, in which he recorded how many kilometers he had covered on foot and how many in the water.

I think I was right to be careful about making recommendations for things to do. Soon, he would have done anything I asked. But that would not have brought him closer to himself. At best it would have augmented the depressive cycle.

We attempted for several weeks to discuss what his work had meant to him. One day, he came to the session and said, "I talked to my wife about this, and she said that I'd been satisfied when I was working, and had been proud to be useful." He had dealt humanely with his employees, and in difficult situations brought them to his own home. He had been particularly proud that his department functioned so well. He recited this like a well-studied homework assignment, as if it were not about himself at all. I expressed my impression of this. He replied that he had forgotten he had been proud, and did not realize it when we were discussing the subject; now he knew. He felt ungrateful. I indicated that although his wife was able to orient him, he still did not feel understood. He agreed. He did not feel understood at all, he just felt ungrateful. But for the first time I really sensed him—as a schoolboy mindlessly reciting his homework; he was simply being obedient and well-behaved, as had been required of him. I described to him what I had perceived. Full of interest, he said, "Yes," he had the same impression. Apparently he now felt understood, because at the end of the session he brought up the subject of "homework" and said the idea was important. He had done a lot of homework, first at school, then later his parents and then his wife had told him what to do. It was easier that way; throughout his life, he had never really said what he himself wanted to say.

The night after this conversation, after eight months of analysis, and fifty-four sessions, he had the first important dream, as he called it.[4]

> A lot of travelling is going on in the dream. First I'm on a train. The world is speeding past. I'm reading the paper, and suddenly I'm worried because I no longer know how to get where I'm going. I don't really remember my destination. I get off at the next station. I'm relieved; the place looks about right. I wait for a bus, then I ride around a city I'm supposed to know, but I don't recognize it. Suddenly, I'm in my car. Now I have a city map and I methodically look for the way. It's much easier, because I can drive wherever I want—except on the train tracks. And, once, I even drive on the train tracks. This traffic violation seems justified to me, because I have to bring medicine to someone as quickly as possible. The path gets narrower and narrower. In the middle of a wooden bridge crossing over a stream, I don't dare drive any farther. But I don't know how to drive back either. Then, suddenly, I'm walking. It's

very slow, but now I can really go wherever I want. I wake up before I reach the goal.

When I asked how he felt when he woke up, the dreamer answered that he had a good feeling that he was about to reach the goal; it would have been nice, but this way the dream was more mysterious.

I let the dreamer relax and asked him to again imagine the distances he had covered and to be aware of himself while doing so. In reexperiencing the dream in his imagination, he realized how worried he had been when he did not know where he was going. He reexperienced the tension between the certainty that he must reach a goal and the uncertainty of the goal's existence. As a consequence, he became very involved with the question of a goal for his life, and particularly with the question, Is there a given goal for every human being?

To an individual who feels empty and disoriented, it is of immense importance to dream about a goal and a direction. Both energy and intuition are necessary to follow a path. The dream presented a new vital consciousness to the dreamer; although we could not overlook the difficulty he had in finding his way, it was, nevertheless, an orientation.

A definite change could be perceived in the behavior of the dream-ego when he was in his car, when he took hold of the steering wheel, and when he oriented himself with a map. He realized with great relief that he could drive almost anywhere.

When the dreamer reexperienced this dream, he emphasized how pleasant it was to have a map, and to have clear orientation once again. He now remembered how often he had lost his way in life, and how he had scolded his wife because it was her responsibility "to read the map." He realized that he could not make his wife responsible because this time she was not even in the car. This detail suddenly seemed very significant to him. At once, he realized that he expected everyone, and especially his wife, to make plans for him, and to recommend goals. He was angry that she was not doing so now, not even thinking of doing it. However, the dream also communicated to the dreamer that it was up to him to find a way, that he had to assume full responsibility. For the moment we did not discuss to what extent his anger toward his wife was directed at me.

In the dream, he had to accept responsibility for the traffic violation. He emphasized that because of a higher law—that of saving another life—he was justified in breaking a lesser law—the traffic regulations. Nonetheless, he wondered what punishment to expect, and said how unfortunate it would be if he were punished, because for so many years he had driven without breaking the law. These concerns stressed how important it was to him to reach the goal in the dream: he, who otherwise firmly followed traffic regulations, actually transgressed them despite the danger of "running into" the traffic patrol. When he was driving his car, as opposed to the other means of transportation he used, the acceptance of his own responsibility became obvious, and also when he transgressed the order otherwise valid and acceptable to him. His interpretation of the tension was, "If I follow an individual path, I might be conflicting with valid regulations." When I asked if he could imagine such a situation, he responded that he could fall in love again. He then jettisoned this prospect because of the complications; but at least a desire had been addressed.

The dreamer drove along the path as far as possible; but, in the middle of a bridge, he dared not go on. When reexperiencing the dream, he described the feeling that overcame him on the bridge. Suddenly he had lost courage; the railing had seemed menacingly close. He might have been able to drive on, but he remembered that in other situations when he had obstinately pushed on, it had taken great effort to venture back.

However, when we examined the situation in the dream, it seemed irrational to stop the car in the middle of the bridge, notwithstanding the fact that it was unclear how he should open the car doors, because the bridge seemed to have a railing. The dream revealed a person who even in tight situations explored every possibility, but who lost courage midway. At the end of the dream, it was significant that he continued on foot; though slow, it was truly his path. Since autonomous decisions were the initial goal of the dream, getting out of the car appeared to be related to the independence of choosing his own path, even if it was very slow and, as the dreamer remarked, might have tired him sooner. The decisive change of the vehicle used on the path toward his goal—which was in fact the path of his life—took place on a bridge. When he reexperienced the dream, the bridge became very important; it was a transition, a connection; he realized there was a bridge across the abyss he feared so much. But the bridge forced him to get out of the car. The bridge must have signified that he was meant to realize his individual strength and the speed practical for him. Now he could no longer try to reach his goal quickly; he had to approach it step by step. Perhaps this was how he could save a human life, as expressed in the dream.

The dream was very important, both as an experience for the analysand and as a turning point in the analytic process. The dreamer was under the impression that he had received a significant message from himself. Additionally, the dream conveyed a feeling that he could and might be autonomous. Both the fascination of having a goal ahead and the fear of missing the goal were apparent. His fantasy life was greatly activated by the dream and his self-consciousness was strengthened. The dream caused him to remember other, more emotional, stories from his life, particularly those pertaining to his wife, whom he had always persuaded to organize his life, and whom he then scolded for doing so. At this point, we were able to address his transference of the situation onto me. The dream also aroused themes pertaining to the future, themes of hope and expectation, of moving toward a new goal. It was very energizing.

I, too, sensed a transformation. All at once, I could see a goal. This was a relief although I still felt some emptiness. I had the feeling—to return to the image of the lifeguard

—that the man now had his head above water, he was able to swim to a goal independently and actively; he rarely went under. In connection with the joy over his autonomy, the analysand suddenly realized that it was psychically appropriate that he had avoided being retrained. For the first time he had retreated. Although he had not directly refused it, which would have been even better, he had retreated.

In an analysis otherwise marked by few dreams, it was an initial dream of sorts. After two years of therapy, he consummated his anger about early retirement and worked on the insult.

In my opinion, the example illustrated that a conclusive symbolic process could not take place until the analyst really sensed the analysand and conveyed this feeling. In some situations, however, it takes a long time to empathize with someone.

Collusive Transference/Countertransference and the Formation of Symbols

Collusive transference/countertransference[5] means that the behavior of the analyst is usually polarized by the behavior of the analysand. Even if the analyst is aware of this process, initial behavior patterns cannot be changed. A relationship pattern repeats stereotypically. The reason for this becomes clear when we refer to a principal complex definition by Jung:

> (The complex) obviously arises from the clash between a demand of adaptation and the individual's constitutional inability to meet the challenge. Seen in this light, the complex is a valuable symptom which helps us to diagnose an individual disposition.[6]

When we consider that the demand of adaptation of which Jung speaks usually comes from others, from people to whom we are close, we have an indication not only of an individual's disposition, but we can also see that complexes illustrate relationships and all the related emotions and stereotypical behavior patterns experienced in childhood and later life.

Since it is frequently two individuals who face each other in childhood relationships—the child and one person to whom it relates—a complex can split in the analytic relationship. The analyst then behaves like the person to whom the child related, and the analysand behaves like he or she did in a certain complex situation. The opposite can also occur. Such situations in analysis are "complex," they follow a stereotypical course; they are emotionally charged and lead to no results. Both the analyst and the analysand fend off such situations, especially as both feel under pressure. Each is caught in a collusive transference/countertransference situation.

I would like to propose the following hypothesis. Before new symbols can be formed, and the complex expressed through imagination, the complex constellation must be recognized as a reflection of the childhood relationship situation and related emotions; the role models involved must be recognized as inner aspects of the analysand. Often, it takes the analyst's experience to bring out these inner aspects.

A complex involving transference/countertransference can just as well be conceived as a process of symbolization, and the analytic situation as the symbol formed. However, the situation must be understood emotionally, otherwise the energy inherent to the complex remains mired in a somewhat childish tug-of-war of transference/countertransference.

Collusive transference/countertransference must be acknowledged. Often quite a bit of involvement is needed to make us aware of it. Once truly understood, that is, once the analysand and his life story are acknowledged, and the analyst understands his own behavior in the unique situation, new symbols can be formed and perceived. However, a great deal of empathy and sensitivity is necessary to understand oneself in these situations.

I will demonstrate my hypothesis with an example of a

therapeutic process and will attempt to describe the process as precisely as possible. But, first, a discussion of guilt.

Thoughts on Guilt. Guilt is a torturous feeling of having failed. To say the least, it is embarrassing. Guilt is accompanied by shame and a fear of being punished. Often, we do not feel guilty until caught. As long as our offense is undetected, we can to a degree work it out by ourselves. Feelings of guilt cause people to "atone" for something. But this is not always possible. Guilt, that torturous feeling, disturbs our sense of harmony and exposes the fact that we are guilty of something we should not have permitted to happen. We have not fulfilled an obligation. Guilt also expresses the grief that we are not as ideal as we thought we were, or the anger that we cannot be as good as we wanted to be.

When we have feelings of guilt, we are at odds with ourselves. To a greater or lesser extent, we suffer an identity problem. We fend off the fear that threatens our identity and places us at odds with ourselves. We seek justification, and look for scapegoats. We could, however, accept guilt, and in so doing gain a more human image of ourselves, an image of someone who can and must be guilty of something.

The Intrapsychic Dynamics. When we are torn by feelings of guilt, a battle is raging in our psyche. We attack ourself and become the victim of our attack. There is a conflict between aggressor and victim. Aggressor, "Why didn't you . . . ," "You always . . ." Victim, "I'm such a horrible person!" "I can't go on living . . . ," and so on. The emotion inherent to the aggressor, which often conceals repressed fear, is aggression. The emotion inherent to the victim is fear, and fear easily turns into aggression. Thus, fear and aggression are both merged in guilt. We are afraid and angry at the same time; this dynamism causes the feeling of being torn apart and leads to the loss of positive self-worth. We then have to somehow manage despite bad feelings; we employ defense mechanisms, or coping mechanisms. Here are a few typical mechanisms:

—Downplaying the situation, "Oh, it isn't all that bad . . ."

—Justification: "But I had to . . ." "I had to do it because . . ." As we know, justification easily launches a vicious circle. We justify our justification, and the justification escalates, because, as in the French saying "Qui s'excuse, s'accuse" (He who excuses himself, accuses himself), it is also an accusation. The justification cycle is a means to defend guilt. However, we might see it as an attempt to empathize with oneself. When we are consumed by guilt, we cannot initially empathize with ourselves in the least; we no longer understand ourselves; we can no longer react compassionately to ourselves, and, instead, react only destructively. But, frequently, the attempt to empathize through justification does not succeed. We then reach for other coping mechanisms.

—Scapegoating: In ancient Judea, a goat was loaded with all the sins of the community and sent into the desert. And thus the sins disappeared from sight. What you do is to look for someone who is guilty of everything, on whom all guilt can be blamed: a vehicle for projection. Then you send him out in the desert; ostracize him, segregate him. This is a fairly common behavior pattern: We look for a guilty person, and a scapegoat can easily be found because someone is always doing something wrong. We can load our guilt onto the scapegoat to alleviate ourselves. The scapegoat is devalued, we are elevated; but when we need to use the scapegoat for a different purpose, things get difficult. If the scapegoat does not help us overcome our guilt, further coping mechanisms can arise.

—Death wish for oneself: Feelings of guilt can escalate so far that we harbor a death wish for ourself. The aggressor within says: "You don't deserve to live!" The death wish might also appear as a fear of dying, such as in fantasies about being in an accident or being attacked. This is motivated by the conviction that we are so guilty that only an anonymous power can destroy us. A total identification with the victim takes place. The aggressor is projected outward.

The coping mechanisms outlined above demonstrate

that in the inner conflict between victim and aggressor, we are sometimes more the aggressor, sometimes more of a victim.

We can also admit to guilt. To admit guilt is usually less dangerous than we presume. We like guilty people. Angels of innocence are annoying. When someone continually professes complete innocence, we seek out his or her flaws. Another reason why it is so hard to bear these angelic innocents is that they emphasize others' guilt.

Guilt and Responsibility. The word "guilt" has two meanings. When we accept responsibility, we speak of guilt. "It's my fault this happened." We also speak of guilt when we fail in a responsibility, in which case we suffer from pangs of guilt. Guilt is related to making an ego-decision against a norm or a law. A norm can be either an inner or an external law. Since we, as personalities, never quite agree with inner and external laws and norms, we are inevitably guilty of something. Consequently, we also inevitably have to deal with guilt. The purpose of guilt is to make us aware of the fact that we must accept responsibility.

Guilt is a feeling that reaches back into the past. It indicates that something was done wrong, but, at the same time, it should light the path to the future and challenge us to consider what responsibility we should accept. Restitution is a forward motion. We sometimes cannot directly atone for the transgression against someone, but we can atone toward others by acknowledging our guilt and by accepting responsibility.

The Role of Empathy. When torn by feelings of guilt, it is helpful to empathize with oneself. When we ask how a circumstance could have come about, it is easier to generate an empathic attitude. We tend to blame each other. This is an unproductive game that can carry on forever. Once we ask how the situation started, and in what way we influenced each other to bring it about, we can treat ourselves, or our partner, with greater compassion. It is crucial that we accept that guilt is human; we inevitably owe something to one other, and always will owe something. This means we must accept our finiteness, and, nonetheless, must accept responsibility for everything for which we can be responsible. We not only owe something to others, but often to ourself.

Dealing with Guilt Unproductively. Sometimes, though the fault may be quite trivial, we agonize over a shortcoming for extended and unproductive periods. We might complain about something we failed to do five years, or maybe weeks ago. To confess guilt in this manner is not empathic; it blocks life. We blame ourself for a situation that may not be entirely our fault. We distort our perception of those things for which we are truly guilty, for which we are repeatedly guilty, and for which we should accept responsibility. To complain about a shortcoming indicates both the aggression which is inherent to feelings of guilt and could provide the impetus to act, and fear which could help us understand ourselves. The blockage prevents us from a greater involvement in life, for the more involved we are in life, the more likely we are to be guilty—guilty for what happens, guilty of failing, guilty if something we have initiated takes a course we had not anticipated.

This unproductive feeling of guilt distorts our perception of those factors for which we are actually to blame. At the same time, it is the expression of a fear of becoming guilty.

Excerpts from a Course of Therapy. A fifty-two-year-old woman's husband died in an automobile accident only a day after she had initiated legal proceedings for divorce and told him about it. They had been married for twenty-eight years and had three children, who were by this time all older than twenty.

The woman sought therapy three weeks after her husband's death. She could not bear it anymore. The only words she could find were, "It's not my fault, it's not my fault!" The analysand was a medium-sized woman, gaunt, her features rather hard. She was dressed in mourning, and was visibly disturbed. I found her sympathetic. I wanted to help her. It was evident from the start, since she was constantly proclaiming her innocence, that she had pronounced guilt feelings. To obtain a divorce, the woman had had to describe her marital relationship in court. At the very beginning of the consultation, she asked me to read the transcript. Normally, I would not do such a thing, but, on impulse, I accepted the pages and began to read. The account depicted her husband as a scapegoat, as the sole and exclusive scapegoat; so much so, that my psychic need for symmetry was acutely disturbed. I had a reaction. I wanted to protest this one-sidedness and refuse to accept it. I sensed an aggression, which I could not understand, toward the woman. I was inclined, in my imagination, to make her into the scapegoat. I became the aggressor. I felt like ostracizing her and wondered if I wanted to work with the woman at all. I thought it abhorrent that I had such feelings about a woman who was in such a terrible situation. But, to a degree, I understood my feelings. I acknowledged the emotions developing inside me, but I said nothing to the woman. When I looked up, she said of her own accord that, at this point, she would write the story differently. Since her husband's death, she no longer regarded him exclusively as a scapegoat. Later it became apparent that she scapegoated her husband's family instead, his colleagues, and the place where he used to work.

The fact that the subject of guilt was so centralized indicated that the woman had to contend primarily with feelings of guilt in the mourning process, and that guilt would be her main problem. But it might have indicated that feeling guilty had always been a problem for her. Loss activates central problems.

She felt a bit better when she became convinced that her husband's colleagues were guilty of his death, for they had once again encouraged him to drink and then to drive. In the end, of course, his parents were guilty for having made him a sissy, and his employers were guilty for having demanded too much of him. The defense mechanism of the projection helped her avoid her feelings of guilt.

I asked her to describe her life with her husband. "When my husband's mother died he needed a new woman." She had been the right age, and she had been single. He had courted her, and she had been attracted to his somewhat melancholy nature, but she never really loved him. "True love only happens in romance novels, right?" I wanted to respond, but I could say nothing. I had the impression I was being sucked into the fatal "we." She felt she had done a good deed by marrying this young man who had become rather lost. Besides, he was pleasant, decent, and hardworking. Everyone else thought so too.

This was followed by a long narrative in which she justified why she had married the man even though she had not really loved him. No new information was added. She kept defending herself for having married him; she even realized she was justifying herself. The justification cycle began. "Now it sounds as though I want to defend myself. I don't have to, of course. I don't need that. In the beginning, things went fairly well. It's just that he was so soft, so spoiled; he needed me to be his mother. Whenever there were problems he got a stomachache, like a child." She remembered how jealous he had been of their three children. She related an episode. "The kids were screaming and I asked him to help me. He just looked at me gloomily and said, 'And me, what about me?' " She had cursed at him and even hit him once; she said, "That kind of thing makes us women boil with rage, doesn't it!?" I felt included in the expression "us women," which implied, You and I are innocent, the others are guilty. Or, As women, we are both innocent victims, even if we attack aggressively or destructively. The division between victim and aggressor became evident. I had the feeling she dominated me swiftly and skillfully, and that I could not intervene. I soon felt like a victim, but not, as is common in the mourning process, doomed by the knowledge that there is no cure for death. Instead, I felt like a victim of her manipulations. I wondered whether her husband might have felt as I did. But I could (should) not articulate this impression. For the time being, I just observed what was happening. Since I did not intervene, I assumed that this was a case of collusive transference and countertransference; the woman was playing the role of the aggressor, and I became the victim. If I had verbalized my interpretation, she would have become the victim. As long as she could delegate the part of the victim to me she would not have to suffer the confrontation between victim and aggressor, nor the disruption it caused.

In addition, the pattern that surfaced in our relationship had to be considered. She was probably familiar with it. In my opinion, the fact that I was unable to address this relationship pattern indicated that bringing it up would unleash anxiety in her and would undermine her defense mechanisms against guilt. I perceived that I disagreed with a few things. First of all, there was this fatal "we," then, my inclination to reject her, and, finally, there was my feeling that I was being rejected. I felt myself in a stranglehold and wondered if she was in the stranglehold of her guilt. I remembered my own vehement feelings of repulsion at the beginning of the consultation.

She described how the marriage had deteriorated. Her husband's colleagues had tempted him with alcohol. She had "tried to keep his head above water," and had taken great pains to help him keep up with his demanding job as an electronics technician. She described her arduous life: she did everything, she raised the kids, she looked out for him, she took care of their home, she worked to pay off the debts from building a new house. In her eyes, he had been completely irresponsible. When I asked what their sex life had been like, she said she had never felt much. Her husband had frequently wanted to cuddle; she had liked that at first, but later it had become a problem. When he wanted to have sex, she didn't feel like it; when she wanted to have sex, he retreated. But, actually, it all fizzled out, and one day she realized she would be crazy to continue in such a marriage to the day she died. Naturally, she didn't get this idea on just any day; it was the day when one of her husband's colleagues told her he found her attractive. She thought, Before my life is really over, something has to happen. Divorce had always been an issue, and a threat. She had always used divorce as a means to threaten him, but this time she meant it. Her husband's reaction was that he complained and drank. She said it wasn't his, but his mother's fault that he complained and drank; his mother had spoiled him. It was his colleagues' fault. Of course, he had been drinking before the accident. "A thousand times I told him not to drink and drive. I warned him, but his colleagues always talked him into it."

And then reflection set in. "I should be relieved. It's better to be a widow than divorced. But I feel so very alone, so helpless, even though I wanted to get rid of him. Now I can't sleep and there's all this confusion and anxiety." I asked her what she thought about when she could not sleep at night. She said she remembered situations with her husband; she thought she heard him coming home and then realized he would never come home again; she was relieved, but sad. "Sometimes I think I drove him to his death. But I have the right to look after myself, too, don't I?" I confirmed that she had decided for divorce out of responsibility to herself, and, finally, I asked if she was guilty of her husband's death. "Guilty, no. Obviously, it was the alcohol. But somehow I am mixed up in it, too."

We have feelings of guilt when there is something for which we should accept responsibility. And we might very well be guilty. I attempted to approach the woman's guilt feelings by addressing the related sense of responsibility, which we both valued. At the same time, I supported her sense of self-worth by intervening, and this meant that she would more than likely be able to accept the challenge of guilt. She could then to a degree appreciate her feelings of guilt. I would like to mention a peculiar point: in Swiss German usage, *Schuld*, guilt, primarily means sharing the causal responsibility, but not exclusively guilt. In terms of semantics, it was unnecessary for her to evade her guilt, though, psychologically, it was of course necessary. Therefore, I responded very carefully to the subject of guilt that she had introduced; she defended herself, and there was a change in the dynamism of the relationship. Previously, we had been in solidarity against some accusing entity; by intervening I had broken the solidarity. From a therapeutic standpoint, it was meaningful that the guilt problem and its aspect of aggressive guilt, the role of the aggressor, was transferred, or projected, onto me. And yet, I accepted her resistance as a sign that it was still too frightening for her to address the problem. I also accepted her telling me for weeks on end about the everyday problems she had to solve, legal problems, problems with the children, who wanted to inherit. Her deceased husband was discredited by the insurance company. They claimed he had been driving while heavily under the influence of alcohol and therefore had been reckless. She, who previously had said the same about him, was outraged, and insisted that he had been a decent man. These accusations from the outside at least put an end to her belief that she was sheer goodness and he, sheer evil; she began to see that he was both good and evil. I had hoped that during this phase of our discussions we would be able to reexamine their relationship in terms of the effect it had on both of them, rather than simply determining who was the guilty party, or the scapegoat. In other words, we could attempt to clarify how each partner had influenced the other, causing what had happened. The understanding that both parties were guilty, though not condemned, might have led to an appreciation for each partner's actions.

It is difficult, however, to address the background and effect of a relationship, because this necessitates the elimination of the repression that conceals the guilt, and the guilt must subsequently be experienced.

The woman began to describe the nature of the relationship. She had been proud when she had her first child. She felt it was her creation. The child needed her and was entirely dependent on her. When she had expressed her feelings, her husband had said that he, too, had done his share. She had argued that the child had grown inside her, and that it would not even exist without her. In retrospect, she realized that she had in fact rejected him. She had not allowed him to share the joy of the child. Yet, it had meant so much to him to belong. In the beginning, when she had put me in my place so quickly, I, too, had felt rejected; I had the feeling she needed me, but would not allow herself to need me. In other words, it seemed to be typical behavior on her part. Why did she behave like this?

Now she saw herself as a terrible, evil woman: guilty, because she had repeatedly rejected her husband. Her unremitting divorce threats had also been a form of rejection. Suddenly everything was her fault, her husband was innocent. She had absolutely no empathy with herself; she shifted all the blame onto herself.

In the twenty-eighth session, after some six months of treatment, she repeated once again, "It's my fault, I'm entirely to blame." I had the impression that our relationship was bogged down, and I said, "I think I can understand the feeling you have very well." I told her about the impressions I had when I first read the transcript of the divorce. I told her of my being almost moved to send her away, and how rotten that had made me feel in light of her terrible situation. We harmonized in our feelings, which effected a marked relief in the woman. She told other stories that illustrated how much it had meant to her husband to belong. He had always wanted to do things with other people; in the family, too, it was important that everyone be together, that, as long as possible, everyone be in one bed, in one tent, that everything be shared. For him, each child's path to independence had been extremely painful. She also believed that the more independent the children became —and she made sure they became independent quickly— the more he drank.

While she related this, her voice took on a scornful tone. I asked her how she had experienced his desire to belong. In the beginning, she had thought it funny, but she had become increasingly touchy about it. Finally, she had taunted him and had done everything she could to prevent togetherness. "It's not his fault. It wasn't his fault; his family was like that. That's why he had to get married as soon as his mother died."

Her own family had emphasized self-sufficiency and independence, and had barely any togetherness, while her husband's family had been very close. She said that at this point she was supported by her husband's, rather than by her family. I suggested that her husband's family must have fascinated her at first, since they behaved so differently toward each other, but that their behavior probably frightened her; perhaps out of fear of becoming a dependent nobody. She went on to say how independence had always been encouraged in her home; it meant one had grown up. Furthermore, in childhood, she and her siblings had not really been part of the village. They had lived on the edge of the village, which in itself signifies a degree of remoteness. They had been the only members of the Reformed Church in an otherwise Catholic area. She was an outsider, she identified with those who had excluded her and caused others to become excluded; at least she had alienated her husband. Apparently, their children had developed normally.

When we examine guilt in terms of the alienator and the alienated, the accuser is the alienator, and the accused is alienated. Since she considered herself guilty, the woman became, as she had been in childhood, the outsider. Many times, she asked me to describe how I had felt in the first session when I had wanted to reject her. I repeated what I had felt, and she maintained that she still felt the same way. I also told her that I understood my reaction and that hers was equally understandable.

I mentioned that sometimes I could plainly see her as a rejected child, and that I understood how miserable she must have felt. This remark caused a memory image to surface. This was the thirty-second session, and it was the first time an image emerged. She saw herself standing outside the kindergarten. All the other children were inside, but she and her siblings could not go because the kindergarten was too far away. It was early summer, and the children were singing a summer song. She was standing outside and wanted very much to join in the song, but she could not. She stood there, miserable, then she ran home to her mother, and told her that she too wanted to go to kindergarten. Her mother said, "You know we don't belong, and we don't want to belong." This statement might have made the child feel special, but, in this case, she felt only anger, despair, and pain. Several similar memories surfaced. Both she and I sensed the pain of the alienated child; we felt very close.

The subject "alienators and alienated" continued to be central. Since the woman never remembered dreams, but was able to recall vivid images from her childhood, and even remembered what the soil had smelled like in front of the kindergarten, I gained the impression that her imagination might lead us into the realm of images. I am particularly interested in images, because they are connected to a dimension of the future.

In the thirty-fifth session, after I had made her relax somewhat, I asked her for images relating to the subject "rejected." I believed the time had come for the complex to be activated in fantasy.

"Rejected . . . I see a blind girl wandering around in a thorny place." (Later she associated "Rapunzel" and "The Girl with No Hands" to this image.)

To the subject "rejector": "The girl is rejected by a bickering old man with a stick."

I asked her to place herself inside either the blind girl or the old man.

The woman could not empathize with herself nor approach her feelings of guilt until she perceived herself as rejector or rejected. Our solidarity was necessary to allow her to accept her imagining.

She identified with the girl. "I'm barefoot and blind, and I'm not used to being blind. It's cold and rainy. I keep bumping into things. My skin is scraped. I feel warmth coming from somewhere; I'll go there. There are houses, but all the doors are locked. I imagine an old man with a stick standing behind a door. He's angry. He punishes. He knows why; he's unshakable. He has decided all girls must do penance. The girl goes away from the door. She accepts, and goes back out in the rain, into the thorns. Without a goal, without orientation. She must do penance. She accepts it."

At this point I intervened in her imagining.[7] "Does the girl know the offense for which she is doing penance?" I asked the question because I had the impression she was suffering for the sake of suffering. While listening, I had suddenly felt the anger that the girl should have felt. When all aggression is projected onto the aggressor, the victim has no aggression at all. If the victim can feel constructive anger, he or she can escape the victim-aggressor game.

The girl did not know her offense, she was simply prepared to do penance. I asked, "Does the old man know her offense?" This question incited a role change in the imagining. At the same time, she was encouraged to be more empathic with herself. The old man had to look it up. He grumbled, "Girls always do something forbidden. Girls must always be punished." He flipped through a book until he finally found the page with the registry of penance, and said profoundly, "Hmmm, hmmm," and fell silent.

The girl decided to do no more penance and left the place. She ran in one direction, thinking that sometime someone would come. She tripped and fell. Slowly daylight came. She lay down on the grass, slept, and felt wonderfully secure.

The imagining lasted from the thirty-fifth to the forty-second session. When the girl finally woke up, she began to see. An old woman was putting herbs on her eyes and feet, speaking words of pity and consolation. The words soothed her like ointment. The girl did not want to wake up at all. But when the woman asked, "Is it true that you still can't see?" she opened her eyes and could see. She did not recognize the old woman.

At first she was surprised and then pleased that there was such a woman in her fantasy. She wished she could have had that kind of a mother, and she would have liked to be a mother like that. We talked for a long time about this woman who was able to accept her suffering and console her. At this point, I interpreted the character for her on a subjective level as her potential for life and emotion. She smiled radiantly and said, "But you know, she's a bit like you." She transferred the herbalist onto me. We were no longer caught up in the complex, in the transference/countertransference game of victim and aggressor.

There is always the question that we might frustrate transference by interpreting symbols on the subjective level. In my experience, transference may often not be addressed directly until the analysand senses that the transference is within him– or herself, and that it is not contradictory to sense a force both in the relationship and in him or herself.

In retrospect, we both wondered about the silly girl who wanted to do penance for no reason other than that she felt she had to do penance. I asked her who in her life would have grumbled the kind of things the old man did in her imagining. This prompted her to remember a pastor who believed all sin came from women; therefore, girls should do penance in advance. Throughout her life, the girl within had the feeling she had done everything wrong and that everything was her fault.

In the imagining, the girl stayed for some time with the kind woman. She grew and learned a good deal. The kind woman was seen as a projection, but the analysand was aware that the woman was a part of herself as well, and occasionally recognized the woman in herself. Neither of us was excluded. In this phase, we still spoke about her being rejected and about her no longer really having to be the outsider.

Once again, she described the nature of her relationship with her husband, but this time she truly had empathy for both herself and her husband. Despite this empathic treatment of the impact of their relationship, the feelings of guilt were much more pronounced, and could be felt with greater intensity. She felt miserably guilty, and said so. I asked her to find a different definition for guilt, because she tended to hide behind the declaration, "I'm so very guilty." She rephrased it, "I gave neither him nor myself what I could have. We could have had security; we could have belonged to each other and still have been separate individuals."

She was still occupied by the question of guilt. Then

she remembered the old man from her imagining. Surely he knew the answer. I was glad she had resumed this part of the imagining. Somehow, the old man had always remained present to me, even when she did not speak of him.

When analysands imagine, the therapists, in a sense, share the imagining. In this case I was happy to see how she matured with the old woman, but still on the periphery of the image was the house with the old man, as if to say, "He may be peripheral, but he must not be forgotten." However, I did not articulate these thoughts to the analysand.

In her imagination, the analysand looked for the old man. She went to his house, but he had gone. A younger man stood there; she asked him where the old man was. "He died." She said she had to know what her offense was. The young man now had the book. Together they looked for her page. When they found it, the man read, "She did not take her feelings seriously." It sounded like a confirmation text.

From then on, imaginings with the old empathic woman and the old man no longer occurred. These imaginings had concluded.

She was then intensely preoccupied with the "confirmation text." To her it was the kind of motto given to one in an initiation rite. She realized that her guilt, and her responsibility, were related to taking her feelings seriously. She contemplated why and in which instances she had failed to take her feelings seriously. Many memories surfaced, and finally she remembered that she had been fully aware that her husband was soft; he had always been that way. She also knew that he tended to drink when he had conflicts; she had noticed that when she first met him. But she had married him anyway. Even when she felt the need for comfort, she believed out of principle in separateness and autonomy.

From this point on she was convinced that she wanted to take her feelings seriously. She could accept that she was guilty, and that she felt guilty about her husband; but she could also understand the structure and nature of their relationship. She would have liked to have a sign from her dead husband that he did not blame her for anything. She hoped to have a dream. She had none. She decided to accept that up to now she could not have acted otherwise, but that in the future she would treat herself differently and take her feelings seriously. Feelings of guilt invariably indicate that something can change in the future.

I initiated a very important separation phase, and the analysis concluded after eighty-six sessions.

The collusive aspect was typical in the transference/countertransference process of this therapy. The role of the victim and the aggressor were interchanged and alternated with solidarity. It is also typical that such division is deprecated, for it goes against one's own wholeness. The process cannot continue until empathy is present, until we can empathize with the division, and, particularly in the realm of negative emotions, until emotional solidarity can develop. In this case, this occurred when the imagining provided a possibility for the analysand to mother herself. It also led her away from girlhood, and allowed a very rigid father figure in herself to die and to be resurrected in a milder form.

In addition, she had gained access to the method of imagination.

Basically, Jung feels that the creative path is the best way to deal with the unconscious. He recommends that we "think through" a fantasy and shape it as if it were an inescapable real–life situation.

> All the difficulties you overcome in such a fantasy are symbolic expressions of psychological difficulties within yourself, and inasmuch as you overcome them in your imagination, you also overcome them in your psyche.

In another passage, Jung says that by practicing the method of imagination we can both analyze the unconscious and give the unconscious the opportunity to analyze the ego-complex.[9] Once we practice imagination, we can easily relate to the constellated complexes through this method and, even outside of the therapeutic situation, allow them to emerge in fantasy.[10]

Archetypal Countertransference as a Fairy-tale Revelation

Marcel was twenty-five years old when he came to me to be "tested." This at least was how he formulated his request on the telephone; I thought that he must want career counseling. When he arrived—medium-height, dark haired, muscular, and athletic—he seemed very tense. He told me that he despised tests and, since he had already lost eight therapists because they moved that he was actually looking for a therapist who would stay in the same area for at least ten years.

The whole situation seemed peculiar to me, and I asked him to describe his therapeutic experiences.

He was dissatisfied with his life and job and had sought therapy since the age of twenty. He had his first anxiety crisis, which he called depression, when he was offered a more responsible position. He worked as a laborer for a state-owned company. During the four years before he commenced therapy with me, he worked only occasionally and, because he believed he suffered from depression, had voluntarily committed himself to psychiatric clinics six times.

The history of his therapeutic experiences revealed that two therapists had abandoned him—both had forgotten scheduled appointments—but that he had left the others. He just quit going.

I confronted him with the negative reality I perceived, "It seems to me you're looking for another therapist to prove she's worthless as well, and to convince yourself that you're incurable." He replied, "I'll prove to you that you're wrong." Then, "I don't feel like telling you my story. I've told it a thousand times. By the way, no one believes my story. It's unbelievable. The doctor at the clinic will send you my case history."

During the first session I had contradictory feelings and impressions. I was curious about Marcel. I sensed a strong vitality, and found him amiable. On the other hand, I sensed within myself a great deal of anger, aggression, and a type of fear with which I was unfamiliar. He conveyed the impression that he approached his problems very energetically, only to retreat at the decisive moment. I told him I saw him as a driver stepping on the gas and braking at the same time. The reason might have been the fear triggered by the confrontation with his problems. He felt understood and said, "I have some confidence in you, but now I've got to go away and decide if I really want to work with you. Maybe you can think about it, too."

Evidently, Marcel was afraid of being pushed away, and did not realize he was doing the pushing. He felt abandoned. I was aware of strong and very contradictory emotions, in particular aggression and fear. He repeatedly sought help that he could not accept. As soon as he felt some trust toward me, he had to go away and think about whether or not he really wanted to work with me. He must have been very frightened of becoming involved in a therapeutic relationship; it was probably a fear of getting too close to me, and, in this respect, to risk being abandoned. Marcel returned to the clinic where he was staying at the time and arranged at once for his case history to be sent to me. He told anyone who would listen that he had found the best therapist in the world, as the doctor informed me. This was a "primitive idealization."

Marcel had been diagnosed a schizoid personality with paranoid tendencies. Some remarks on his case history: He was the elder of two children in a very problematic family. His mother, a paranoid schizophrenic, had been committed on several occasions, the first time when Marcel was three years old and his sister one. His father was an aggressive alcoholic. Between his sixth and fifteenth year, Marcel and his sister were brought to a home managed by nuns. The prevailing pedagogic climate seemed extremely severe to him. When he finished school, he worked as a temporary laborer. He tried on several occasions to take on an apprenticeship, but every time he applied to a prospective master, he invented a biography rather than have to tell his real story. He was too ashamed of his background. Inevitably he then got his various biographies mixed up and, consequently, was described as a liar in his case history. I think it was not a question of lies, but, rather, of a splitting and the associated negation.

Some considerations for diagnosis: The first crisis occurred when he was about to work independently, in other words, at the moment of separation from his coworkers. Periods of separation and the challenge of more autonomy were frightening to him. Splitting and denial were evident as defense mechanisms, as were omnipotence fantasies and devaluation strategies. I will later discuss the situation of "transference/countertransference."

My preliminary diagnostic reflections led me to see Marcel as a borderline paranoid personality.

In the second session he told me that he had thought about working with me and that he believed we could work extremely well together. He believed that we could succeed in curing him in a very short time. In any case, he was determined to work with me very intensively, and he wanted to prove his good will by letting me in on two secrets. The first secret: he was enormously frightened of getting sick, which was why he never touched doorknobs or shook hands with others. Later, during the course of therapy, this secret led me to work on the patient's physical ego, in order to make him aware of his body and, in particular, to allow him to sense his hidden aggression as a strength.

The second secret: The "whole world" thought his illness was related to his mother's illness, but that wasn't true. He recounted, "When I was a child, it was very difficult for me whenever the police came to take my mother away. But it was also difficult when my mother spoke to people I couldn't see. It was very frightening." While he was telling me this, the horror of it was still written on his face.

"But my mother is a very sweet person. I love her a lot. I remember how carefully she washed us. She washed our feet with Vim." (Vim is an abrasive scouring powder.) "I'm very important to my mother. I have to make sure she takes her medicine."

He proceeded: "While I was telling you that, I had the following fantasy. I'm in the mountains, I'm on a meadow at the edge of a forest. It's fall, like now. There's a little river; it's a very nice place. It's good to be alone. I don't want to see anyone."

And then he added in a threatening tone: "If anyone comes, I'll beat them up, especially if it's a woman."

I: "Is anyone coming?"

He: "No, no one. This is boring. Why don't you come?"

I: "I don't like to be beaten up."

Marcel: "You may come, but I decide the distance."

I: "All right. I'm approaching."

Marcel: "Now we're two hundred meters apart. That's good."

I: "It's nice here. We're above the fog."

Marcel (triumphant): "You have to go down. Go down into the fog. You'll be cold."

I: "I guess you didn't like it when I talked about the fog? I did that because it's not possible that it's so beautiful, that your situation is this peaceful, that you feel so good. It *is* boring. And then, you already told me a secret. The secret is very important to me. I believe that you have a good relationship to your mother, but it must be difficult to live with her and take care of her. I'm still uncertain about it, that's what the fog is."

He listened intently, then he said: "I'll punish you anyway."

I: "You're punishing me because I won't do what you want? Do you punish people when you're afraid? It's frightening to see something for what it is. I understand that very well."

Marcel: "I'm always very aggressive. I'm always mad. I'm always afraid. And now you've destroyed my fantasy. I'm going to punish you. But let's go into the fog. The session is over. Don't forget my secrets."

The mailman was standing outside the door to the office. The analysand spoke to him as if nothing had happened.

What had happened? When he spoke about the secret regarding his mother, he tried to close his eyes to the difficulties and the fears he must have had in dealing with her; he produced a very peaceful fantasy. However, his isolation, particularly regarding women, immediately became clear. He transferred his fear of women, his desire for them, and the related aggression, onto me. In addition, a distance-closeness problem was evident. He wanted everyone to be close to him, but it was extremely important to him that he determined the distance. To approach him was like approaching a frightened animal. My interpretation helped him express his fear and acknowledge that he was still angry. Thus, my explanation strengthened his ego to a degree. This confirmed my hypothesis that Marcel's case had more to do with a psychic problem and borderline condition than a beginning psychosis. On the plane of transference, a tendency to splitting was apparent. On the one hand, I was someone who was able to share his loneliness, or a good person; but as soon as I did not do what he wanted, I immediately became a bad person whom he had to fight and punish. This indicated a projected identification connected to a fantasy of omnipotence that concealed powerlessness and helpless fear. It also became clear that he was easily able to split off whatever happened in therapy and react inconspicuously in everyday reality.

For my own part, I felt intense anger when he told me I could go down into the fog where it was cold. It was not so much the words, it was the way he said it, and the malicious, sadistic grin I thought I had seen on his face. I had partially interpreted my anger as a countertransference brought on by his own anger. Naturally, part of the anger was my own against men who order women around. Feelings of countertransference are never entirely free of emotions from our personal background. I understood that, as long as he controlled those around him, Marcel could endure his fears. The defense mechanism of the projected identification was evident. He experienced aspects of his personality in those to whom he related and, in order to remain "whole," he had to control them, or at least prevent the negative aspects from uncontrollably turning against him. There was definitely a connection with the experience that his mother could not control her fears and that, in childhood, he had been at the mercy of her fears.

During the following five sessions, Marcel spoke of his daily life and his problems at work. The goal was to find a job he liked that also suited his abilities. In order to deal with the problem, he—having already received disability benefits—had been assigned to a vocational counselor by the welfare office. He repeatedly discussed with me what the counselor had found out. In this situation, I was given the role of the good father, while the job counselor was the evil father. I saw Marcel about every two weeks. I chose this rhythm for the sessions because individuals with a borderline condition develop a great fear of fusion and therefore are forced to act very destructively if the sessions occur too frequently. He told me in our first conversation that the therapist whom he had seen only every two or three weeks had achieved the best results.

In the eighth session, about three months into therapy, Marcel arrived and said, "I'm very dissatisfied with you. Things can't continue this way!"

I: "You want to punish me?"

Marcel: "I'll tell you a story. Do you know which one?"

I: "I'm not clairvoyant."

Marcel: "Precisely. That's the problem. You're not even clairvoyant, poor thing."

On the one hand, I was amused by the demand that I be clairvoyant, and on the other hand, I asked myself what this was all about. I became irritated and sensed a fear that I could not explain growing inside me.

Marcel: "You're in a bad mood today, I can see it clearly. Unfortunately, I can't be considerate of your bad mood.

I'm sorry, I have to tell you my story. I invented it at home: I'm in a cave, and you live in a farmhouse not far from the cave. I'm alone. It's boring. I go outside, I see you working in the garden. I ask if I can help you, and I decide you need a fence, so I build one. In the evening you go back to your house. You invite me to come over. I want to drink milk, and you bring me milk. I want to go back to my cave, but it's cold, and you invite me to stay in your guest room. In the morning you get a phone call; you have to go away. I'm still asleep. You write me a note. I make breakfast. After you've returned, we eat together."

While he related the story, he attentively looked at me, and I, according to agreement, did not look at him; he did not like to be looked at. I was to look at him only when he specifically allowed it.

He continued: "You wash the dishes, I make my bed, then I go back to my cave. You can call if you need anything from me. And now I'm talking about you: You're a whore. Your hairs should be pulled out one by one, then you should be thrown into a dungeon. There are many different kinds of whores, like the nuns at my boarding school, and the ones who want to sleep with every man. It's unbearable that my sister is a prostitute. I can't stand it. My mother must suffer so."

I: "Does your mother realize it?"

He: "No, it's me who suffers. I'm responsible for my sister. I was always responsible for my sister."

I explained to him that it must have been immensely important to his sister that he took over the responsibility for her, but that now she had to live her own life and we had to accept it, even if we doubted that what she was doing was good.

Marcel had this fantasy between the seventh and eighth session. He indulged in fantasies involving me as the good, nurturing mother. I gave him milk, and I had a garden. He identified with me; he knew what was happening, he knew what I needed. In his fantasy I needed a fence. In other words, he felt the need for boundaries; perhaps our relationship had to be protected, or we needed to deal with boundaries more closely in the context of our relationship. He reserved for himself the opportunity to retreat into a cave. And, naturally, the question arose why he picked this of all symbols. The cave is one of the symbols for the mother archetype; it means both protection and constriction. It is a place of transformation, the earth's uterus. His coming to me, then, could be a path to autonomy. He described his cave as a cold place, a possibility to put distance between the warm and living mother and himself. In his fantasy, he also revealed that he would have to help me help him. Helping to be helped might be a relationship motif from his childhood. It is a common relationship pattern in society.

In his fantasy, the idea of potential fusion was evident, but at least he permitted me to have a degree of autonomy; he even dared to fantasize that I trusted him enough to go away and return.

On the whole, the fantasy expressed a good deal of trust and closeness. He saw me as the nurturing mother who also permitted autonomy. He demonstrated that he could fulfill his basic human needs in the relationship; he presented himself as a protector, but this probably was the only prospect for him to establish a relationship.

After he had elaborated the fantasy at home he brought it to the session and said he was not satisfied with me at all, and demanded that I be clairvoyant. Here the split once again became obvious. He had fantasized only about the positive aspects of the relationship, and I imagine he was very frightened that I might reject him and his fantasy, or that his desire to fuse with me as the good mother might have become too strong. The fence might also have been a barrier against regression or against overly compassionate feelings.

In the midst of his dialogue he said: "And now I'm talking about you," as if he had not been speaking of me up to that point. This was correct inasmuch as I was at that moment essentially an object of transference. He called me a whore—bad enough—then said my hairs should be pulled out one by one; to me, this was a sadistic image.

These images indicated that he had sexual fantasies involving me, which he did not dare express. By tearing out my hair he probably wanted to rob me of my erotic energy as well; I had already become dangerous to him in various aspects.

In my reaction I did not interpret the progress expressed in the fantasy, nor the evident split. Perhaps I should have done so. That he spoke of his sister out of the blue, of yet another humiliating secret regarding the fact that she is a prostitute, showed that he also projected his sister onto me.

In the following sessions he spoke much and often about his sister. He tried to understand why she was a prostitute. By speaking of her, he inevitably spoke of his sad experiences at the boarding school. He described himself as someone overcome by constant and desperate anger. On the one hand, I sympathized with his anger, while on the other, his childhood experiences made me very sad. At one time I had tears in my eyes; he must have noticed, for he began to cry. The next time he came, it was the beginning of December; he inquired how long I would be going away at Christmas. Then he looked at me severely and said, "You made me cry last time. Don't do that! I must not lose my cool! I'll whip you with chains! I'll tie you up in chains and beat you! I'll take an iron rod and beat you some more! Your blood will flow, your blood will flow . . . I'll drive you before me like an animal . . ."

Here I interrupted and said: "Stop, I've had enough, I can't stand it!"

I was frightened and was tempted to react with primitive sadistic means and just throw him out. I was afraid for my life. This fear expressed itself in my fantasy that he might at any moment pull a pistol out of his pocket and kill me. I speculated how I could disarm him. While I was occupied with my fantasy, I saw that his face showed great fear. I realized that I had to protect him; he was at least as frightened of me as I of him. I explained that we had just experienced his maniacal rage, his destructive rage, and that it had frightened both him and me. Such situations triggered an intense, primordial fear and anger, which controlled both of us. I also told him that this kind of anger and fear occurred as a defense against tenderness. I explained that he had expressed very primordial aggressive and sexual drives, and that it was natural that they were frightening, even to me, but that I also believed our relationship was good enough so that he could express his fantasies. However, I had to have the opportunity to say "stop."

Whereupon Marcel said, "Please forgive me. You know, it's not I who made those fantasies. It's a very big man who makes them."

I: "Can you see this man in your fantasy?" (I deliberately added "in your fantasy" because I had the impression that he was confusing the concrete situation with the fantasy.)

Marcel: "The man is big, sort of like a giant, very serious, very demanding. He wants me not to cry, he wants me to have a good job, he wants me not to be afraid, he wants me to do things like all the other young people do."

I: "You feel pretty much terrorized by him?"

Marcel: "Yes, he terrorizes me. He doesn't help me. No one ever helped me in my whole life. My father was always drunk. I had to protect my mother from him. He didn't help me. He wanted me to stay with mother. When I was eighteen he criticized me for not having a good job. What should I do if this man terrorizes me again, or if I terrorize you again?"

I: "When the man starts to terrorize you, tell me right away, and we'll try to understand what is frightening you. You terrorize when you're afraid, and you're afraid when you think you might lose me, as for instance when the Christmas vacation is about to start. And you're also frightened when I get too close. I think we should keep an eye on this man. Maybe we can tame him."

My sadness had created a great closeness between us, and perhaps a closeness between him and his self. He was afraid of being swallowed by such feelings, which was why he created a destructive fantasy of omnipotence. My intervention was hardly professional. I had not considered whether it really was the right moment to make him aware of the fact that I was a real person outside of his system; but my reaction was the only one possible for me. What was interesting was his reaction to my intervention. He differentiated between himself and this big man who terrorized him. A differentiation between the ego and the non-ego took place, a separation, and at the same time he felt responsible for the big man. Maybe the situation would have developed otherwise if I had noticed that the transference attack was really a declaration of love that he had to fend off. Had I let him know that then, a different process would probably have been initiated. However, I was not aware of it at the time.

In Marcel's fantasies at the beginning of the course of therapy, the characteristic manifestations of transference seen in borderline patients, as defined by Rohde-Dachser based on Kernberg, were obvious. Essentially, they are as follows:[11]

—Therapy and therapist are expected to have magical powers.

—A diminished ability to differentiate between fantasy and concrete situations.

—Episodes of transference that are excessively aggressive and characterized by distrust and an extensive fear of being rejected.

—Abrupt change in the emotional tone of the transference going as far as a transference psychosis. I reacted to these transferences with special countertransferences that are also typical to borderline condition. Many different feelings of countertransference were apparent within a single session; they changed abruptly.

—Subliminal aggression. It was always in the room.

—On my part, too, mechanisms of projected identification were activated; primordial fears and aggressions were triggered and turned against the analysand.

On the one hand, the feeling of closeness, my fear, and my resistance against these primordial feelings and, on the other, my refusal to accept his transferences had caused

Marcel to distance himself from the big man who terrorized him. Repeatedly, Marcel was able to describe his fear of the man, but we did not get anywhere. For weeks we were occupied with the man without anything major happening. I became increasingly worried. I attempted to concentrate more on myself and hoped for an inspiration. In this situation I thought of the fairy tale about Blue Beard, and I told Marcel the story.

The idea of a fairy tale in a certain analytic situation is a special form of countertransference; it is an archetypal countertransference. With this inspiration I was implying that I was ready to accept this "inner" man into an area of our relationship to which we could both refer. It was also a means to place his personal story, his personal suffering, within a greater context. Personal suffering is reflected in common human experience. The fairy tale also has the advantage of demonstrating how to deal with a given problem, in this case Blue Beard's dominion. It turned out that the solution offered in the fairy tale was a way out both for Marcel and myself.

BLUE BEARD[12]

There was a man who had fine houses, both in town and country, a deal of silver and gold plate, embroidered furniture, and coaches gilded all over with gold. But this man was so unlucky as to have a blue beard, which made him so frightfully ugly that all the women and girls ran away from him.

One of his neighbors, a lady of quality, had two daughters who were perfect beauties. He desired of her one of them in marriage, leaving to her choice which of the two she would bestow on him. They would neither of them have him, and sent him backward and forward from one another, not being able to bear the thoughts of marrying a man who had a blue beard, and what besides gave them disgust and aversion was his having already been married to several wives, and nobody ever knew what became of them.

Blue Beard, to engage their affection, took them, with the lady their mother and three or four ladies of their acquaintance, with other young people of the neighborhood, to one of his country seats, where they stayed a whole week.

There was nothing then to be seen but parties of pleasure, hunting, fishing, dancing, mirth, and feasting. Nobody went to bed, but all passed the night in rallying and joking with each other. In short, everything succeeded so well that the youngest daughter began to think the master of the house not to have a beard so very blue, and that he was a mighty civil gentleman.

As soon as they returned home, the marriage was concluded. About a month afterward, Blue Beard told his wife that he was obliged to take a country journey for six weeks at least, about affairs of very great consequence, desiring her to divert herself in his absence, to send for her friends and acquaintances, to carry them into the country, if she pleased, and to make good cheer wherever she was.

"Here," said he, "are the keys of the two great wardrobes, wherein I have my best furniture; these are of my silver and gold plate, which is not every day in use; these open my strongboxes, which hold my money, both gold and silver; these my caskets of jewels; and this is the master-key to all my apartments. But for this little one here, it is the key of the closet at the end of the great gallery on the ground floor. Open them all; go into all and every one of them, except that little closet, which I forbid you, and forbid it in such a manner that, if you happen to open it, there's nothing but what you may expect from my just anger and resentment."

She promised to observe, very exactly, whatever he had ordered; then he, after having embraced her, got into his coach and proceeded on his journey.

Her neighbors and good friends did not stay to be sent for by the new married lady, so great was their impatience to see all the rich furniture of her house, not daring to come while her husband was there, because of his blue beard, which frightened them. They ran through all the rooms, closets, and wardrobes, which were all so fine and rich that they seemed to surpass one another.

After that they went up into the two great rooms, where were the best and richest furniture; they could not sufficiently admire the number and beauty of the tapestry, beds, couches, cabinets, stands, tables, and looking glasses, in which you might see yourself from head to foot; some of them were framed with glass, others with silver, plain and gilded, the finest and most magnificent ever were seen.

They ceased not to extol and envy the happiness of their friend, who in the meantime in no way diverted herself in looking upon all these rich things, because of the impatience she had to go and open the closet on the ground floor. She was so much pressed by her curiosity that, without considering that it was very uncivil to leave her company, she went down a little back staircase, and with such excessive haste that she had twice or thrice like to have broken her neck.

Being come to the closet door, she made a stop for some time, thinking upon her husband's orders, and considering what unhappiness might attend her if she was disobedient; but the temptation was so strong she could not overcome it. She then took the little key, and opened it, trembling, but could not at first see anything plainly, because the windows were shut. After some moments she began to perceive that the floor was all covered over with clotted blood, on which lay the bodies of several dead women, ranged against the walls. (These were all the wives whom Blue Beard had married and murdered, one after another.) She thought she should have died for fear, and the key, which she pulled out of the lock, fell out of her hand.

After having somewhat recovered her surprise, she took up the key, locked the door, and went upstairs into her chamber to recover herself; but she could not, so much was she frightened. Having observed that the key of the closet was stained with blood, she tried two or three times to wipe it off, but the blood would not come out; in vain did she wash it, and even rub it with soap and sand, the blood still remained, for the key was magical and she could never make it quite clean; when the blood was gone off from one side, it came again on the other.

Blue Beard returned from his journey the same evening, and said he had received letters upon the road, informing him that the affair he went about was ended to his advantage. His wife did all she could to convince him she was extremely glad of his speedy return.

Next morning he asked her for the keys, which she gave him, but with such a trembling hand that he easily guessed what had happened.

"What!" said he, "is not the key of my closet among the rest?"

"I must certainly," said she, "have left it above upon the table."

"Fail not," said Blue Beard, "to bring it me presently."

After several goings backward and forward she was forced to bring him the key. Blue Beard, having very attentively considered it, said to his wife,

"How comes this blood upon the key?"

"I do not know," cried the poor woman, paler than death.

"You do not know!" replied Blue Beard. "I very well know. You were resolved to go into the closet, were you not? Mighty well, madam; you shall go in, and take your place among the ladies you saw there."

Upon this she threw herself at her husband's feet, and begged his pardon with all the signs of a true repentance, vowing that she would never more be disobedient. She would have melted a rock, so beautiful and sorrowful was she; but Blue Beard had a heart harder than any rock!

"You must die, madam," said he, "and that presently."

"Since I must die," answered she (looking upon him with her eyes all bathed in tears), "give me some little time to say my prayers."

"I give you," replied Blue Beard, "half a quarter of an hour, but not one moment more."

When she was alone she called out to her sister, and said to her:

"Sister Anne" (for that was her name), "go up, I beg you, upon the top of the tower, and look if my brothers are not coming; they promised me that they would come today, and if you see them, give them a sign to make haste."

Her sister Anne went up upon the top of the tower, and the poor afflicted wife cried out from time to time:

"Anne, sister Anne, do you see anyone coming?"

And sister Anne said:

"I see nothing but the sun, which makes a dust, and the grass, which looks green."

In the meanwhile Blue Beard, holding a great saber in his hand, cried out as loud as he could bawl to his wife:

"Come down instantly, or I shall come up to you."

"One moment longer, if you please," said his wife; and then she cried out very softly, "Anne, sister Anne, do you see anybody coming?"

And sister Anne answered:

"I see nothing but the sun, which makes a dust, and the grass, which is green."

"Come down quickly," cried Blue Beard, "or I will come up to you."

"I am coming," answered his wife; and then she cried, "Anne, sister Anne, do you not see anyone coming?"

"I see," replied sister Anne, "a great dust, which comes on this side here."

"Are they my brothers?"

"Alas! no, my dear sister, I see a flock of sheep."

"Will you not come down?" cried Blue Beard.

"One moment longer," said his wife, and then she cried out: "Anne, sister Anne, do you see nobody coming?"

"I see," said she, "two horsemen, but they are yet a great way off."

"God be praised," replied the poor wife joyfully: "they are my brothers; I will make them a sign, as well as I can, for them to make haste."

Then Blue Beard bawled out so loud that he made the whole house tremble. The distressed wife came down, and threw herself at his feet, all in tears, with her hair about her shoulders.

"This signifies nothing," says Blue Beard; "you must die"; then, taking hold of her hair with one hand, and lifting up the sword with the other, he was going to take off her head. The poor lady, turning about to him, and looking at him with dying eyes, desired him to afford her one little moment to recollect herself.

"No, no," said he, "recommend thyself to God," and was just ready to strike . . .

At this very instant there was such a loud knocking at the gate that Blue Beard made a sudden stop. The gate was opened, and presently entered two horsemen, who, drawing their swords, ran directly to Blue Beard. He knew them to be his wife's brothers, one a dragoon, the other a musketeer; so that he ran away immediately to save himself; but the two brothers pursued so close that they overtook him before he could get to the steps of the porch, when they ran their swords through his body and left him dead.

> The poor wife was almost as dead as her husband, and had not strength enough to rise and welcome her brothers.
> Blue Beard had no heirs, and so his wife became mistress of all his estate. She made use of one part of it to marry her sister Anne to a young gentleman who had loved her a long while; another part to buy captains' commissions for her brothers, and the rest to marry herself to a very worthy gentleman, who made her forget the ill time she had passed with Blue Beard.

Contrary to his usual habits, for the analysand normally disliked it when I spoke, Marcel listened very attentively. When the story was over, he said it was about himself. It was the very same Blue Beard with whom he was in constant battle. He soon realized that the brothers at the end of the fairy tale would fight against him. Though Marcel emphasized that his big man did not have a blue beard, he said he easily could have one. By relating Blue Beard to his male figure, we clearly addressed a perspective of interpretation in the fairy tale. The objective was to put a stop to Blue Beard's plans. In light of the end, when the brothers closed in on Blue Beard and killed him, the interpretation had to do with the transformation of destructiveness into active aggression. This interpretative perspective was important for the analysand. He noted that Blue Beard must have been a very powerful and wealthy man, but that women could not bear to be with him. Marcel sensed that the fantasies he had devised were the same as those described in "Blue Beard." In his projection onto the fairy tale, it was substantially easier for him to stand up for his fantasies and deal with them. He thought Blue Beard was sadistic. He thoroughly condemned the women who got involved with him, for they did it only for the money. Marcel sensed the fact that the women all had a bad feeling at first and did not want to have anything to do with Blue Beard, as was expressed in the beginning of the fairy tale. He was undecided as to whether he should have been angry at the women or just at Blue Beard. We discussed how Blue Beard butchered his wives only when they found out his secret. Marcel became agitated over this and said he'd kill everyone who knew his secrets, and that it was important for him to keep his secrets. I reminded Marcel that we were speaking not of him, but of Blue Beard. He calmed down.

The fairy tale effected a kind of triangulation. Problems that had previously been projected onto our relationship could now be seen projected onto the fairy tale; there they could be addressed and acknowledged as Marcel's personal problems only to the extent that he could tolerate them.

For about six months we worked on the fairy tale. We spoke of his everyday life, and the apprenticeship he had started. Often we resorted to fragments of the Blue Beard story. Marcel suggested ideas and repeatedly brought up the dead bodies. He saw himself cut to pieces and he occasionally mentioned that he must have been very frightened of women if he needed to butcher them.

After a few weeks, he lost interest in the dead bodies; he began to take an interest in the behavior of the youngest daughter. I had been aware for some time that I was in the position of this young woman who, in an effort to escape Blue Beard, turned to other powers and hoped for her brothers to deliver her. I realized it because—and this also is a form of countertransference—the second part of the fairy tale was always very much on my mind even when Marcel spoke of Blue Beard and the dead bodies; I always knew that the woman must not get involved, and that, at the same time, she must not blind herself to Blue Beard's destructiveness.

In our version of the story, the heroine turned to her sister. The sister represented that aspect of the heroine not under the spell of Blue Beard. The sister was only the mediator to the valiant brothers. This passage was important; it helped me, and probably the analysand, to go through with the entire Blue Beard theme.

As with all work using fairy tales, this story allowed him to face his problem, and at the same time to distance himself enough to prevent it from crippling him.

When he first took an interest in Blue Beard's wife, I asked Marcel to imagine the green grass and the shining sun. He recognized this as an immense contrast to the death chamber down in the castle. He coined the term "death chamber," and it seemed very meaningful to me, since a death god is of course lurking in Blue Beard, while Marcel's destructiveness concealed a fear of death. When we related the fairy tale to the analysand's individual problems, we did not include the component of "Blue Beard the Death God." I asked him to see the green grass and the shining sun, alternately with Blue Beard sharpening his knife. He succeeded in imagining both images and withstood the tension. Soon the brothers were activated in his imagination, and he repeatedly described them with great love. The appearance of the brothers, for which he had been intensely yearning, signalled an important turning point. Once he had imaginatively succeeded in allowing the brothers to close in on Blue Beard and kill him, he was convinced that he had slain the Blue Beard within him as well.

During the period when we were working on the fairy tale there were hardly any instances of transference attacks. Whenever I got too close with a statement and he wrinkled his forehead or got that certain tone of voice, I reminded him of the fairy tale.

A symbolic process, such as expressed in a fairy tale, can take on the function of a transition object. Working with fairy tales can relieve the burden on the relationship with the therapist. Instead of looking at each other, we look at a third party. In this case, it seemed particularly sensible, because the destructive man had to be observed and transformed. But working with fairy tales can also be seen as an effort to indicate what is behind the relationship, what is behind concrete, everyday reality. Finally, it indicates the overall primary cause accessible in the symbol, and particularly in the symbolic processes expressed in fairy tales. In this respect, I see the supporting elements of the collective unconscious, which become accessible to us in fairy tales and myths, and which we can provide to others so that the problem might be reworked. And this also has an effect on the structure of the ego.

In the period that followed, the therapy entered calmer waters. The brothers from "Blue Beard" were still important to Marcel. He speculated how they could help him, how they might behave in certain situations; and at times he was able, instead of being destructive, to actively charge ahead; this pleased him.

This example illustrates how my idea of introducing a fairy tale, which offered the analysand the opportunity to work out inner conflicts, and also to develop new perspectives, was related to turbulent transference/countertransference processes typical in individuals with a borderline condition.

These three cases serve to illustrate that situations in which true transformation can be perceived in the therapeutic process are also related to the formation of new symbols. The symbols, in turn, are clearly related to special situations of transference and countertransference as an essential aspect of the therapeutic relationship. This hypothesis was examined by Riedel, among others, based on a rather long series of paintings that were spontaneously created in a course of analysis.[13] Processes of symbolization and relationship are intermeshed in therapy. Practical cases of therapeutic work confirm the significance of Jung's statement: "Individuation . . . is in the first place an internal and subjective process of integration, and in the second it is an equally indispensable process of objective relationship."[14]

NOTES

Chapter 1. Aspects of the Human Concept

1. Jung, "A Study in the Process of Individuation," CW 9 (I), par. 530.
2. Jung, "Psychology of the Transference," CW 16, par. 445.
3. Jung, "Psychology of the Transference," CW 16, par. 454.
4. Jung, "Psychotherapy Today," CW 16, par. 227.
5. Jung, "Psychology of the Transference," CW 16, par. 400.
6. Jung, "The Alchemical Interpretation of the Fish," CW 9 (II), par. 257.
7. Jung, "The Transcendent Function," CW 8, par. 159.
8. Jung, "The Conjunction," CW 14, par. 760.
9. Jung, "The Psychology of the Child Archetype," CW 9 (I), par. 291.
10. Cf. Kast, *The Nature of Loving*.
11. Jung, *Psychological Types*, CW 6, par. 891.
12. Jung, "Psychology of the Transference," CW 16, par. 416.
13. Jung, *Letters*, vol. 2, p. 297.

Chapter 2. Aspects of the Symbol

1. For this and the following definitions, cf. the entry for "symbol" in Lurker, pp. 551 ff.
2. Riedel, *Bilder*, pp. 38–39.
3. Cf. Kast, *A Time to Mourn*.
4. Cf. the fairy tale "The Girl with the Little Moon on Her Forehead." In *Märchen aus dem Iran*.
5. Cf. Kast, *Märchen als Therapie*.
6. Cf. Kast, *Imagination*.
7. Cf. Mahler et al.
8. Jung, "The Aims of Psychotherapy," CW 16, par. 99.
9. Cf. Fromm, p. 53: "To be creative means to consider the whole process of life as a process of birth, and not to take

any stage of life as a final stage. Most people die before they are fully born. Creativeness means to be born before one dies."
10. Jung, "The Transcendent Function," CW 8, par. 131 ff.
11. Cf. Matussek.
12. Jung, "The Transcendent Function," CW 8, pars. 159–60.

Chapter 3. Aspects of the Complex

1. Jung, "Problems of Modern Psychotherapy," CW 16, par. 125.
2. Jung, "The Psychology of Dementia Praecox," esp. "The Feeling-Toned Complex and Its General Effects on the Psyche," CW 3, par. 77–106.
3. Jung, "A Review of the Complex Theory," CW 8, par. 210.
4. Cf. these comments to Kast, "Die Bedeutung der Symbole."
5. Kast, *Das Assoziationsexperiment*, pp. 19 ff. and Jung, "A Review of the Complex Theory."
6. Cf. Grof.
7. Jung, "A Psychological Theory of Types," CW 6, par. 926.
8. Jung, "A Review of the Complex Theory," CW 8, par. 200.
9. Cf. Jung, "Experimental Observations," CW 2, and Kast, *Das Assoziationsexperiment*.
10. Jung, "A Review of the Complex Theory," CW 8, par. 210.
11. Jung, "A Psychological Theory of Types," CW 6, par. 925.
12. Jung, "A Psychological Theory of Types," CW 6, par. 926.
13. Jung, "The Psychology of Dementia Praecox," CW 3, par. 140.
14. Jung, "A Review of the Complex Theory," CW 8, par. 203.
15. Jung, "The Structure and Dynamics of the Psyche," CW 8, pars. 207–08.
16. Jung, "A Review of the Complex Theory," CW 8, par. 204.
17. Jung, "A Psychological Theory of Types," CW 6, par. 923.
18. Jung, "Problems of Modern Psychotherapy," CW 16, par. 125.
19. Cf. Kast, *Imagination*.
20. Cf. Riedel, *Farben*.
21. Cf. Riedel, *Bilder*.

Chapter 4. Aspects of the Ego Complex

1. Jung, "A Psychological Theory of Types," CW 6, par. 923.
2. Jung, "The Psychological Foundations of Belief in Spirits," CW 8, par. 582.
3. Ibid., par. 580.
4. Jung, "The Psychology of Dementia Praecox," CW 3, par. 82–83.
5. Jung, "The Ego," CW 9 (II), pars. 3, 4.
6. The *shadow* designates aspects of ourselves that we cannot accept; these aspects do not agree with our ego ideal, and are often in disagreement with the values established by society. We therefore repress them and prefer to see them projected onto other people, where we can fight them. Along with the personal shadow, there is also the collective shadow.

   On the personal shadow: A person who likes to be generous has a selfish aspect in his or her shadow. Though he or she will not notice it, someone who likes to appear unaggressive may be aggressive when his or her shadow is constellated. The shadow can be experienced if we are attentive; perhaps we wish to respond pleasantly to a person who secretly angers us, but the anger can be detected in our voice. If we recognize our harsh tone and choose not to repress it, we have to modify our self-image of a friendly person. Because we like to resemble our ideal image, this is not a simple matter. If we feel that we do not resemble it, we consequently react with insecurity and anxiety.

   In dreams, we may encounter our shadow as thieves, murderers, idlers, sadists, or greedy people. If while dreaming, or when remembering the dream, we sense an almost uncontrollable revulsion, it undoubtedly has to do with our shadow. This does not imply that we are murderers, it is rather an indication that we can experience the characteristics we associate with murderers. The difference between ourselves and a murderer is that by conscious control we can prevent the eruption of homicidal impulses. But it is quite sensible to be aware that in the face of a certain situation we can be murderously angry or completely destructive; we are not as balanced as we wish to believe.

   We are not only what we would like to be. The shadow confronts us with the fact that the very thing we consciously oppose is present within our psyche. However, we do not at first encounter our shadow within our psyche, but projected onto other people. We spend much time criticizing the dishonest practices of some contemporaries. We relish describing their actions, we condemn them, and prove that we are the better person. By taking an interest in the individual onto whom we project our shadow—who may very well have dishonest habits—we animate our shadow only in part. By morally condemning this person, we become detached. We may for the moment be relieved because our shadow is not quite as repressed, but we avoid the responsibility for our shadow. This moral conflict does not have to be endured. To become aware of one's shadow means that we must ask why we are so incensed about others' dishonesty, even though we may not have been directly harmed. But we rarely pose this question. Often, we project our shadow onto people who are far away, where our shadow would be least dangerous. We project it onto strangers, onto people in foreign countries, and onto minorities. We falsely attribute characteristics that can lead to prejudices—such as, Italians are noisy. We should examine where these characteristics can be found in our lives. Perhaps we have a side that wants to be a bit louder, more vivacious, and less controlled than standards permit. Therefore, shadow acceptance is the realization that the shadow is a part of us, and that we can avoid projecting it. This causes conflict, and offends our sense of self-worth. But, once accepted, it brings relief and freedom and strengthens our sense of self-worth. Shadow acceptance implies conflict—because we must accept that we have aspects we deeply abhor, and cannot conceal, because they become visible in our actions. It offends our sense of self-worth, if self-worth exclusively depends on identification with positive imaginings. By accepting the shadow, we experience relief because we no longer need to repress certain aspects of ourselves that are often connected with great vitality; we no longer need to be better than we are. The shadow is not only what we think to be morally evil. Though there might be dangerous aspects to the shadow, it often contains something exceptionally vital.

Shadow acceptance has far-reaching consequences. When we are familiar with our shadow and accept its existence, we can expect the presence of a shadow in other people. We will treat weaknesses and faults with greater tolerance and benevolence. If the shadow were a collectively approved value, it would be easier to justify flaws. This tolerance or solidarity would extend to minority groups; shadow acceptance would have sociopsychological consequences. We are sometimes greatly troubled by minorities, for they embody the shadow of the establishment. Therefore, shadow acceptance is a prerequisite for democracy and solidarity. Shadow acceptance would be important on a political level; in time, we will be forced to practice it. We project our shadow onto people who are far away, so that, whatever happens, it will not come back. As a result, we fear them and call up entire armies against possible attack. We fear them instead of our shadow. But the world is getting smaller; without much effort, we can travel far. We cannot avoid meeting, seeing, perhaps even loving, people from the ethnic groups onto which we projected certain characteristics, and then we will realize: They're not like that at all! What do we do with our shadow then? The solution is to accept the shadow.

The desire to live with our shadow cannot mean that we allow every shadow aspect into our lives unchecked. Concealed in the shadow are a good deal of energy and love of life. How many enjoyable things we have condemned—perhaps we could retrieve the lost enjoyment. But it is the moral problem with which we must deal responsibly. It is our responsibility to become increasingly aware of our shadow, and to deal with the shadow once we are aware of it. To accept our shadow, we need other virtues beyond responsibility. Every conscious attitude pushes other values into the "shadow"—the confrontation between the ego ideal and the shadow has to be repeatedly endured.

7. Jung, *Two Essays on Analytical Psychology*, CW 7, par. 303.
8. Cf. Erikson.
9. Cf. Mahler et al.
10. Cf. Bürgin and Stern.
11. Cf. Rohde-Dachser, "Abschied."
12. Cf. Bürgin.
13. Cf. on this subject "Critical Appraisal: The Anima and Animus Concept," in Kast, *The Nature of Loving*. Jung's descriptions of anima and animus varied widely over the years, but they are always archetypal images that mediate between consciousness and the unconscious. One definition, published in 1928, specifies, "If I were to attempt to put in a nutshell the difference between man and woman in this respect, what it is that characterizes the animus as opposed to the anima, I can only say this: as the anima produces *moods*, the animus produces *opinions*." (*Two Essays on Analytical Psychology*, CW 7, par. 331). This definition can be supplemented by a statement in the commentary on *The Secret of the Golden Flower*, 1929, "Just as the anima of a man consists of inferior relatedness, full of affect, so the animus of a woman causes inferior judgements, or better,

opinions." (*Alchemical Studies*, CW 13, p. 60.) In 1956, he says, "The anima is indeed the archetype of life itself, which is beyond all meaning and moral categories." (*Mysterium Coniunctionis*, CW 14 (II), par. 312). And in a letter of 1957, "(The anima) symbolizes the function of relationship. The animus is the image of spiritual forces in a woman, symbolized by a masculine figure. If a man or a woman is unconscious of these inner forces, they appear in a projection." (*Letters*, vol. 2, p. 402)

The young Jung sees a distorted anima and animus; the old Jung sees within animus and anima potentials beyond pathology. One reason why animus and anima are distorted is that they are still related to the parent complexes; another reason is that they are repressed because both are often associated with desires and strong emotions; this is why we have a tendency to fight them. An intercepted anima or animus becomes a distorted anima or animus. As with anything repressed or split off, these archetypal symbols push their way into consciousness and cause sudden ill-temper, not infrequently arising from a fantasy that cannot be indulged.

Whenever Jung discusses what animus and anima have in common, he describes them as archetypal images, which, like all archetypal images, mediate between consciousness and the unconscious; the creative aspect of the unconscious is made conscious principally by the animus and the anima.

Since the animus and the anima are archetypes, they affect consciousness as archetypal images. They seem compelling, numinous, and are often surrounded by an atmosphere of secrecy, unconditionality and, finally, emotional consequence. Thus, we can speak of animus and anima only when an emotional experience with interior images or projections onto other people is present.

Where is the difference? Jung's definitions make it clear that the animus is projected onto a man or men, while the anima is projected onto a woman or women. By the way, Jung reasons that men have an anima and women an animus because the factor that produces projection in male children is the mother, and in female children, the father. If we consider animus and anima as archetypes, and to my knowledge Jung never speaks of sexually specific archetypes, the question arises whether animus/anima might not be images that can be perceived and experienced by both sexes. If Jung's considerations are based on the fact that the father is the first factor to produce projection in a girl, I believe that he has in this instance conceived the woman's psychology to be the opposite of the man's; and this is in no way acceptable. "The first factor to produce projection," for either a woman or a man, could be the mother, and perhaps even both parents. This is why I believe that both anima and animus appear in men as well as in women, and that they represent aspects of the male and female psyche.

Let us proceed from the observable facts: To me, it seems obvious that men can be fascinated by women, and women by men, without this attraction necessarily having the numinous implications that animus and anima are being projected.

To my knowledge, there are typical anima figures that appear in dreams, desires, and fantasies of both men and women, such as nymphs, a fascinating little girl, mermaids, good fairies, witches, whores, saints, and so on. These figures are anima figures only when they are accompanied by a passionate feeling, usually a feeling of desire. In the same way, fascinating animus figures, such as the mysterious stranger, the divine youth, the fascinating thinker, a deity throwing lightning bolts, or a mysterious, Christ-like man, appear in the dreams, fantasies and projections of both men and women. Emotionally, animus figures impart enthusiasm and inspiration rather than the spiritual fascination that anima figures tend to arouse. When I asked colleagues which emotions they associated with animus and anima I came to the following conclusions. Everyone agreed that the anima makes us more alive. Expressions like "spiritual expansion," "desire to unite," "a yearning for symbiosis, and the feeling of never being able to achieve symbiosis" were associated with the anima. Some emphasized that this desire belonged more to the religious sphere; the sexual domain was also taken into account. "It is a desire to have not only sex, but to immerse oneself in physicality, where sexuality can become all-embracing and make us whole." But being overcome by art, painting, poetry and the whole phenomenon of losing oneself, were all described as emotions that can be experienced when the anima is constellated. In terms of space, the emotion called forth by an anima constellation was compared with the horizontal; it is an emotion of expanding oneself, of being inside life, of being able to let be, and of serenity. Within this expansion, then, lies the potential to relate to a myriad of things.

At first, expressions like "spiritual concentration," and "being inspired" were used for the emotion related to the constellated animus, then "tingling inside, exhilarated by stimulation," and "relating things with each other," and "fascination with words." The emotion connected with the animus causes us to grasp, to want to grasp, "what it is that holds the world together on the inside." It leads us to get to the bottom of things and find a solution by understanding the pith of the matter. In space, this emotion was clearly equated with the vertical. The desires and basic human needs related to the emotions that belong to the animus and anima definitely seem human; both appear in men and in women.

Usually, we encounter the animus and anima in projected form; we are fascinated by other people, and tend to fantasize about other individuals and about our relationship to them, therefore these fantasies express a retroactive bond with our deeper psyche.

The unification of animus and anima, either intrapsychic or in a fantasized relationship to an actual person, is accompanied by a vital feeling of spiritual-psychic inspiration, which often cannot be distinguished from the feeling of love.

14. Cf. Kast, *A Time to Mourn*.
15. Cf. Kast, *The Creative Leap*.
16. Cf. Kast, *The Nature of Loving*.
17. Cf. Rauchfleisch, p. 145.
18. Kast, *The Creative Leap*.
19. Cf. Jacoby, *Individuation und Narziβmus*.
20. Cf. Krapp.
21. Neumann, *The Great Mother*.
22. Cf. de Coulon.
23. Mentzos.
24. Neumann, *The Child*.

Chapter 5. Aspects of the Archetype

1. Jung, "Synchronicity: An Acausal Connecting Principle," CW 8, par. 856.
2. Cf. Jung's foreword in Jacoby's *Psychotherapeuten sind auch Menschen*.
3. Jung, "The Psychology of the Child Archetype," CW 9 (I), par. 262.
4. Jung, "Concerning the Archetypes and the Anima Concept," CW 9 (I), par. 118.
5. Jung, "Medicine and Psychotherapy," CW 16, par. 206.
6. Jung, "On the Nature of the Psyche," CW 8, par. 404.

NOTES

7. Jung, "Psychological Aspects of the Mother Archetype," CW 9 (I), par. 152.
8. Jung, "On the Nature of the Psyche," CW 8, par. 417.
9. Ibid., par. 414.
10. Von Franz, *Number and Time*.
11. Jung, "The Phenomenology of the Spirit in Fairytales," CW 9 (I), par. 393.
12. Jung, "The Structure of the Psyche," CW 8, par. 339.
13. Jung, "Archetypes of the Collective Unconscious," CW 9 (I), par. 3.
14. Jung, "Psychology and Literature," CW 15, par. 160.
15. Jung, "Archetypes of the Collective Unconscious," CW 9 (I), pars. 44–45.
16. Jung, "On the Relation of Analytical Psychology to Poetry," CW 15, par. 129.
17. Cf. Schwarzenau.
18. Cf. Bloch.
19. Jung, "The Structure of the Psyche," CW 8, par. 339.
20. Jung, "On the Relation of Analytical Psychology to Poetry," CW 15, par. 130.
21. Jung, "Archetypes of the Collective Unconscious," CW 9 (I), pars. 44–45.
22. Jung, "The Practical Use of Dream-Analysis," CW 16, par. 340.
23. Cf. Kast, *Imagination*.
24. Cf. "Dreams as Guides during the Process of Mourning" in Kast, *A Time to Mourn*.
25. Jung, *Psychological Types*, CW 6, par. 789.
26. Jung, "The Conjunction," CW 14, par. 760.
27. Jung, *Two Essays on Analytical Psychology*, CW 7, par. 303.
28. Jung, "The Fish in Alchemy," CW 9 (II), par. 203.
29. Jung, "The Alchemical Interpretation of the Fish," CW 9 (II), par. 257.
30. Jung, "The Mana-Personality," CW 7, par. 404.
31. Jung, "The Alchemical Interpretation of the Fish," CW 9 (II), par. 257.
32. Jung, "Psychology of the Transference," CW 16, pars. 502–03.
33. Jung, "The Conjunction," CW 14, par. 778.
34. Ibid.
35. Jung, *Psychological Types*, CW 6, par. 789.
36. Lurker, p. 352.
37. *Ibid.*, p. 353.
38. Jung, "Individual Dream Symbolism in Relation to Alchemy," CW 12, par. 46, n. 3.

39. Riedel, *Formen*, p. 90.
40. Jung, *Letters*, vol. I, 1906–1950, p. 172.
41. Jung, "A Study in the Process of Individuation," CW 9 (I), picture 19.
42. Jung, "The Psychology of the Child Archetype," CW 9 (I), par. 267.
43. Jung, "Concerning Mandala Symbolism," CW 9 (I), par. 714.
44. Jung, "King and Queen," CW 16, par. 448.
45. Ibid., par. 445.
46. Cf. Evers.
47. Cf. Koch.
48. Cf. von Franz, "The Process of Individuation."
49. Jung, "Religious Ideas in Alchemy," CW 12, fig. 231.
50. Jung, "The Philosophical Tree," CW 13, illus. 22.
51. Jung, "Synchronicity: An Acausal Connecting Principle," CW 8, par. 858.
52. Capra, p. 363.
53. Cf. von Uexküll.
54. Jung, "The Psychology of the Child Archetype," CW 9 (I), par. 290.
55. Cf. Overbeck.
56. Ibid.
57. Cf. Kast, *Imagination*, pp. 30, 64, and 172 in the German original. English translation forthcoming from Fromm International.
58. Cf. Middendorf.
59. Cf. Frank and Vaitl, pp. 97 ff., and Ahrens, pp. 339 ff.
60. Cf. Studt.
61. In German, the word *Krebs* means both "cancer" and "crab."
62. Kast, *Imagination*, pp. 60 ff. in the German original.

Chapter 6. Transference, Countertransference, and the Formation of New Symbols

1. For the sake of linguistic clarity, the distinction between male and female analysts and analysands has been omitted on the following pages.
2. Jung, "Psychology of the Transference," CW 16, par. 422.
3. Cf. also Jacoby, *Psychotherapeuten sind auch Menschen*.
4. Cf. Kast, *Traumbild Auto* for a detailed interpretation of this dream.
5. Cf. Willi.
6. Jung, "A Psychological Theory of Types," CW 6, par. 926.

7. Cf. Kast, *Imagination*.
8. Jung, *Letters*, vol. I, 1906–1950, p. 109.
9. Jung, *Letters*, vol. I, 1906–1950, p. 460.
10. Cf. Kast, *Imagination as a Space of Freedom*. In this book, I have attempted to provide a method for the practice of imagination and suggest how to advance from imagination to active imagination, which observes the theory of the formation of symbols.
11. Cf. Rohde-Dachser and Kernberg.
12. By Charles Perrault.
13. Cf. Riedel, *Die Symbolbildung*.
14. Jung, "King and Queen," CW 16, par. 448.

BIBLIOGRAPHY

Ahrens, Stephan. "Zur Affektverarbeitung von Ulcus-Patienten —ein Beitrag zur 'Alexithymie'-Diskussion." In *Psychosomatik in Forschung und Praxis*, edited by Hans H. Studt. Munich, Vienna, Baltimore: Urban und Schwarzenberg, 1983.

Anderson, Harold Homer, ed. *Creativity and Its Cultivation*. New York: Harper & Row, 1959.

Barz, Helmut; Kast, Verena; and Nager, Frank. *Heilung und Wandlung: C. G. Jung und die Medizin*. Zurich and Munich: Artemis, 1986.

Bloch, Ernst. *The Principle of Hope*. 3 vols. Cambridge: MIT Press, 1986.

Bürgin, Dieter. "Die Bedeutung der affektiven Austauschvorgänge für den Aufbau des Selbst in der Kindheit." In *Allmacht und Ohnmacht: Das Konzept des Narziβmus in Theorie und Praxis*, edited by Udo Rauchfleisch. Bern: Huber, 1987.

Capra, Fritjof. *The Turning Point: Science, Society and the Rising Culture*. New York: Simon & Schuster, 1982.

Coulon, N. de. "La cure de packs, une application des idées de Winnicott en clinique psychiatrique." In *L'Information Psychiatrique*, vol. 61, no. 2, Février 1985.

Evers, Tilman. *Mythos und Emanzipation: Eine kritische Annäherung an C. G. Jung*. Hamburg: Junius, 1987.

Frank, R., and Vaitl, D. "Alexithymie: Differentialdiagnostische Analyse aud verhaltenstherapeutischer Sicht." In *Psychosomatik in Forschung und Praxis*, edited by Hans H. Studt. Munich, Vienna, Baltimore: Urban und Schwarzenberg, 1983.

BIBLIOGRAPHY

Franz, Marie-Louise von. "The Process of Individuation." In *Man and His Symbols*, conceived and edited by Carl Gustav Jung. New York, London, Toronto, Sydney, Auckland: Doubleday, Anchor Books, 1984.

———. *Number and Time*. Evanston: Northwestern University Press, 1974.

Fromm, Erich. "The Creative Attitude." In *Creativity and Its Cultivation*, edited by Harold Homer Anderson, New York: Harper & Row, 1959.

Grof, Stanislav. *Realms of the Unconscious*. New York: Dutton, 1976.

Jacoby, Jolande. *Complex, Archetype, Symbol in the Psychology of C. G. Jung*. Bollingen Series LVII. Princeton: Princeton University Press, 1959.

———. *Individuation und Narziβmus: Psychologie des Selbst bei C. G. Jung und H. Kohut*. Munich: Pfeiffer, 1985.

———. *Psychotherapeuten sind auch Menschen*. Olten: Walter, 1987.

Jung, Carl Gustav. *Collected Works* (= CW). Edited by Gerhard Adler et al. Bollingen Series XX. Princeton: Princeton University Press, 1954 ff. The following volumes were used in particular:
CW 2: *Experimental Researches*. 2nd ed., 1970.
CW 3: *Psychogenesis of Mental Disease*. 1960.
CW 6: *Psychological Types*. 1971.
CW 7: *Two Essays on Analytical Psychology*. 2nd ed., 1966.
CW 8: *The Structure and Dynamics of the Psyche*. 2nd ed., 1968.
CW 9, Part 1: *The Archetypes and the Collective Unconscious*. 2nd ed., 1968.
CW 9, Part 2: *Aion*. 2nd ed., 1968.
CW 12: *Psychology and Alchemy*. 2nd ed., 1967.
CW 13: *Alchemical Studies*. 1968.
CW 14: *Mysterium Coniunctionis*. 2nd ed., 1970.
CW 15: *The Spirit in Man, Art, and Literature*. 1966.
CW 16: *The Practice of Psychotherapy*. 2nd ed., 1966.

———. *Letters*. Edited by Gerhard Adler and Aniela Jaffé. 2 vols. Bollingen Series XCV. Princeton: Princeton University Press, 1963 and 1973.

———. *Man and His Symbols*. New York, London, Toronto, Sydney, Auckland: Doubleday, Anchor Books, 1984.

Kast, Verena. *Das Assoziationsexperiment in der therapeutischen Praxis*. 2nd ed. Fellbach: Bonz, 1988.

———. *A Time to Mourn: Growing through the Grief Process*. Einsiedeln: Daimon, 1989.

———. *The Nature of Loving: Patterns of Human Relationship*. Wilmette: Chiron Publications, 1986.

———. "Die Bedeutung der Symbole im therapeutischen Prozeβ." In *Heilung und Wandlung: C. G. Jung und die Medizin*, edited by Helmut Barz, Verena Kast, and Frank Nager. Zurich and Munich: Artemis, 1986.

———. *Märchen als Therapie*. Olten: Walter, 1986. 3rd ed., 1989.

———. *Imagination as Space of Freedom: Dialogue between the Ego and the Unconscious*. New York: Fromm International (in print).

———. *The Creative Leap: Psychological Transformation through Crisis*. Wilmette: Chiron Publications, 1990.

———. *Traumbild Auto: Vom alltäglichen Unterwegssein*. Olten: Walter, 1987.

Kernberg, Otto F. *Borderline Conditions and Pathological Narcissism*. Northvale: Aronson, 1985.

Koch, Karl. *Der Baumtest*. Bern: Huber, 1982.

Krapp, Manfred. "Gestaltungstherapie als Beitrag zur Psychotherapie psychotischer Patienten." In *Zeitschrift für Analytische Psychologie*, vol. 20, no. 1, 1989, pp. 32–57.

Lurker, Manfred. *Wörterbuch der Symbolik*. Stuttgart: Kröner, 1979.

Märchen aus dem Iran. Jena: Diederichs, 1939.

Mahler, Margaret S.; Pine, Fred; and Bergmann, A. *The Psychological Birth of the Human Infant.* New York: Basic, 1975.

Matussek, D. *Kreativität als Chance.* Munich: Piper, 1974.

Mentzos, Stavros. *Neurotische Konfliktverarbeitung.* Munich: Kindler, 1982.

Middendorf, Ilse. *Der erfahrbare Atem: Eine Atemlehre.* Paderborn: Junfermann, 1984.

Neumann, Erich: *The Great Mother: An Analysis of the Archetype.* Bollingen Series XLVII. Princeton: Princeton University Press, 1964.

———. *The Child.* Boston: Shambhala Publications, 1990.

Overbeck, Gert: *Krankheit als Anpassung: Der sozio-psychosomatische Zirkel.* Frankfurt/M.: Suhrkamp, 1984.

Perrault, Charles. "Blue Beard." In *Best-loved Folktales of the World*, selected and edited by Joanna Cole. Garden City: Doubleday, 1982.

Rauchfleisch, Udo, ed. *Allmacht und Ohnmacht: Das Konzept des Narzißmus in Theorie und Praxis.* Bern: Huber, 1978.

Rohde-Dachser, Christa. *Das Borderline-Syndrom.* Bern, Stuttgart, Vienna: Huber, 1979.

———. "Abschied von der Schuld der Mütter." Lecture held in Lindau during the 39. *Lindauer Psychotherapiewochen*, 1989.

Riedel, Ingrid. "Farben." In *Religion, Gesellschaft, Kunst und Psychotherapie.* Stuttgart: Kreuz, 1983. 7th ed., 1989.

———. *Formen: Kreis, Kreuz, Dreieck, Quadrat, Spirale.* Stuttgart: Kreuz, 1985.

———. *Bilder in Therapie, Kunst und Religion.* Stuttgart: Kreuz, 1988.

———. "The Formation of Symbols in the Analytical Relationship." In *Personal and Archetypal Dynamics in the Analytical Relationship*, edited by Mary Ann Mattoon. Einsiedeln: Daimon, 1990.

Schwarzenau, Paul. *Das göttliche Kind: Der Mythos vom Neubeginn*. Stuttgart: Kreuz, 1984.

Stern, Daniel. *The First Relationship: Infant and Mother*. Edited by Jerome Bruner et al. Cambridge: Harvard University Press, 1977.

Studt, Hans H. *Psychosomatik in Forschung und Praxis*. Munich, Vienna, Baltimore: Urban und Schwarzenberg, 1983.

Uexküll, Theodor von. *Psychosomatische Medizin*. Munich, Vienna, Baltimore: Urban und Schwarzenberg, 1983.

Willi, Jürg. *Die Zweierbeziehung*. Reinbek bei Hamburg: Rowohlt, 1975.

INDEX

Acceptance, 69, 74, 76
Adolescence, 60
Adaptation, 34, 38, 157
Adulthood, young, 61
    later, 65
Affect, 48
Age, old, 65
Aggression, aggressiveness, 42, 57, 63, 68, 141, 159, 171
Aggressor-victim theme, 34, 43, 159ff., 171
    and division, 164ff.
Aging, 63, 65ff.
Alchemy, 128
Amplification, 93, 103ff.
Analysis, turning points in, 146–157
Analytic relationship *see* relationship
Anger *see* rage
Anima/animus, 60, 62, 114, 199ff.
    as archetypal union, 64
    definition, 199ff.
    unification of, 202
Animus *see* anima
Anima and animus figures, 201
Anxiety, 61, 67, 69, 81
Apathy, 101
Archetypal constellation, 93, 97ff., 123, 125, 129
    and relationship, 97ff.
    experience, 99–102

Archetypal countertransference, 175, 186
Archetypal images *see* images
Archetypal imaginings, 91–94
Archetypal material, 80
Archetypal mother, 25
Archetypal motif, 81, 94, 110
Archetypal plane of transference, 24
Archetypal structure, 126ff.
Archetypal union, 64
Archetype, 32, 47, 90–142
    concept of, 95ff.
    dynamic nature of, 91ff.
    effect (simultaneous effectiveness of various), 90ff., 127ff.
    of death, 65
    of parents, 61
    of the divine child, 62, 64, 94, 111
    of the hero, 3, 60ff., 127ff.
    of the self, 5ff., 106–108 (dynamic aspect), 108, 111 (structural aspect), 108, 111, 122
    of the wise old man or woman, 65, 127
    structuring factor, 91
Aristotle, 1
Association (dream analysis), 103ff.
Association studies, 97
Association test, 32, 37, 40, 48, 51, 68

INDEX

Attention, 67
Authority complex, 55, 125
Autonomy, 2, 78, 92, 139, 141
   developing, 3, 56
   experiencing, 56
Avicenna, 128
Awareness, 53

Becoming who one is, 2, 53
Behavior (stereotypical, patterns of), 35, 70, 76
Bloch, Ernst, 95ff.
Bodily sensations, 52, 54
Body and ego complex, 51, 57, 105, 134
   and psyche and environment, 130ff.
   and soul, 129
Borderline condition, 180, 185, 193
Boundaries, 53, 114
   perceiving, 53
   traversing, 114, 115
Buddha, 94

Capra, Fritjof, 128
Caring, 64
Child, 34, 57–58, 77, 86, 99, 158
   as archetype *see* archetype
   as divine child *see* archetype, symbol
   as symbol, 16, 94, 112
Childhood, 16, 33, 57–59, 86ff., 158
   phases of development, 57
   situations that mould our personality, 54, 58, 78
Circle, 5, 108, 111
COEX systems, 33
Coherence (of ego complex), 53, 58, 61, 69, 80, 85–89, 111, 112, 134

Collective symbol, 82
Collective unconscious *see* unconscious
Color (suggesting a meaning), 11
   black, 20, 138
   green, 48, 137
   orange, 41
   red, 11, 138
   purple, 41
   yellow, golden, 20, 48
Compensation, 70–79
   as attitude, 76–79
   classic, 70
   destructive rage as, 73ff.
   through devaluation, 74ff.
   through fantasies of grandeur, 70ff.
   through idealized parent figures, 71ff., 77
   through mirror identification, 72, 78
Compensatory reaction (from the unconscious), 93, 98
Complex, 31–50, 85, 90, 92, 95, 97, 102, 134, 147
   age-related, 39
   and ego complex, 37, 39, 51
   "being ignored", 34
   definition, 157
   description, 37–48
   identification with, 44
   landscape of, 33, 40, 48, 67
   signs of, 48
   typical, 90
   with empowering influences, 48–50
Complex identity, 45
Complex reaction, 36, 68
Compulsive neurosis, 95
Concepts, formation of, 67

Conflict, 74, 84, 133ff.
    between aggressor and victim, 159
    moral, 198
Consciousness, 66–68, 85, 93, 97
    conscious attitude, 98
    coming to, 20, 56, 58ff., 60, 66ff.
Consolidation phase, 59, 61
Constellation *see* archetype, ego complex
Continuity, 53, 65
Control, 36
Coping mechanism *see* defense mechanism
Cosmos, 6
Countertransference, 87, 143–147, 151, 185
    archetypal, 175, 186
    illusory, 146
    feelings of, 179
    see transference
Countertransference image, 150ff.
Countertransference reaction, 130, 150
Creativity, 28, 64
Cross, 5, 108

Death, 64, 81, 129, 138
    and rebirth, 81ff., 121
Death wish (for oneself), 160
Death-mother, 20, 139
Defense mechanism, 17, 35, 61, 67, 69, 84, 120, 159–161, 177
    developed early in life, 84
Defense process, 23
Demand of adaptation, 34, 38, 157
Denial, 84, 177
Depression, 101, 148
Depressive circle/cycle, 76, 152

Depressive tendencies, 72
Depth psychology, 10
Destructive rage, 73ff.
Destructiveness, 73, 85
Devaluation, 74ff., 151
Devaluation strategy, 76, 177
Development, 56
    human, 57
    spontaneous, 58
Developmental psychology, 56, 59
Dismemberment (as motif), 81
Divine child *see* archetype, symbol
Dorn, 6
Dream, dreams, 3, 15, 40, 46ff., 70, 72, 75, 80ff., 88, 98, 101, 103, 122, 123, 150, 153–157, 197
    series of, 105ff.
Dream analysis, 102–106
Dream-ego, 70, 104, 154

Ego, 51ff., 57ff., 64, 79, 83, 85, 92, 107, 120
    and self, 66, 120
    development of, 88
    expansion of, 64
    strong, 83
    weak, 83
Ego-activity, 52
Ego complex, 33, 37, 39, 41, 44, 68–89, 106
    and body *see* body
    and identity, 52–57
    and other complexes, 66, 104
    and self, 6, 67, 106
    as central complex, 52, 54, 66, 85
    basis, 52, 54
    becoming conscious, 56, 57ff., 62
    coherence, 53, 58, 61,

69, 80, 85–89, 111, 112, 134
constellation, 68–70
definition, 51ff.
fragmentation, 39, 79–85, 87
ideal typical development, 60–66
in terms of developmental psychology, 57–66
reestablishing coherence, 85–89
restitution, 80
Ego-consciousness, 98, 106
Ego-fragmentation, 80ff. *see* fragmentation
Ego function, 35, 52, 66–68, 79, 83, 87, 110
disturbed, 67ff., 81, 88
primarily autonomous, 67
Ego-ideal, 54, 199
Ego-self axis, 89, 110, 112
Ego-strength, 83ff.
Ego-weakness, 83ff.
Emotion, 31ff., 35ff., 37, 48, 54, 57, 69, 79, 93, 107, 128, 131ff., 134, 200
Emotional dependability, 86
Emotional disposition, 101ff.
Empathy, 85, 158, 174, 201ff.
Existential fear, 82
Expansion phase, 59ff., 65
Expression, displaying, 48

Fairy tales, 12, 80, 98, 175, 186
"Blue Beard," 186–190
"The Girl with the Little Moon on Her Forehead," 19
working on, 192
Family-complex, 97
Fantasies of omnipotence or grandeur, 85

compensation through, 70, 77
Fantasy, 32, 40, 54, 71, 85, 92, 96, 122, 135, 146, 174, 178
destruction, destructive rage, destructiveness, 73ff., 85
of a suprapersonal character, 90
Fate, 93, 132
Father, 41, 43, 45, 47, 71, 72, 98, 140
Father archetype, 98
Father complex, 40–48, 55, 59, 67, 71, 79, 90
series of paintings relating to, 40–47
Fear, 35, 64, 82, 84, 159
Fear of death, 64, 138, 160
Feeling
emptiness, 148
recognizing, 85ff.
Fertility, 82
Formation of symbols, 31, 40, 131, 143, 146, 158, 193
and collusive transference/countertransference, 157ff.
and psychosomatic disturbance, 136–142
as a process, ix, 18, 23ff., 26ff., 29, 104ff., 106, 192
in psychosomatic disturbance, 136–142
relating to a father complex, 40–48
relating to a mother complex, 18–27
spontaneous, 11ff.
Fragmentation, 39, 79–85, 87
Franz, Marie-Louise von, 91, 115

Freud, Sigmund, 55
Fromm, Erich, 28

General psychovegetative syndrome, 136
Gestalt therapy, 80
Geulincx, 129
God, gods, 107
Grandiose self, 70ff.
   in the child, 70, 76
Green complex, 48
Grof, Stanislav, 33
Group, 80
Growth process, 114, 118
Guilt, 132, 160, 167
   and responsibility, 161, 167
   defense mechanism, 160
Guilt feeling, 73, 133, 159–170, 173
   Subject "alienator and alienated", 170
   psychic dynamism, 159–161
   dealing with, 202ff.

Hands, implication/meaning of, 137
Hate, 128
Hathor, 116, 118
Helper complex, 55
Helplessness, 93
Hermes, 94
Hero *see* archetype
Hippocrates, 128
Hope, 82, 92
Human being, eternal, 6, 107
   uniqueness, 2
Human concept, 9
   aspects, 1ff.
   of fairy tales, 98

I Ching, 126, 129
I-you relationship, 78, 113
Idealization, primitive, 176
Identification
   projected, 179
   with a complex, 44, 47
Identity, 39, 44ff., 60ff., 68, 83, 159
   basis, 52
   boundary, 53
   development, 52ff.
   experience, 52–55
   insecurity, 60
Identity crisis, 61
Illness, 61, 131–135
   as a dynamic imbalance, 131, 133
   psychosomatic, 130, 132, 134, 136
Illusionary countertransference, 146
Image/picture/painting, 18, 32ff., 40ff., 80, 88, 91, 103, 111, 124
   archetypal, 22, 24, 92ff., 96, 99, 103
   of parents, 71
   of the old man or woman, 64, 127
   of tree as a symbol, 115–120
   relaxing, 135, 141
   sadistic, 182
   series of, dream as, 103
   series of, relating to a father complex, 40–47
   series of, relating to a mother complex, 18–27
   series of, relating to psychosomatic disturbances, 136–142
Imagination, 40, 103, 105, 134ff., 173ff.
Impotence (powerlessness), 70
Incubation phase, 29
Individuation, 5, 7, 112, 116
   impulse toward, 116
Individuation process, 1–4,

27, 85, 96, 110ff., 112–122
  and self, 106–108
  as a goal, 1, 5
  as a process differentiating one's quality and as a gradual approach, 2
  as a process of integration and relationship, 3ff., 104, 112ff., 193
  emancipatory aspect, 114
  repercussions, 113
Inferiority complex, 33
Information, 103
Insult, 69, 70, 73, 79, 147
Integration *see* individuation
Interpretation, 4, 17, 40, 103–106, 130
Interpretation of dreams, 102–106
Intersubjectivity (preverbal), 58
Introspection, process of, 113
Isis, 81, 116

Jealousy, 63, 76
Jesus, 94
Joy, 48ff.
Jung, Carl Gustav, ix, 1, 2–7, 15, 27ff., 31, 33, 37–40, 51ff., 57, 85, 90–93, 95, 97ff., 106ff., 108ff., 112–114, 124, 126, 129, 131, 143ff., 174, 193, 199ff.
Jungian psychology, 15, 27, 40, 66, 88, 96, 104, 129, 131, 134
  view of humanity, 1, 2, 6
Jungian therapy, 15, 27
Justification, vicious cycle of, 160, 164

Kali, 139
Kernberg, Otto F., 185

Koch, C., 115
Krishna, 94

Leibniz, Gottfried Wilhelm von, 129
Limitations (perceiving), 53, 63, 69
Liberation, 7
Longing, 5
Loss, 18, 79, 81, 83, 163
Love, 5, 63, 128
Love, being in (as complex), 50

Magic, acts of, 127
Mandala, 108–112, 122
  classic, 110
Maternal archetype, 19, 98, 100, 116, 120, 122
  positive (good), 19, 22, 25, 48, 98
  negative (devouring), 22, 25, 140
Memory, 67, 81, 87
Mercurius (as virgin), 116
Middle age, 62ff.
Mind and matter, 128
Mirror identification, 72ff.
Mother, 41, 45, 59, 74, 89, 97, 98, 140
Mother and father matrix, 59, 61
Mother complex, 41, 55, 59, 98, 122, 140
  series of paintings relating to, 18–27
Mother goddess, 116
Motif, archetypal, 81, 94, 110
  mythological, 82, 90, 102, 104
Motor functions, 67
Mourning, process of, 19, 81, 163
Mourning, work of, 60, 63, 83

Mythological motif, 82, 90, 102, 104
Mythology, 94, 116

Narcissistic disturbance, 65, 76
Narcissistic insult, 65, 125
Narcissistic longing, 77
Narcissistic upgrading, 72
Neumann, Erich, 88
Neurosis, ix, 38
Night sea journey, 102
Number, 11
Numinosity, 93
Nut, 116, 118

Occasionalism, 129
Omnipotence, 70, 77 see fantasies of grandeur
Omnipotence and impotence, 70
Oracular methods, 129
Order, causal and acausal, 129
Orientation, 67
Osiris, 81
Overbeck, Gert, 132, 134

Pain, 138ff.
Painting see image
Parental complex, 38, 53, 55, 59, 66
Parental figure, 71ff., 77
Parents, 58ff., 98, 140
Perception (distorted), 67, 81
Persona, 2, 114
Physical self/ego, 57, 66, 82
Picture see image
Pindar, 1
Plotinus, 128
Preestablished harmony, 129
Primordial fears, needs, 140
Primordial images, 93
Primordial longings, 140
Process, therapeutic, 78, 126
  collective-archetypal, 92

Projection, 15, 34, 45, 57, 60, 62, 67
Psyche, 51, 131
  and matter, 128
  as a self-regulating system, 5, 29, 40, 47, 70, 79, 87, 125
  counterregulation, 87
Psychodynamics of suicide cases, 74
  of compulsive neurosis, 95
Psychosomatic disturbance, 136–142
  series of images for, 136–142
Psychosomatic idea, 132
Psychosomatics, 130ff.
Psychovegetative syndrome, general, 136

Quadrangle, 108, 110

Rage, anger, 54, 69, 73–74, 150, 171
Rauchfleisch, Udo, 70
Reality, 10, 67
Realization of the self, 5, 108, 111
  drive toward, 5, 114
Rebirth, 82
Regression, 139
Relationship, 53, 60, 62, 64, 72, 74, 98–102, 112ff., 167
  analytic, ix, 77, 88, 111, 143ff., 158
  and individuation, 112
  defining, 112ff.
  I-you relationship, 53, 78, 113, 104
  patterns of, 40, 42, 86, 142, 157
  patterns of in childhood, 34, 86

therapeutic, 48, 76, 78, 104, 143, 147, 193
Responsibility, 64, 133, 161
Restitution, process of, 79ff.
Riedel, Ingrid, 109, 193
Rohde-Dachser, Christa, 185

Scapegoat, scapegoating, 160, 163
Self, 5–7, 56–57, 59, 64, 106
 and individuation process, 106–108
 as Anthropos, 6
 as archetype, *see* archetype
 as central archetype, 5, 106ff.
 as unified duality, 108
 definitions, 106ff.
 "my self," 6
 relation to ego complex, 6, 67, 106
 self-defeat, 69
 symbol, 6
Self-healing, 111
Self-image, 54, 122
 idealized, 54ff.
Self-regulation of the psyche *see* psyche
Self-worth, feeling of, sense of, 33, 52, 63, 68ff., 74–76, 198
Sensation, 67
Separation-individuation phase, 26
Seth, 81
Shadow, 54, 114, 197–199
 projection of, 198
Shadow acceptance, 198
Shame, 24, 35, 69, 73
Sign, 10ff., 14
Sphere, 5
Splinter psyche, 39, 45
Splitting, 84, 177
Square, 109
Squared circle, 108, 122

Suicide (psychodynamics), 74
Super-ego, 55
Superiority complex, 33
Symbiosis (on an archetypal plane), 23
Symbol, ix, 8–30, 40, 90, 97, 102–106, 114, 143
 ability to formulate, 31, 40, 131, 143, 146, 158, 193
 accepting, 15–18
 and complex, 31ff.
 and goal of therapy, 27–30
 appearance, 11–12, 147
 as a common object, 8ff.
 "billy-goat," 11
 "calf," "cow," 19–27, 111
 "cave," 182
 "child," 16, 94, 111
 collective, 82
 compression of associations within, 17
 concept, 10ff.
 "crocodile," 45
 dealing with, 102–106
 developmental dimension, 104ff.
 "divine child," 94
 form of interpretation, 4, 46
 formation of *see* formation of symbols
 "king," 108
 mandala, 108–112, 122
 "octopus," 139, 141
 personal, 90, 102
 "raven," 18
 "ring," 9, 11
 "rooster," 41
 "self," 6
 symptom as, 131, 135–137
 "tree," 2, 112, 114–122
Symbolic act, 14–15
Symbolizing attitude, 135

Symbols, 76–78, 130
    tendency to formulate, 130
Symptom (as symbol), 131, 135–137
Synchronicity, 123–130
    and psychosomatics, 130–142
Szondi, Leopold, 97

Tarot, 129
Theory of learning, 38
Theory of systems, 128
Therapeutic process, 78, 126
Therapeutic relationship *see* relationship
Therapy, goal of, ix, 27ff., 93, 143, 148
Thinking *see* thought
Thought/thinking, 67
    causal, 131–132
    synchronistic, 126, 129, 132
Total being, totality, 5, 7, 57, 62, 64, 128
Transference, 34, 43, 78, 101, 122
    in borderline patients, 185
    plane of symbolic, 24
Transference/countertransference, ix, 76, 78, 101, 146
    and relationship, 144
    collusive, 146, 157, 165
    schematic for, 144
Transference/countertransference process, 174
Transformation, 1, 63
Transformation myth, 81ff.
Transformation process, 60
Transition in life, 60, 128
Transition object, 192
Tree as Arbor Philosophica, 115, 116
    as mother symbol, 117
    as projection carrier, 114–122
Tree goddess, 116
Tree nymph, 116
Tree of life, 115, 116
Tree test, 114
Triangle, 5, 138
Triangulation, 191
Turning points in analysis, 146–157

Uexküll, Theodor von, 130, 132
Unconscious, the, ix, 3, 15, 32, 47, 53, 87, 92, 96, 105–106, 120, 174
    activating the, 143
    collective, 19, 92, 97, 192
    family unconscious, 97
    integration, 85
    personal, 97, 145
    shared, 145
    societal, 97
Upheaval (as fragmentation), 79
Utopia, 7, 60, 63, 96

Vagina dentata, 139
Victim *see* aggressor, conflict
Vitality, 52

Weakness, 93
Whole, wholeness, 5, 7, 57, 62, 64, 128
Wise old man or woman *see* archetype
Witch, 99
Word association test, 32, 37, 40, 48, 51, 68
World Ash Yggdrasil, 115

Yin and Yang, 111, 122